Hindutva and National Renaissance

BY THE SAME AUTHOR

Ayodhya: Ram Temple and Hindu Rennaissance

The Ideology of India's Modern Right

Hindus Under Siege: The Way Out

Sri Lanka in Crisis: India's Options

Terrorism in India: A Strategy of Deterrence for India's National Security

Rama Setu: Symbol of National Unity

Corruption and Corporate Governance in India: Satyam, Spectrum and Sundaram

Economic Development and Reforms in India and China

India's China Strategic Perspective

Virat Hindu Identity: Concept and its Power

Building the Sri Rama Temple in Ayodhya

2G Spectrum Scam

Hindutva and National Renaissance

Subramanian Swamy

President of Janata Party and
Former Union Cabinet Minister of Commerce, Law and Justice
Government of India

HAR-ANAND
PUBLICATIONS PVT LTD

Reprint, 2024

Published by Ashok Gosain and Ashish Gosain for
HAR-ANAND PUBLICATIONS PVT LTD
E-49/3, Okhla Industrial Area, Phase-II, New Delhi-110020
Tel: 41603490
E-mail: info@haranandbooks.com/haranand@rediffmail.com
Shop online at: www.haranandbooks.com

@haranand_publications
Har Anand Publications

Printed in India

PREFACE

Since becoming free of British Imperialist rule in 1947, India's ideological space had been for most of the more than six decades period circumscribed by an essentially Left--leaning socialist secular framework, with very little room left in the mainstream of thought for any other significantly different ideological perspective rooted in our Hindu civilisational past.

The central feature of the last sixty or more years in the progressive dehumanization of the individual in Indian Society. No society can be strong, however impressive the infrastructure, if the individual is dehumanized or demoralized.

No doubt, the country's commitment to democracy and national unity is largely intact. But this is a cause for superficial satisfaction. Even these commitments are being weakened every day through wrong policies and corrupt machinations. If the electoral system becomes undermined through corrupt practices, how long can democracy last? If region after region becomes infected by terrorism then what is the future of national unity? And who is primarily accountable for all this, to fix responsibility and to remedy the situation?

The old Sanskrit adage "*Yatha Raja Tatha Praja*" (As the leader, so the people) applies to the present depressing situation. It is my contention that the failure of leadership to foster a clear concept of national identity is the key factor responsible for the present morass.

Unless therefore the inspirational quality of leadership in India is raised, things cannot improve substantially. In other words, India's growth and well-being will depend upon three factors: how professional and well-trained its leadership is, its definition of identity and common inspiration and purpose for the nation, and how it seeks to fulfill its goals.

The leadership in a society is in five sectors: political, administrative, industrial, academic, and defence. These are five wheels that move the engine of our national development.

At the apex is naturally the political leadership, "the steering wheel", because in a democracy, it represents the people, therefore, the mainspring of policy initiation and provides the overall direction to the other sectors. Representing the people it has a feel for their aspirations, which it articulates, and then generates ideas through the other sectors of leadership to make plans for the future and ensure their efficient implementation.

India has an abundance of both natural and human resources, in fact a surplus of the latter, so that they emigrate abroad in large numbers, at all levels of scientific, technological, managerial and general skills. Our administrators, industrial executives, scientists and technologists, and defence officers are all carefully and competitively selected and intensively trained at our many institutions of excellence. They have basically high levels of competence and integrity, despite their relatively low salaries and the demands or influence of the political apparatus that forces or cajoles some of them into lowering their integrity.

However, their standards are high enough for them to be in demand abroad. These standards are maintained by inputs throughout their career that keep them up to date with changes at home and abroad. They are in fact remarkably well-exposed to world developments in knowledge in their fields.

As Dr. Prakash Tandon, an erudite former Chairman of the State Trading Corporation had observed long before the IT revolution: "India can be justly proud of its standards, which are they envy of many developing countries. See our professionals all over the world, never can one be more than a few moments away from an Indian face in any campus in the USA, Canada, the U.K., Australia and in some countries in Europe. They are there as teachers, researchers, students and visitors, carefully picked by these institutions who appreciate their ability and industry. Few let down India; most do it credit".

These other sectors of leadership all depend, however, upon the inspirational quality of political leadership for their effective functioning. Deprived of good political leadership, their effectiveness can vary from the mediocre to the negative. And this is where our incongruence begins. Our fifth wheel, the steering wheel, has usually no professional training, no careful selection and no post-experience inputs; in fact, its members can begin life and go through it completely innocent of knowledge, much more so of modern knowledge. Many have just a native cunning, a capacity to influence, to manipulate, and a shrewd, deep sense of opportunism. Coming from the grassroots, they are the grassroots and remain at that level. This is no more acceptable because in a modern state in a globalization process, the task of leadership is very demanding, which requires a great deal of erudition, articulation and sophistication.

The task of the political leadership, is to identify the people's problems, wants and aspirations, which in a poor country are many and in a democracy more so. Having identified them, its next task is to consult the different sectors of leadership to find answers and solutions. It must bear in mind, however that the country's needs are so large that its resources will not match them for a long time to come.

The planning and implementing leadership must, therefore, use the available resources optimally, while it is the political leadership's task to persuade the people not to pitch their expectations too high and at the same time sacrifice some of the gains of today for investment in more growth tomorrow. Close coordination is necessary between sectors to ensure this.

In actual practice, political leaders in India to gain easy popularity, have consistently promised the people the moon, and when they cannot, blame the administrators, industry, and everyone else; they prevent him from fulfilling promises they complain! We have recently had some very unedifying examples of ministers calling their administrators names that would really have better fitted themselves.

At the base of this opportunism is the politicians' lack of professionalism. They do not perceive the implications of their promises. Instead of asking for sweat and tears, they talk euphorically with a reckless disregard of what is possible. Professionalism would enable them to look at people's problems objectively, their needs critically and analytically, and work out with the other sectors, solutions that are possible.

The nation therefore is a vehicle with four sound wheels, each wheel representing highly professional and competent sectors of leadership, with a fifth wheel—the steering wheel, which is eccentric and of indifferent calibre, in which the process of knowledge and professionalism has not even begun. The result is that the vehicle does not move properly, and hence veers and lurches from time to time.

Thus the first objective of the nation should be to correct this defective fifth wheel by inducing and encouraging into its leadership persons with professional competence in fields such as economics, management, engineering, medicine, law and journalism. This effort should be especially at the district level so that professional competence in local leadership can be ushered at the grassroots.

The task will not be easy as professionals will have to make a sacrifice of their career to a great extent. But the rejuvenation necessary in Indian politics cannot come about unless this professionalism and managerial expertise are available. It is only if this strata is encouraged to enter politics and extolled if they do, that the people's cynicism about the current political leadership, and the nation's capacity to change and reach a higher standard of living, will be altered, and thus public confidence restored.

Such cynicism and apathy as we see today had prevailed in the early part of this century too. People then were not even confident that *Swaraj* (self-rule) was viable as a concept. Most had thought of the British as necessary to administer the country, as well as being unshakeable fixtures in India. But with the induction of a large number of professionals, especially from the legal profession, we Indian people began to develop confidence that we could rule ourselves. That was the great contribution of the freedom struggle and the inspiration of Gandhiji.

There is thus a need for a patriotic political coalition today which can mobilize and emplace professionals in politics. This cannot be done overnight. It may take years, but it is worth the investment today.

This is needed as a prerequisite for the successful functioning of our democratic system, because at the core it is always a comparatively small number of persons who at any given time are mandated for moulding the contours of national policy. Even Parliament of both Houses together consists only of 780 MPs in a nation of 1.03 billion people who steer national policies. And of these 780, about 30 are effective in doing so. As politics in Indian society is in such a predominant position, it is in the political sphere where competent leadership becomes most essential, but is today least available.

The responsibilities of leadership in a democratic system are greater than in an authoritarian one, because while in the latter, responsibility is concentrated in one or a few persons upon whose bidding the rest of society must act, in a democracy this authority is shared by a wider spectrum of political functionaries. In a democracy furthermore an added dimension is the fact that authority periodically, if not quinquinally, is accountable however imperfectly to the electorate.

There are three essential qualities for effective democratic leadership: *vision, dynamism and integrity.* By vision it is meant the ability to take not merely a regional or party view of issues but to look upon them in a national perspective in a vast and varied country, even as it is inevitable that elected representatives will be committed to certain regional problems and demands. This regional commitment is necessary if they are to be truly representative of their electorate, but it is nevertheless a test of true leadership to be able to place them in a national perspective and have the courage to subordinate the smaller interest to the larger whenever the necessity for this arises. In fact the whole concept of national integration tends to lose its meaning if regional claims are pressed in such a manner as to weaken the national interest and integrity.

The second essential ingredient of effective leadership is dynamism, by which I mean the ability to function actively both in the physical and the intellectual sense. Placed as we are at a crucial juncture of our national history, the emergence of a more dynamic leadership both at the Centre and in the States is a prerequisite for a real breakthrough to progress.

This is not to argue that youth and dynamism necessarily go together. All of us know many 'young' politicians who lack vitality due to their dissoluteness, while some elderly persons Morarji Desai and Charan Singh were examples of those who retained an essentially youthful vitality and probity until the very end. It all depends on the lifestyle one leads. Dynamism is essentially thus youthful moral vitality and decisiveness, without ambivalence and procrastination, and with a capacity to take calculated risks.

Dynamism hence implies the intellectual capacity to think and act in bold terms. The world in which we live is globalizing at a fast pace. In the last three or four decades science and technology have transformed the face of this planet, and today mankind stands at the crossroads in which one path could lead to death and destruction while the other points the way to a possible unprecedented progress and prosperity.

At a time like this our political leadership must possess the intellectual equipment and dynamism necessary to grasp the immensity of the challenge and boldly take the decisions that are required. The impact of change on a traditional society sets up tensions which call for a high degree of political acumen if the two extremes of continued stagnation and violent revolution are to be avoided. Decision-making is an essential component of dynamism, and with its checks and balances it becomes all the more necessary that in a democracy, leadership should possess the courage and the capacity to take firm decisions upon important matters without dithering or prevarication.

The third ingredient of true leadership is integrity. In one dimension this implies honesty in financial matters. It should be unnecessary to stress this, but corruption at various levels of society continues to be one of the gravest challenges that democracy faces in this country. India is already ranked near the bottom of nations by a corruption index complied by Transparency International. But integrity is also required in a deeper sense is as much as it represents a genuine commitment to democratic ideals and fundamental rights, and not merely to the outward forms of democracy. A democratic leader has to justify in every way the confidence of his electorate, and must have the capacity to share their pain and sorrow, their hopes and aspirations. This genuine empathy is not possible unless he possesses integrity in this sense of the term.

Integrity would also imply the inner strength and equilibrium which enables one to meet with equanimity the alarms and set backs of contemporary politics. All who have been in public life know of those moments when the problems surrounding them appear insurmountable, and their means to deal with them grossly inadequate. There are times when darkness gathers such as during the Emergency (1975-77), and one despairs whether the dawn will ever break out. It is at such times that one has to call upon those inner reserves of strength and power with which every human being is potentially equipped but which requires a spiritual evolution to realise.

In the Bhagavad Gita the importance of leadership is enunciated as follows:

Yadyad aacharti sreshthah tattadevetaro janah
Sa yat pramaanam Kurute Lokastadanuvartate

'Always will people imitate a leader, following the example set by his action.'

The *first prerequisite* thus for a leader is to have a 'spiritual' commitment to democracy and public welfare. This essentially indefinable quality combines a dedication to the public good, not merely on the intellectual and emotional planes but on a higher moral and spiritual level; a commitment to the development of all that is best in our culture and heritage, and a special concern for the welfare of the backward and weaker sections of society.

Without this quality of governance norms as the first prerequisite, leadership is always in danger of degenerating into sheer opportunism and the quest for personal power, both of which are disastrous for democracy.

Second, is the capacity to communicate, not only with colleagues but more importantly with the masses, whose sanction is crucial in the democratic process. In a country as large as ours, with an infinite variety of custom and tradition, language and culture, and an electorate still largely uneducated, this capacity is extremely important at the national level. A leader, though he should certainly have a strong political base in his own region or caste must be able to communicate with a much broader segment of the nation, not merely on the verbal plane but emotionally and intellectually.

Third prerequisite is that the leader should have the courage to subordinate lesser interests to the larger national good. In India, with it's diversities it is all too easy to get involved in local issues, sometimes to the detriment of that larger national integration that essential in a truly great nation. A national leader must have this perspective in mind, and weigh every decision and every move against this standard. This indeed is one of the important ways in which our much talked of national unity and purpose can be strengthened.

In Rig Veda, it is beautifully stated:

Aham Nijah Paravetee Ganana Laguh Chetahsam Udaar Charitaanamtu Vasudeva Kutumbakam

"Do not have the petty thoughts of what is mine and what is not. Have the larger vision of the world as one family". This sloka incidentally is engraved outside the Central Hall of Parliament.

Fourth, decision-making is often an excruciatingly hard task, as it is seldom a question of a clear choice between right and wrong, good and evil. Rather it implies a careful weighing of various alternatives and a delicate assessment of the complex risk involved. At some stage or the other, however, a clear-cut decision has to be taken, even at the cost of incurring the hostility or displeasure of a section of public opinion. This capacity to take clear decision is one of the essential functions of a leader. Too often do we allow a policy of drift and indefinite postponement to hamstring our thrust towards progress, and it has been proved time and again that in the long run, taking no risk can become the most risky thing to do.

Fifth, is the necessity to have a clear scale of priorities regarding the various issues to be tackled since so much is desirable to do and yet so little is possible. We can make the best use of our limited means only if we have a clear picture as to the ends which must receive priority, otherwise there is the danger of getting bogged down in a vast series of undertakings which fritter away our resources without achieving any substantial result. While expert advice is extremely valuable in the context, the ultimate choice is for political leadership to lay down a coherent scale of priorities which is most suited to national requirements at any given time.

Sixth, a national leader must be aware of the broad implications of the scientific methods in decision making such as information technology that is transforming the world before our very eyes, and hence must be intellectually equipped to harness such a technology in reaching efficient decisions.

Seventh, national leader should also have a lively awareness of the globe beyond the frontiers of India. Indeed one who knows only India lacks an important dimension which is of tremendous value in the task of providing dynamic leadership. This assumes special significance in the context of what is called globalization. Willy-nilly, we are being driven to accept the concept of a new world order through such institutions as the UN and the WTO. The establishment of such an order, however, necessitates enlightened leadership in the nations of the world, and we in India must necessarily play a leading role in the globalization process.

These three ingredients and seven prerequisites of leadership emplaced in a person make him or her a national leader. But the right leader of the nation for the moment in history must have an ideology and an agenda for the nation consistent with the true identity of the nation.

The world has seen three main ideologies in the nineteenth and twentieth centuries. These are Capitalism, Communism, and Democratic Socialism. The United States, the U.K. and some West European countries have practiced Capitalism. The USSR was a prominent Communist country and China remains one. Scandinavian nations have adopted Democratic Socialism. All three are inappropriate and unsuitable for Indian identity.

All three ideologies are one-dimensional and materialist in character. Although through them, some nations have been able to raise the standards of living of their peoples, the countries adopting these ideologies have failed to make their people happy. In the United States and Europe, the economic prosperity achieved has been admired by all, but the social problems created in the process have begun to raise serious questions about whether the achieved economic growth is worth the price paid by society. The movement for environmental protection, anti-pollution measures etc., have all meant putting a brake on this kind of growth. But more surprising is the rise in the number of people in these countries who are becoming adherents of spiritual practices such as meditation and Yoga, and are adopting *gurus* from India.

A certain consensus is taking shape all over the world that material progress has to blend with spiritual values to make national development meaningful to the people. This the age-old contribution of Hindu civilization. Pure material progress produces new kinds of exploitation replacing the old degeneration of human decencies, leading to a "rat race". On the other hand a purely spiritually minded society is not a viable concept. Society needs to eat and live tolerably well. Material progress is thus necessary, but it must not be an end in itself. Therefore a blend is necessary, between pursuit of material progress and the adherence to spiritual and moral values. This should be our goal in renaissance or what in India we call as *sanatana dharma.*

Hitherto, in the course of the last nearly six decades, we have tried to develop democracy *without* dharma. This is what we have called "secular" politics. Secularism has meant for us not so much separation of religion from the State but anything that is anti-religious or unreligious. But the State cannot leave religion alone. It has to enact laws that regulate and sometimes even interfere with religion. The Hindu Code is an example. The Hindu Endowments and Charitable Trusts Acts in many states is another example. Various laws restricting religious processions or take-over of temple lands are examples of other such interference. In secular India, the state has to treated religion as merely a law and order problem. Thus, even *not* implementing the Constitutional Directive Principle of uniform civil code has been avoided as a "secular" ideal to obviate a law and order problem.

Religion has thus not been thought of as a force for shaping a moral society. Such negative thinking is considered as constituting "secularism". But this approach is erroneous. Sri Aurobindo said: "All great movements of life in India have begun with the new spiritual thought and usually a new religious activity". Even Jawaharlal Nehru ultimately acknowledged this in his foreword to one of Dr. Karan Singh book as follows: "It is significant to note that great political mass movements in India have had a spiritual background behind them."

A society based on dharma is vitally needed at this moment in our history, because there is a dimension to the current national crisis, namely, the moral decay and the decline of character in our society which if not stemmed, will slowly poison to death our nation. This decay and decline is visible in every aspect of our lifepoliticians defecting for office and cash, bureaucrats taking bribes, teachers selling exam questions, students passing by cheating, businessmen adulterating products, lawyers cheating clients, doctors betraying their patients etc. To some extent such degeneration is there in every society, but the alarming aspect in India is the pace of this decay and the spread of it. Consequent to this decay is the wave of dangerous cynicism amongst the youth.

This moral decay has to be stemmed. A renaissance of values in society has to take place. How will this renaissance come about? And which leader shall be its instrument? For this, a leader shall be one who is committed to an ideology and determined to implement an agenda for renaissance. What are the items of this agenda?

In India, the majority is the conglomerate Hindu community which represents about 81% of the total Indian population, while minorities are constituted by Muslims [13%] and Christians [3%]. Sikhs, Jains, Parsis, and some other small religious groups, represent the remaining three percent. Though these groups are also considered minorities, but are really so close to the majority community in culture that they are considered as partners of Hindu society. Unlike Islam and Christianity, these minority religions were born as dissenting theologies of Hinduism. They share the core concepts with Hindus such as re-incarnation, equality of all religions, and ability to meet God in this life. That they feel increasingly alienated from Hindu society nowadays is also the consequence of India's identity crisis.

To research, propound, and propagate a new ideological framework that can unite the nation, make the people strive to global greatness and struggle for world power, the Centre for National Renaissance has been set up in New Delhi to be funded by the Naveen Hindustan Trust. My colleagues and I who constitute the Centre's Board of Governors have an established and acknowledged record of dissenting from the past ideological framework of the nation. This dissent has taken even the form of struggle and we have suffered denial in our professional life from the state. We were denounced as conservatives or reactionaries. But we never wavered, convinced that the day will dawn when an alternative ideology of national renaissance will be needed by the country. The new millennium has ushered in that dawn.

We own the Hindutva ideology. We do not promise to create heaven on earth through our ideology. We know that it cannot be done by anyone. Instead as *Hindutvavadis* we promise change while preserving the best in our past. We dare to change the things that we must and can, and await the moment when we can change that we must but cannot for now. The wisdom of the ideology lies delineating which is which. That is, we are not revolutionaries, nor are we libertarian anarchists, but we are for consistent if only gradual change brought about by the individual himself driven by his own interests in the milieu of voluntary social actions and norms. We do believe that the individual can be and should be motivated by incentives, by equipping him with fundamental concepts of his individual, social and national identity, and empowered by adequate education.

The ideological framework of Hindutva to achieve national renaissance, which thus the Centre proposes to research, articulate and propagate in an intellectually challenging way, has the following markers:

(a) The Hindutva based state is to be minimalist in regulatory interventions in social and economic matters, maximalist in the maintenance of law and order, in opposing terrorism, and optimalist in providing the quality of life needs, while being politically accountable to the people in a democracy.

(b) A social ethos based on the Hindu concepts of trusteeship of wealth, philanthropy and voluntary group action is encouraged by religious sanction for the better distribution of income and for minimizing economic contradictions and deprivation.

(c) The key goal of the state is to empower the individual through a modern education that blends the essential concepts of spiritual commitment of *Sanatana Dharma* with material pursuits, to enable the individual to be self-reliant and yet have strong character. The state is thus guided by Integral Humanism.

(d) The individual is persuaded by the state by incentives and not by coercion. That the state will make no promise to the people without specifying the sacrifice to be made.

(e) India can make rapid economic progress to become a developed country only through a globally competitive economy which requires assured access to the markets and technological innovations of the United States and its allies. This has concomitant political obligations which must be accepted as essential for national renaissance.

(f) Such rapid progress would require a national security strategy for a peaceful environment which necessacitates strong security ties with such as of those countries with which India has no intrinisic clash of interests.

(g) At present, generally the Indian has loyalty to the family but is apathetic to the community where he lives. The Indian does not easily acknowledge the accomplishment of others, respects intellectual endeavour but not dignity of labour, and is more concerned with form than content. Moreover, an Indian feels less accountable for his actions the higher he rises in authority. These are character flaws that have come from two centuries of deprivation and are incompatible with a people forming a great nation. These flaws can be rectified by developing a strong and coherent concept of national identity whose defining characteristics can be culled from a correct perception of Indian history.

This is an enormous but glorious task that we have undertaken to do. The Centre for National Renaissance therefore seeks ties with other like-minded institutions, think tanks, and international conservative foundations to benefit from their experience and thus be enabled to perform this momentous task.

The study is, therefore, undertaken to inform the dimensions of possible research for future scholars of the Centre. Although the views expressed herein are the author's, nevertheless the broad ideological framework is the *raison d'etre* of the Centre.

In this book, I have tried to blend my knowledge of politics as a practitioner with my familiarity with the academia as a former professor. I have propounded these eight Fundamentals to offer the native Indian a recipe for restoring the nation's glory through a renaissance. By accepting and owning these Fundamentals the vision of why we are Indians becomes patent and crystal clear.

I claim here no originality or research in writing this work. Instead, I have digested the existing literature on the subject and written the book with my own focus on Hindutva as a weapon of mass churning and upsurge in the society, to make Hindus rise above their petty local, linguistic and caste loyalities and weld themselves into a *virat akhand* Hindustani society, and thus make India a great country again.

SUBRAMANIAN SWAMY

For want of knowledge,
wisdom was lost

For want of wisdom,
character was lost

For want of character,
momentum was lost

For want of momentum,
wealth was lost

For want of wealth,
The down-trodden were lost.

All for want of knowledge was lost

Mahatma Jyotiba Phule

YOU ARE A VIRAT HINDU

If you can keep your head when all about you
Are losing theirs and blaming it on you,
If you can trust yourself when all men doubt you,
But make allowance for their doubting too,
If you can wait and not be tired by waiting,
Or being lied about, don't deal in lies,
Or being hated don't give way to hating,
And yet don't look too good, nor talk too wise;

If you can dream—and not make dreams your master
If you can think—and not make thoughts your aim,
If you can meet with Triumph and Disaster
And treat those two imposters just the same;
If you bear to hear the truth you're spoken
Twisted by knaves to make a trap for fools,
Or watch the things you gave your life to, broken,
And stoop and build' em up with worn-out tools;

If you can make one heap of all your winnings
And risk it on one turn of pitch-and-toss,
And lose, and start again at your beginnings
And never breathe a word about your loss,
If you can force your heart and nerve and sinews
To serve your turn long after they are gone
And so hold on when there is nothing in you
Except the Will which says to them: "Hold on!"

If you can talk with crowds and keep your virtue,
Or walk with kings—nor lose the common touch,

If neither foes nor loving friends can hurt you,
If all men count with you, but none too much;
If you can fill the unforgiving minute
With sixty seconds' worth of distance run,
Yours is the Earth and everything that's in it,
And—which is more—you'll be a Man, my son!

["If" of Rudyard Kipling; Title changed by this Author]

CONTENTS

Chapter I

INTRODUCTION

With the dismantling of the USSR into sixteen sovereign countries in 1991, and the balkanization of Yugoslavia into four in 1995, it is now clear that a nation's political ideology cannot by itself create social cohesion and preserve its integrity. Nor have we seen that even a cohesive religion can, by itself, be the glue to keep a people together as a nation, as demonstrated in Pakistan in 1971 and Indonesia recently. Race also cannot be a sufficient adhesive as shown by the prolonged conflicts in Sri Lanka and Nigeria, where a people of one race have been divided in civil war.

Hence we need to ponder what *has so far kept* for ten or more milleniums, and what *will keep* in the future, India together as a nation. Paradoxically, despite India's impressive record of keeping its integrity intact it has been long predicted, from Winston Churchill to Richard Nixon to recent Chinese blogs, that India is an artificial union that will disintegrate sooner or later. Churchill had predicted that it would take three years from 1947, while Nixon felt that dismemberment could be induced from outside. Chinese blogs think it is imminent.

But India has survived all the Cassandras, and since the British 'imposed' Partition of 1947 Indian territory has not shrunk since, even if every inch of it is *not yet* within its control. If at all, the geographical span of India has marginally increased with the merger of Sikkim in 1974. In 1962, 1977, and 1984 Indians have dramatically and publicly demonstrated their intrinsic unity and emotional solidarity.

From a study of nations that remain united and contrasted with those which have disintegrated, it seems that the crucial element for national integrity is the concept of 'who we are' that the people within a geo-political boundary accept. This concept however has to be nurtured, renewed, continually enriched and given substance. Such a concept however cannot be forced down the throats of a people, as the examples of USSR and Yugoslavia demonstrate or allow the concept as it did in Hitler's Germany to derail a society. At the same time the concept cannot be amorphous, meaning all things to all men, and without a time frame for its acceptance.

The late Dr. Samuel Huntington, a Harvard professor, has recently published a study (titled: *Who Are We?*) about the concept of US as a nation and its viability. He argues that the US as a nation is rooted in the 'American identity' which is constituted in two dimensions: *salience and substance. Salience* is the importance of one's national identity over other sub-national identities (of language, region, profession etc.), while *substance* is what one thinks he or she has in common and that which distinguishes this commonality from that of other peoples.

He suggests that a people with both, a definite salience and rich substance, will remain a nation, while others will not. Hence, Dr. Huntington argues, the US has remained a nation because salience over the last two and quarter centuries has been clearly defined and renewed. He thinks that the most recent renewal emerged out of the American sentiment against the terrorist atrocity on September 11, 2001 (now abbreviated the 9/11). The patriotic sentiment upsurged amongst the American people, dwarfing all other sub-national identities.

American identity is also sustained by the substance rooted in 'American creed', or what in popular parlance is called the 'American way'. Paraphrasing Dr. Huntington, the 'American creed' may be identified as (i) Anglo-Protestant work ethic (such as sticking to contracts, punctuality, word as bond, honouring IOUs etc.). (ii) Christianity-religious belief in God, in good being rewarded and evil being punished by Him. (iii) English language. (iv) Rule of law and equality before it. (v) Individualism and the pursuit of happiness. Dr. Huntington quotes a 1931 judgment of the Supreme Court in which the apex Court held that US is a Christian nation, and hence he advocates that acceptance of that is part of the American creed. We shall apply the concepts of salience and substance to Indian identity in the next chapter.

Since Independence from colonial rule, in 1947 Indians have been grappling with the question of 'who are we'? *This as-yet-unanswered question represents India's identity crisis.* The failure to date, to resolve this crisis, has not only confused the majority but confounded the minorities as well. However, without a resolution of the crisis, which requires an explicit clear answer to this question, the majority will never understand how to relate to the legacy of the nation, and to the minorities. Minorities would understand how to adjust with the majority only if this identity crisis is resolved. In other words, the present dysfunctional perceptional mismatch in understanding of who are we as a people, is behind most of the communal tension and inter-community distrust in the country. It also weakens India's integrity.

Unless we settle this question clearly, finally, unambiguously, and authoritatively as to who we are, Indians will flounder, flip-flop, and generally be devoid of healthy patriotism. The core fundamentals of the Indian nation are: to know our identity through a correct perception of our history, and to restructure our society on that basis. To achieve such a reform and usher a renaissance, of course, requires a complete de-falsification of Indian history, rejecting that portion that has been deliberately contrived by British imperialists and their compradors, and to correct the currently erroneously perceived linkages to our past.

A society based on dharma is vitally needed at this moment in our history, because there is a dimension to the current national crisis, namely, the moral decay and the decline of character in our society, symbolized by the epidemic of corruption, which if not stemmed, will slowly poison to death our nation. This decay and decline is visible in every aspect of our life- politicians defecting for office and cash, bureaucrats taking bribes, teachers selling exam questions, students passing by cheating, businessmen adulterating products, lawyers cheating clients, doctors betraying their patients etc.. To some extent such degeneration is there in every society, but the alarming aspect in India is the pace of this decay and the spread of it. Consequent to this decay is the rising wave of dangerous cynicism amongst the youth.

This moral decay has to be stemmed to safeguard India's integrity. A renaissance of values in society has to take place. How will this renaissance come about, and what shall be its instrument, on which we commit to an ideology and a determination to implement an agenda for renaissance. And what are the items of this agenda?

In India, the majority is the Hindu community which represents about 81% of the total Indian population, while minorities are constituted by Muslims (13%) and Christians (3%). Sikhs, Jains, Parsis, and some other small religious groups, represent the remaining three percent. These groups are also considered minorities by the government, but are really so close to the majority community in culture that they are considered as partners of Hindu society. Unlike Islam and Christianity, these minority religions are born as dissenting theologies of Hinduism. They share the distinct core concepts of Hindus such as re-incarnation, equality of all religions, respect for the cow, and ability by penance to meet God in this very life. That they feel increasingly alienated from Hindu society now a days is also the consequence of India's identity crisis.

The India of today would *not have been in existence* had the past attempts to divide Hindus succeeded. Over the last five centuries, there had been attempts to divide the Hindu community into castes and races, by targeted persecution, and by religious conversion, which attempts if had been successful, would have made the Islamic faith the single largest community in India. The religious tax 'jazia' was one such instrument to widen the caste gulf. Hindus bore it and by and large did not succumb to it.

In the early 20th century, a sinister attempt to divide the Hindu community on caste basis was made in 1932 when the British imperialists offered the scheduled castes a separate electorate. But shrewdly understanding the conspiracy to divide India, Mahatma Gandhi by his fast unto death and Dr. Ambedkar by his visionary rejection of separate electorate, foiled the attempt by signing the Poona Pact.

But the possibility that such attempts at dividing India socially maybe made again in the future, cannot be ruled out. Recently, under an implicit direction from Ms. Sonia Gandhi, a Congress leader from Kamataka, H. Hanumanthappa threatened to "fight-to-the-finish a struggle" to get separate electorate for scheduled castes. Indian patriots will have to watch such attempts very carefully. Segmentation, fragmentation, and finally balkanization have been part of the historical process in many countries to destroy national identity and thereby cause the political division of the nation itself.

The majority-minority question has dogged India for the last six decades and more in years of Independence. Paradoxically, the Hindus despite being over 80% are suffering from a complex, because Hindus of today are being confused by others on whether the Republic of India founded in 1947 is a legatee of the ancient Hindu India, or a new nation altogether forged as a by-product of British rule. This confusion, as we noted earlier, is at the core of the identity crisis. The confusion will however disappear if we decide which of these two we are.

Indian history books written by the British authors under the imperialist's patronage, and digested by the English educated intellectuals in India, have sought to foist the second concept. They have made out that India is a fusion of foreign invaders, first the Dravidians, then the Aryans, and then others. The British, they argued, gave us a central government which India never before had.

All this is of course bogus history, as Dr. B. R. Ambedkar in his forgotten writings on India history, has clearly shown.

Writing a research paper in 1916 titled "Castes in India; Their Mechanism, Genesis, and Development" for an Anthropology Department seminar at the prestigious Columbia University in New York, Dr. Ambedkar stated:

> "I venture to say that there is no country that can rival the Indian Peninsula with respect to the unity of its culture. It has not only a geographical unity, but it has over and above all a deeper and much more fundamental unity—the indubitable cultural unity that cover the land from end to end" *(Indian Antiquary. vol. XLI May, 1917, p. 84).*

Dr. Ambedkar said 90 years ago what is most relevant to say today. He understood and had the courage and erudition to say that the British had manipulated our history to suit their ends.

In 1947, the nation had no doubt inherited a host of dehumanizing feature such as poverty, communal antagonisms and human bondage of various kinds. However, human capital in the form of dedicated tested leadership and a heightened mass consciousness had been accumulated during the freedom struggle. But since then, because of the policies and programmes adopted by the Government and the political culture of the parties in power, this human capital has now been largely depleted. The inherited dehumanizing features have become further entrenched. The moral fibre of Indian society thus is weaker today than it was in 1947.

Since becoming free of British imperialist rule in 1947, India's ideological space had been for five decades circumscribed by a Left-leaning secular framework, with very little room left due to the patronage of the State, in the mainstream of thought for any other significantly different ideological perspective. Because of a dominant government controlling the commanding heights of the economy, ruled by a party that became increasingly authoritarian, any serious secular ideological challenge to this established thought was crushed at the nascent stage. Even when the nation faced a grave economic crisis, as in 1991, that required some dismantling of the oppressive regulatory system, it was dressed up as a natural evolution of the same framework.

But the author of this reform who dared to deviate more than necessary, namely. Prime Minister Narasimha Rao was disowned by his party and the Left, and then pilloried, defamed and criminally prosecuted till his heart gave out. Even in his last rites, he was not honoured. Instead he was made an example of, for other who doubted this framework.

In this suffocating atmosphere, only a right wing religious radical stance found a footing and gradually expanded onto the center stage of the national ideological platform. But within six years, that too fizzled out because of the leadership's inexplicable reluctance to make a clean and clear ideological break with the past and a pathetic craving for legitimacy from the Left leaning Socialist 'secular' Establishment.

But now, both the Left leaning secular socialists and the confused religious right have had their innings, and are unlike to regain the center stage. What remains today is an ideological mish mash that needs to be swept out. Till a new ideological framework is designed and presented with clarity to the people, the present hybrid ideological *ad hocism* will continue. This confused state of affairs however cannot steer the nation to new heights and world power status.

To research, propound, and propagate a new ideological framework that can unite the nation, make the people strive to global greatness and struggle for world power, the Centre for National Renaissance has been set up in New Delhi to be funded by the Naveen Hindustan Trust. My colleagues and I who constitute the Centre's Board of Governors have an established and an acknowledged record of dissenting from the past Left leaning ideological framework of the nation. This dissent has sometimes taken the form of struggle, and for that we have suffered denial of our due in our professional life, imposed by the state. We also were denounced as conservatives or reactionaries. But we have never wavered, convinced that the day will dawn when an alternative ideology of national renaissance will be needed by the country. Happily the new millennium has ushered in that dawn.

If the epithet of being a 'conservative' in ideology means we do not promise to create heaven on earth, then we are Conservatives. Conservatives promise change while preserving the best in our past. That is, we dare to change the things that we must and can, and await the moment when we can change that we must but cannot for now. The wisdom of an ideology lies delineating which is which. That is, we are not revolutionaries, nor are we libertarian anarchists, but we are for consistent, if only gradual, change brought about by the individual himself driven by his own interests, in the milieu of voluntary social actions and norms. We do believe that the individual can be and should be motivated by incentives, by equipping him with fundamental concepts of his individual, social and national identity, and empowered by adequate education.

The ideological framework to achieve national renaissance, which thus the Centre proposes to research, articulate and propagate in an intellectual challenging way, has the following markers:

(a) The state is to be minimalist in regulatory interventions in social and economic matters, maximalist in the maintenance of law and order, in opposing terrorism, and optimalist in providing the quality of life needs, while being politically accountable to the people in a democracy.

(b) A social ethos based on the concepts of trusteeship of wealth, philanthropy and voluntary group action is encouraged by religious sanction for the better distribution of income and for minimizing economic contradictions and deprivation.

(c) The key goal of the state is to empower the individual through a modern education that blends the essential concepts of spiritual commitment with material pursuits to enable the individual to be self-reliant and yet have strong character.

(d) The individual is persuaded by the state by incentives and not by coercion. The state will hence make no promise to the people without specifying the sacrifices to be made.

(e) India can make rapid economic progress to become a developed country only through a globally competitive economy that requires assured access to the markets and technological innovations of the United States and its allies. This has concomitant political obligations that must be accepted as essential for national renaissance.

(f) Such rapid progress would require a national security strategy for a peaceful environment which necessitates strong security ties with India's neighbours and with such of those countries with which India has no intrinsic clash of interests.

(g) At present, generally the Indian has loyalty to the family but is apathetic to the community where he lives. The Indian does not easily acknowledge the accomplishment of others. He respects intellectual endeavour but not dignity of labour, and is more concerned with form than content in personal and professional discourse. Moreover, an Indian feels less accountable for his actions the higher he rises in authority. These character flaws have come from four centuries of deprivation and colonialism. These flaws are incompatible with a people forming a great nation and can be rectified by developing a strong and coherent concept of national identity whose defining characteristics can be culled from a correct perception of India history.

I am persuaded that for defining our identity which factors in national integrity, it is essential to invoke our time tested ethos of Hindutva, the *Hinduness* imbibed in all of us. To elaborate this ethos, I have chosen to write this book titled: Hindutva and National Renaissance. The new Indian mindset must have the Hindutva architecture.

Chapter II

THE CONCEPT OF HINDUTVA

Hindutva is a concept that reflects the broad spiritual ethos of India, an ethos fostered by many great rishis, yogis and sanyasis, and their diverse teachings *but in one spiritual vision*. The word *Hindutva* was first explicitly used by Veer Savarkar to define nationalism. The word itself was popularized in mid-nineteenth century meaning "Hinduness."

In the context of the Hindu political struggle against British colonial rule, Sri Aurobindo gave the clearest exposition of national renaissance emanating from and founded in *Sanatana Dharma,* thus giving content and root meaning to Hindutva. Veer Savarkar gave it political currency.

In this study, we have essentially followed Sri Aurobindo's formulation of Hindutva, which though having the same goal as Savarkar's, is more broad-based. Hinduness springs from Sanatana Dharma in Sri Aurobindo's broader formulation as also in Savarkar's narrower formulation. In the final analysis, Hindutva as interpreted here conforms to Vedanta as propounded by Swami Vivekananda, and as also as re-interpreted by Gandhi, Golwalkar and Upadhyaya.

The Hindutva inspiration was the emotional spearhead for the first major nationalist struggle—the *Swadeshi* Movement, in which Aurobindo was a prime mover—the movement that followed the Partition of Bengal in 1905 but preceded Savarkar's writings. Taken together, today Hindutva is a multi-facet concept of identity, socio-constitutional order, modernity, our civilization history, economic philosophy and governance.

Sanatana Dharma is eternal because it is based *not* upon the teachings of a single preceptor of a chosen prophet but on the collective accumulated wisdom and inspiration of great seers and sages from the dawn of civilization. Hindu theology and scriptures therefore are accumulated revealed knowledge and not revelations of any prophet that was taken down by scribes or followers. In case of the Bible, St. Paul who compiled it had never met Jesus Christ, and therein lies an unresolved controversy on what Jesus actually said!

This unique feature of focusing on the message and its truth rather than the authority of the messenger brings *Sanatana Dharma* proximate to a science, and spiritually its logic akin to the scientific inquiry. In science also, a principle or a theory must stand or fall on its own merit and not on the authority of anyone. If Newton and Einstein are considered great scientists, it is because of the validity of their scientific theories. In that sense, science is also *apaurusheya*. Gravitation and Relativity are eternal laws of nature and existed long before Newton and Einstein 'discovered' it. These are cosmic laws that happened to be discovered by the scientific 'sages' Newton and Einstein. Their greatness lies in the fact that they discovered and revealed great scientific truths. But no one invokes Newton or Einstein as authority to 'prove' the truth of laws of nature. These laws stand on their own merit.

This is the greatest difference between *Sanatana Dharma* and religions like Christianity and Islam. In a document titled "Declaration of Lord Jesus," the Vatican proclaims non-Christians to be in a "gravely deficient situation" and that even non-Catholic churches have "defects" *because they do not acknowledge the primacy of the Pope and his infallibility.* This of course means that the Vatican refuses to acknowledge the spiritual right of the Hindus to their beliefs and practices! Christianity consigns all non-Christians to hell, and the only way they can save themselves from hell is by becoming Christians, preferably Catholics, and by submitting to the Pope.

A Hindu thus even if he lives a life of virtue, is still consigned to hell by Christianity because he refuses to acknowledge Jesus as the only savior and the Pope as his representative on earth. The same is true of Islam; one must submit to Prophet Muhammad as the last, in effect the only prophet, in order to be saved. Belief in God means nothing without belief in Christ as the savior or Muhammad as the Last Prophet.

Even one who believes in God but does not accept Jesus or Muhammad as intermediary is considered a non-believer and therefore a sinner or a Kafir. These two major religions simply do not tolerate pluralism. This is what makes both Christianity and Islam *exclusive*, what makes Hinduism pluralistic and tolerant, and *therefore Hindutva naturally inclusive*.

Hinduism recognizes no intermediary as the exclusive messenger of God. In fact the Rigveda itself says: '*ekam sat, vipra bahuda vadanti*,' meaning "cosmic truth is one, but the wise express it in many ways." The contrast between exclusivism and pluralism becomes clear when we compare what Krishna and Jesus Christ said.

Krishna in the *Bhagavadgita* says: "All creatures great and small – I am equal to all. I hate none nor have I any favourites … He that worships other gods with devotion, worships me." Jesus on the other is quoted as saying: "He that is not with me is against me."

Moreover, a Christian devotee cannot directly know God, but can only pray to God and go through the intermediary—who jealously guards his exclusive access to God. Those who try otherwise, even if a priest, is ex-communicated as was done in the case of Rev. Don Mario Muzzoleni, as he himself records in his recent book.

Don Mario Mazzoleni was a Catholic priest in Rome. He went in search of the Ultimate Truth and reached Sathya Sai Baba. He then spent 12 years studying the miracles at Puttaparti of Sathya Sai Baba and wrote a book called *A Catholic Priest Meets Sai Baba*. Bishop Monsignor Roberto Amadei of the Vatican then summoned him and expressed disapproval as seen below from an extract of the book [see pages 268-69]:

Bishop: They have telephoned me from Rome to tell me about this book of yours. You uphold some ideas which are not in line with those of the Church. For example, the Christ, for us, is Jesus Christ, and there cannot be anyone else. You made a distinction between Jesus and the Christ.

Mario: Yes, but I mean to say that there is a difference between the human and the divine nature of Jesus Christ: the first is the container, the other is the content; the first is illusory, the second is real.

Bishop: This is precisely the point of real divergence between what you say and the official doctrine of the church, the Magisterium. I cannot agree with your opinion. You end up putting Christ and Sai Baba on the same plane!

Mario: Not exactly in those terms, but I understand that it would be easy to interpret it that way. I know that it is difficult to explain it, especially with centuries of interpretations behind us, but, Monsignor, who can deny God permission to take whatever form He wishes whenever He wishes?

Bishop: Mario, God cannot contradict Himself. If He has revealed to us that He has come as savior only in Jesus Christ, He cannot break His word.

"The conversation continued. Bishop maintained that the Truth was revealed in toto and once and for all, by Christ, etc.. Nor did Jesus disappear as man: he is as eternal as the Christ, to the point that the two go together. I looked at him, puzzled; then I asked him:"

Mario: Are you maintaining that the body of Jesus still exists? But where, Monsignor?

Bishop: For example, in the Eucharist.

Mario: Tell that to any child, and he will tell you that he sees nothing but a piece of bread. I ask you please to tell me where the true body of Jesus, in flesh and blood, could be hidden or manifest.

Bishop: See Mario, here too you are not in agreement with the Church…

Mario: By why, Monsignor? Has the Church never made mistakes in its thought?

Bishop: Let's not get into that; it is beside the point.

Mario: Why do we have to come to a point where I am told 'Let's not get into that'? (it wasn't the first time that phrase had come up). Monsignor, permit me to ask you a provocative question. Our Scriptures tell us that the Christ will come again. How will we recognize Him?

Bishop: (after a moment of hesitation and confusion) That will happen at the end of history, when humanity will have finished its existence.

Mario: Even the astronomers say that this Universe is unbelievably vast and in continuous expansion; do you really believe that only the history of our tiny human race is marked by a single, definitive close?

Bishop: There is no other worlds. Therefore, that is how it is.

Mario: There is no need to posit the existence of other worlds … Besides, if humanity ends for good all at once, what would be the purpose of Christ returning in the flesh, in all His glory? To show Himself to whom?

"The bishop touched on a number of other themes, in the effort to convince me that I was wrong. It was not really an interrogation; rather he was sounding me out to see if I really thought as I wrote; and it became evident that indeed I did. My position seemed irredeemable, and all vestige of hope was lost when he subtly suggested that I change my mind, and I assured him that I would never, never at any time, betray what I felt and continue to feel in my conscience."

On May 24, 1992 Don Mario Mazzoleni was excommunicated from Catholic Church for his relationship with Sathya Sai Baba and for writing the book.

Hinduism is the exact opposite of this dogmatism and straitjacketing. Anyone can know God and no jealous intermediary can block his way. And the Hindu tradition has methods like yoga and meditation, guided if you like, through a guru to facilitate one to reach God. Further, this spiritual freedom extends even to atheism. One can be a non-believer (*nastik*), even an atheist and still claim to be a Hindu.

In addition, there is nothing to stop a Hindu from revering Jesus as the Son of God or Muhammad as a Prophet. In contrast, a Christian or a Muslim revering Rama or Krishna would be condemned to death as a Kafir or burnt on the stakes as Joan of Arc was, as a pagan possessed by the devil, or the enemy.

The main objective, in fact, of the *Sanatana Dharma* is to unfold the tremendous multi-dimensional potentialities of human intelligence, step by step, from the outer physical body level to subtle inner mental to intellectual and ultimately to the highest spiritual level, leading to Enlightenment and Self Realization. The human being is constituted by soul, mind and body, parallel in functions to a company incorporated constituted by a proprietor, manager and workers.

The ultimate goal of human life is to experience a deep sense of fulfillment. All else e.g., position, purse, power, prestige, prize, profession etc., are at best, simply the means to that goal which fulfillment be achieved only by acquiring and cultivating the ingredients of *Dharma* because the human, unlike the animal, can reason logically deductively and inductively to conceptualise, analyse, and theorise.

Besides the eternal and universal human values and norms in *Sanatana Dharma* prescription for other aspects of human life as well are embedded. *Sanatana Dharma* as expressed in different parts of the Vedas, has prescriptions for individuals living in different roles, e.g. as a mother (Matridharma), a father (Pitridharma), children (Putri/Putradhrma), a king (Rajadharma), a Guru (Gurudharma), a student (Shishyadharma), a woman (Naridharma), a husband (Patidharma) etc. *Sanatana Dharma* has provision as well for emergencies (Apatdharma) of different kinds. The Vedas are the basic and primary sources of *Sanatana Dharma* and are regarded as the roots of Dharma {*Vedokhilo dharmamulam* in Manusmriti 2/6}.

Thus scientific foundation and spirit of inquiry of Hindu theology has once again begun to find favour abroad. As Lisa Miller, a senior journalist with Newsweek [August 24-31, 2009] writes:

> "America is not a Christian nation. We are, it is true, a nation founded by Christians, and according to a 2008 survey, 76 percent of us continue to identify as Christian (still, that's the lowest percentage in American history). Of course, we are not a Hindu—or Muslim, or Jewish, or Wiccan—nation, either. A million-plus Hindus live in the United States, a fraction of the billion who live on earth. But recent poll data show that conceptually, at least, we are slowly becoming more like Hindus and less like traditional Christians in the ways we think about God, our selves, each other, and eternity."
>
> "The Rig Veda, the most ancient Hindu scripture, says this: "Truth is One, but the sages speak of it by many names." A Hindu believes there are many paths to God. Jesus is one way, the Qur'an is another, yoga practice is a third. None is better than any other; all are equal. The most traditional, conservative Christians have not been taught to think like this. They learn in Sunday school that their religion is true, and others are false. Jesus said, "I am the way, the truth, and the life. No one comes to the father except through me."
>
> "Americans are no longer buying it. According to a 2008 Pew Forum survey, 65 percent of us believe that "many religions can lead to eternal life"—including 37 percent of white evangelicals, the group most likely to believe that salvation is theirs alone. Also, the number of people who seek spiritual truth

outside church is growing. Thirty percent of Americans call themselves "spiritual, not religious," according to a 2009 NEWSWEEK Poll, up from 24 percent in 2005. Stephen Prothero, religion professor at Boston University, has long framed the American propensity for "the divine-deli-cafeteria religion" as "very much in the spirit of Hinduism. You're not picking and choosing from different religions, because they're all the same," he says. "It isn't about orthodoxy. It's about whatever works. If going to yoga works, great—and if going to Catholic mass works, great. And if going to Catholic mass plus the yoga plus the Buddhist retreat works, that's great, too."

"Then there's the question of what happens when you die. Christians traditionally believe that bodies and souls are sacred, that together they make up the "self," and that at the end of time they will be reunited in the Resurrection. You need both, in other words, and you need them forever. Hindus believe no such thing. At death, the body burns on a pyre, while the spirit—where identity resides—escapes. In reincarnation, central to Hinduism, selves come back to earth again and again in different bodies. So here is another way in which Americans are becoming more Hindu: 24 percent of Americans say they believe in reincarnation, according to a 2008 Harris poll. So agnostic are we about the ultimate fates of our bodies that we're burning them—like Hindus—after death. More than a third of Americans now choose cremation, according to the Cremation Association of North America, up from 6 percent in 1975. Let us all say 'Om'."

The Vedas are accepted as Divine Revelations by Hindu saints and sages who evolved and got purified by long and intensive penance, yoga, and meditation. These women and men of wisdom were called Rishikas (females) and Rishis (males).

Vedas are four in number - Rigveda, Yajurveda, Samaveda and Atharvaveda. The *Rigveda* directs the society to move and work in harmony, talk in harmony, practice Dharma for God Realization as the knowledgeable people of yore move from untruth to Truth; from darkness to Light and from morality to Immorality {Brihadaranyaka Upanishad, 1.3.28}. *Yajurveda* declared that the whole world is permeated by Almighty; therefore to enjoy it with sense of detachment and never to covet others property (First mantra of *Ishavasyopanisad*). The *Samaveda* advises that one should pray to the Lord who is Truth, Knowledge, Light, Protector of Dharma and the Savior from misery and diseases. *Atharvaveda* in essence seeks to lead humanity to peace through Enlightenment. The Vedas have six Vedangas, which help understanding the Vedas in proper perspective, and Upavedas, which explain and supplement the knowledge about different aspects of human life.

From the very beginning of creation, women and men have been treated on the basis of gender equality within the fold of the *Sanatana Dharma*. The Lord, it is said, got divided into two equal parts—one female and the other male from a genderless form. This is called *Arthanarishwar* with half male and half-female figure of Lord Shiva and Mother Parvati combined in one figure.

Thus accepting the concept that the genderless original Divine having been divided into two halves, one female and one male, the Vedas glorify both these manifestations in forms of female and male. For example, in Purusha Sukta and Rigveda one finds glorification of the Divine in male form whereas in the Devi Sukta of Atharvaveda the female form is equally glorified. Similarly in Vagambhrinisukta of Rigveda (10.10.125), all male gods pray to Devi and on being asked who she was, she says that she is Brahma (the same is said about the male Divine) and it is from her that both the Prakriti (the female element) and Purusha (the male element of Consciousness) and the whole creation has emerged. In other words, she herself is both Prakriti and Purusha, the visible physical Brahma and the invisible abstract Brahma, Rudra Shakti etc., In short it is Devi who is the source of power of all gods. Fire, Sun, Indra etc; and also that Brahma, Vishnu and Shiva as creator, maintainer and destroyer respectively all draw power from Shakti Devi to play their role. Shrisukta of Rigveda equally represents the grandeur and all-powerful nature of Almighty Goddess. In short Devi is Lakshmi the goddess of wealth, Saraswati goddess of knowledge and Mahakali goddess of destruction (of evils), all in one and the source of power and inspiration for all other gods and their activities.

Hinduism and its scriptures on yoga have a moral code. Twenty ethical guidelines called *yamas* and *niyamas*, "restraints and observances." These "dos" and "don'ts" are found in the ancient Vedas, in other holy texts expounding the path of yoga.

The yamas and niyamas are a common-sense code recorded in the section of the Vedas, called Upanishads, namely the Shandilya and the Varuha. They are also found in the Hatha Yoga, Pradipika by Gorakhnatha, the Tirumantiram of Tirumular and in the Yoga Sutras of Patanjali. The yamas and niyamas have been preserved through the centuries as the foundation, the first and second stage, of the eight staged practice of yoga.

Sage Patanjali said "these yamas are not limited by class, country, time (past, present or future) or situation. Hence they are called the universal great vows." The science of yama and niyama are the means to control the vitarkas, the cruel thoughts, which when acted upon result in injury to others, untruthfulness, hoarding, discontent, indolence or selfishness. For each vitarka possessed, you can create its opposite through yama and niyama, and make your life successful.

The ten yamas, the do nots, harness the instinctive nature, with its governing impulses of fear, anger, jealousy, selfishness, greed and lust. Second are illustrated the ten niyamas, the do's, the religious observances that cultivate and bring forth the refined soul qualities, lifting awareness into the consciousness of the higher charkas of love, compassion, selflessness, intelligence and bliss. Together the yamas and niyamas provide the foundation to support our yoga practice so that attainments in higher consciousness can be sustained.

Now, what has this all have to do with Hindutva?

Humans and animals have many common emotions such as hunger, fear, jealousy. But humans can reason and discriminate [vivek], theorise, deduce and invent which animals cannot. Humans have developed a complex behavioural system to regulate their lives. From very ancient times our maharshis have emphasized that humans must conduct their lives on a value system called *sanatana dharma*. That is the value system that we seek to nurture today on the basis of our ancient wisdom in order to optimize our social behavior, or in other words, the quality of being Hindu, or or possessing the attribute *Hindutva.*

That value system imparts a distinct quality that distinguishes the Hindu. Hindutva has stood our society a great deal of good because our Hindu civilisation is the longest continuous one. Today globalization seems to be eroding it, and Hindu civilization is under siege from hostile forces from terrorism and religious conversion. *Hence the concern for a national renaissance.*

What are these values, how they are being eroded, and what can be done about it? Hindu value system is a balance between hard skills (such as learning arts and science) and soft skills (such as morals and spirituality).

We find these values conceptually elaborated by Lord Krishna in the *Bhagvat Gita* and the practice of it as propounded by Patanjali in his *Yogasutras*. But we cannot simply read the texts and learn these gems of wisdom, because these have to be re-interpreted in the modern context by our spiritual gurus of today, as Swami Dayananda Sarasvati is doing.

Sanatana Dharma is an enlightened code of living which if we follow will keep us happy, stress free, and enable us to make progress in life without bitterness. The present life of materialism without regard to its harmony with spiritual values is disastrous and cause of unhappiness and life-threatening stress.

The first of such a code is: *never to complain about unfairness of life*. We however do so because of jealousy. But we do not complain when we get something good that we know we do not deserve. The same way we should not complain when we get something bad that we feel is unfair. According to Krishna, we deserve both, only that we do not realize it. If we understood the Law of *Karma* properly then we will not complain ever.

In modern language, God maintains an account of everybody's good and bad deeds i.e., *karmas,* and rewards and punishes accordingly in his discretion on timing, and scheme of things. That is, there is no direct linear relationship between effort and success. Krishna in fact says you have freedom of action and an unfettered right to work for a goal, but no right to expect that you will achieve or deserve that goal. For your efforts, you will be rewarded, if not in achieving your goal, but in some other place or venture where you have made no effort. Hence, work for a goal that you want but do not be attached to attaining it or miserable for failing to reach your goal.

There is no simple logical reason why or why not you attain a goal. It is a divine calculus of *karma*—accounting that decides the outcome. *This is the meaning of destiny.*

If we follow this principle then we shall never be stressed by failure or jealous of others who may achieve the goal you want to achieve. This is why US business firms today are teaching their executives Karma and Gita to reduce stress [as reported in *Business Week* magazine in 2007].

But in our country we are fast forgetting this dictum and are searching for short-cuts to a fast buck by cheating, fraud and corruption because our values have eroded to the point where we think that means do not matter, only results do if it means more money; the exact opposite of Gita's lessons. No wonder, Transparency International classes us as the most corrupt nation today. In 1947 we were more honest even when we were poorer.

Doing wrong things and going to temples to seek forgiveness, according to *Sanatana Dharma*, will not spare us. Bhismacharya's example is there—his suffering for the injustice done by him to Amba. Somewhere and sometime in this life, or next, we will pay or be rewarded for our karmas. Thus if one life is not enough to pay for or be rewarded to exhaust our past and this life's *Karmas* then we shall enter in the cycle of re-birth till it is all exhausted.

God thus in *Sanatana Dharma* does not favour anyone. If you pray to God for rewards very sincerely then he may re-schedule your good *karma* rewards but not erase your bad *karmas*. Its bad consequences will be postponed to later life. It is better therefore to exhaust all your bad karmas in early life so that we can enjoy good fortune in later life. But today, we burn out our youth in a promiscuous life, and then are miserable in old age.

You can pray for collective good of course. But the secret of a good life is to keep doing good all the time. Of course you must defend yourselves against evil, even by dubious means, for which we have *apatdharma* that needs social or collective sanction.

Second, a value that is prescribed in the Gita is to develop an evenness towards opposites like happy outcomes and unhappy ones, between pain and pleasure, profit and loss, good and bad news. We should not jump with joy at success and celebrate in wild weekend parties, and collapse with grief from failure, and drown oneself in whisky. Moreover, it is difficult to say when success is embedded in failure and vice versa. Hence take it all cheerfully advises Lord Krishna. But today we find only these extremes in behaviour, due to globalization of cultures, which has meant mostly westernization and pure materialism.

Third, value was built in the now discredited *Varna* social system. In it pristine purity, *Varna* system decentralized power: of knowledge, weapons, wealth, land, and enhanced nobility and the value of learning. Those in the pursuit of learning could not possess weapons, wealth or land. *Varna* has however today degenerated into a birth-based oppressive system and cannot be repaired. It has to be scrapped [see Chapter III].

Fourth, another value is courage which is even more important than achieving victory. Rana Pratap is revered, even though he lost, but Man Singh, his cousin, is despised even though he was secure. Same is true of Rani Lakshmi Bai and Netaji Subhash Bose.

Fifth, value is sacrifice for others without expecting a reward. This is called *nishkam karma*. You may be rewarded, but to make sacrifices expecting a reward is *infra dig*.

The single most important theme of Hinduism is the freedom of the spirit. Just as science insists on freedom in exploring the physical world, *Sanatana Dharma* embodies freedom in the exploration of the spiritual realm. But to do so requires mental and physical discipline, and this the yamas and niyamas provide—the code by which the freedom to attain spiritual enlightenment and bliss can be enjoyed. This is also Hindutva, the quality to attain mental clarity and bliss.

The spiritual tradition of *Sanatana Dharma*, which we call Hinduism includes the code of *Raj Dharma* and *Kshatra Dharma* that is needed to defend the nation. That is also part of Hindutva. This dharma is needed to defend society against hostile forces seeking to destroy society, especially its spiritual foundation. This is what happened during the medieval period when Islamic warriors tried to uproot Hinduism from its soil. But thanks to the heroism of both rulers and the common people, Hindutva defeated these forces and saved *Sanatana Dharma*. That is how today we are still overwhelmingly Hindu in numbers.

It is therefore of paramount importance today to understand what the role of Hindutva can play in the 21st century in defending the country against threats. This part of *Sanatana Dharma* is called *Kshatra dharma*. Those engaged in the defence of *Sanatana Dharama* are called *Kshatriyas*.

A *Kshatriya* does not necessarily fight with weapons. The intellect is an important as the gun. As Sri Aurobindo put it, what characterizes a *Kshatriya* is the *kshatriya spirit* which for the intellectual means: "We should be absolutely unsparing in our attack on whatever obstructs the growth of the nation, and never be afraid to call a spade a spade. Excessive good nature will never do... in serious politics. Respect of persons must give way to truth and conscience.... What India needs especially at this moment is aggressive virtues, the spirit of soaring idealism, bold creation, fearless resistance, courageous attack on the passive tamasic inertia that we already have too much."

His words ring true today. It was this 'tamasic inertia' as Sri Aurobindo called it that gave rise to endless appeasement of evil in the name of *ahimsa* – i.e., non-violence and compromise. Instead evil must always be resisted—by non-violence if possible or by force if necessary—but never appeased. At the intellectual level, this calls for taking, as also defending, currently unpopular positions without the slightest equivocation. It may also call for attacking fashionable ideas, such as free sex, as harmful to society. A *Kshatriya* must fight on all planes against such ideas. *This Kshatriya spirit is a part of Hindutva.*

Vidyaranya, Ramdas, Swami Vivekananda and Sri Aurobindo were sages, but they were also *Kshatriyas* in the intellectual field. They fought hostile forces—whether soldiers or propagandists like missionaries—with uncompromising force. Their weapons were truth and the power of intellect. Sri Aurobindo thus defined Indian nationalism in spiritual terms, which he received as a message in a Yogic meditation. He expressed it in public in his famous Uttarapara speech as follows:

> "It is this dharma that I am raising up before the world, it is this that I have perfected and developed through the *Rishis,* saints and Avatars, and is now going forth to do my work among the nations....... *When therefore it is said that India shall rise, it is Sanatana Dharma that shall rise.* When it is said that India shall be great, it is *Sanatana Dharma* that shall be great. When it is said that India shall expand and extend itself, it is *Sanatana Dharma* that shall expand and extent itself all over the world. It is for the Dharma and by the Dharma that India exists... *I say no*

longer that nationalism is a creed, a religion, a faith: I say that it is Sanatana Dharma which for us is the nationalism."

So the message clear: India and *Sanatana Dharma* exist for each other. *Sanatana Dharma* is our nationalism and our nationalism is *Sanatana Dharma*. Hindutva is the practical and political manifestation of *Sanatana Dharma*. It exists to defend *Sanatana Dharma*, while threatening no one unilaterally. This was the Hindustan that Sri Aurobindo and many other sages had dreamt about. It should also be our dream and goal today.

Vedic civilization endured for many centuries while providing prosperity and justice to all. This happened because it was based on a balance between power and dharma achieved through a collaboration between the rulers and the sages (or kings and rishis) of the land. The two of course can be separated but this understanding of the *Rishi* and King alliance propounded in the Rigveda can serve as a guide and inspiration to the future for India and the polity.

I want to emphasize that we use the terms 'Brahmana' and 'Kshatriya' to mean those who perform those functions, and not the illegitimate concept "castes" based on birth, as is held today. In fact English language commentaries on Hinduism do not even make a distinction between varna [four fold] and jati [innumerable] systems.

Krishna in the *Bhagavadgita* [Chapter IV, sloka 13] says: '*caturvarnyam maya srishtam guna-karma vibhagashah*'. This means: "The four classification (*varna*) are made by me based on character (*guna*) and duties (*karma*)." In due course, this became perverted as 'caste' based on birth—which we hold as a serious corruption of our dharma. By Krishna's call in the Gita, *Dr. Ambedkar was a Brahmin regardless of his birth,* because of his intellectual leadership and shunning of wealth. But yet we call him of Scheduled Caste. Instead he should be called Maharishi Ambedkar.

We owe it to Dr. M. V. Nadkarni for a brilliant study titled: "Is Caste System Intrinsic to Hinduism?" [*Economic and Political Weekly*,

November 8, 2003] wherein he has proved beyond anyone reasonable doubt that "it is necessary to demolish the myth that caste system is an intrinsic part of Hinduism." Dr. Nadkarni further argues very convincingly that "the caste system emerged and survived due to totally different factors, which had nothing to do with Hindu religion." He concludes his study with a highly perceptive remark that the caste sytem "has collapsed today because all its functions have collapsed. It has lost whatever relevance, role, utility, and justification it may have had."

The caste system was never meant to create a Brahmin hegemony or was conceived as birth based. Brahmins were those venerated because they led a simple life and were devoted education and religious theology. But to become a *rishi,* it was not necessary to be born of Brahmin parents. Valmiki, Veda Vyasa, Vishwamitra, and Kalidasa were not born in Brahmin families. Nor were Brahmins above the law. Ravana, a scholar of repute had to pay a heavy price for his abduction of Rama's wife. Caste identification instead was by gunas [virtues], as Lord Krishna told Arjuna according to the Uttara Gita, besides in the Gita [IV/13].

Nor the recent researches on DNA of Indians show any racial differences amongst castes. So why tolerate a system which at the very least is obsolete and a stumbling block in the way of total Hindu unity? I urge all the dharma gurus and acharyas, to find a way to campaign for the abolition of the caste system so that we may achieve a renaissance in Hinduism, or require that varna discipline prescribed, be followed strictly to be entitled to be of a particular varna.

True Brahman or spiritual knowledge always creates the appropriate Kshatra for social manifestation. The spiritual elite of a culture creates the appropriate intellectual and political elite to manifest it in the outer world. This was the Vedic ideal represented by the alliance of the Brahmin and the Kshatriya, particularly the king (raja) and his chief priest (purohita). The Brahmin without the Kshatriya is lame; the Kshatriya without the Brahmin is blind.

Yet, the Brahmins and Kshatriyas had their differences as well. The king with his prowess and passion has a natural pride that resists the truthful guidance of the genuine Brahmin, who ideally is motivated by selflessness and a spirituality that monitors and guides the ruler to function as a servant of the people.

The alliance of Brahama and Kshatra, therefore, is always difficult. Sometimes the Brahma Shakti, or power of spiritual knowledge, must subordinate and control the Kshatra Shakti, or political power, if it is impetuous, if not imperious. The Vedic Rishis sought to create the appropriate Kshatriya to support dharma but if they failed, the Rishis would withdraw support from the Kshatriya and try to create a new and better Kshatriya order. This is illustrated by the Brahmins killing Raja Vena, and then creating Adi Raja Prithu, the first national king of Hindustan.

In the *Kali Yuga*, a crass materialistic age, the Kshatriya Shakti or political force is dominated by greed and arrogance, and will not ordinarily follow any higher spiritual guidance. This is what we generally see in the world today, with political leaders ignoring any spiritual values. Instead they promote cultures of violence, sensation and self-indulgence that does not awaken the deeper and more refined impulses of humanity. This occurs when spirituality gets reduced to religious dogma or to mere superstition, rather than to a practical means of Self-realization, which is the real spiritual quest of *Sanatana Dharma*.

Brahma and Kshatra thus have an organic interrelationship as between the head and arms of the body. They should work best together for the good of humanity, by resolving their inherent tendency to conflict. The Kshatriya represents the height of worldly power. The Brahmin represents its subordination to a transcendent goal.

Even in Vedic times the Kshatriya or political class sometimes resisted spiritual guidance. This led to various conflicts between the Brahmins and the Kshatriyas, in which the Rishis had to oppose various kings, including those they once supported. The reverse of this also happened: sometimes Brahmins fell into the lure of worldly power. This led to instances in which the Brahmins became corrupt, and hence dharmic kings had to resist their own supposed guides who had become tainted with pride and greed. The Vedas record these Brahmin-Kshatriya conflicts, as well as their harmonies and alliances. Drona and Asvatthama are examples of Brahmins who were lured by wealth and power.

When kings refused to accept the guidance of their *purohita*, the spiritual idea of the kingdom failed. We find in the stories of Parashurama, the great Brahmin warrior who defeated the Kshatriyas or kingly families, or in the rivalry between Vasistha, the pure Brahmin, and Vishwamitra, the king who wanted to become a Brahmin, and became *sarvocha maharishi*. It even occurred when the Rishi Bharadvaja took over the throne from King Bharata, whose own sons could not demonstrate fitness to rule.

The Hindu idea of the dharmic king is also very different from a theocracy, or a rule by the church. The purohit never represented a church, institution or dogma. He functioned as an advisor, not as a censor or 'thought police'. One of the functions of the purohit was to make sure that the king was fit, not only politically but also spiritually. Thus, King Bharata disinherited his own sons as unfit to rule. Sagara disinherited his own son Asamanjas and made his grandson Anshuman his heir, who went on to become a great ruler. The Vedic idea of a dharmic king had a democratic side to it. The purohit—as *puro hita*—represented the people's interest. The rishis, therefore, gave the kings their privileges and enjoyments, but balanced these with duties and respect for the sages and the Dharma.

There are only skeletal remains of our glorious civilization that was once scientifically most advanced, and educated and wealthy. The present generation of Hindus therefore has to reconstruct this civilization and rebuild the cultural edifice from these skeletal remains. *This is what we call as national renaissance.*

Hindus have suffered from the long arduous journey of a thousand years of brutality, persecution and oppression of foreigners.

But Hindus have survived even if they have lost a lot. The biggest loss imposed by this past has been of our identity. Forgetting the old wounds, taking control of the life as it is, by learning from this bitter experience, the Indian psyche has now slowly started recognizing the need for an identity.

The question "Who are we?" is the first step in this search for that identity. It is an attempt to seek the foundation stone for a new Hindu Renaissance which is necessary for discarding dysfunctional trappings of the past. We are on the verge of an Indian cultural revolution that draws its sustenance and roots from our glorious past centuries of achievements, and of valour while in bondage.

In his "Paper on Hinduism" read at the World's Parliament of Religions, Chicago on 19th Sept 1983, Swami Vivekananda emphasized the common points agreed by all the Indian-born religions (or Indic religions): "From the high spiritual flights of the Vedanta philosophy, of which the latest discoveries of science seem like echoes, to the low ideas of idolatry with its multifarious mythology, the agnosticism of Buddhists, and the atheism of the Jains, each and all have a place in the Hindu's religion."

Swami Vivekananda thus listed seven common points of Indic religions:

1. Religion is received through revelation, the Vedas. By Vedas no books are meant. They mean the accumulated treasury of spiritual laws discovered by different sages in different bodies.
2. Creation is without beginning or end. Creation and creator can be likened to two lines without beginning and without end.
3. We are a spirit living in a body. We are not the body.
4. The present is determined by our past actions and the future by the present. There must have been causes before the present birth to make a man miserable or happy and those were his past actions. Also the natural habits of a new-born soul must have come from past lives.
5. The soul in its very essence is free, unbounded, holy, pure and

perfect. But the soul will go on evolving up or reverting back from birth to birth and death to death.

6. Worship Him, the God Almighty, through love, love for the love's sake without pre-conditions or expectation.
7. The whole object is by constant struggle to become perfect, to become divine, to reach God and see God. We can have the experience of God in this life.

Hindu is one, the Indian Constitution adopted on November 26, 1949 states, *who is not* a Muslim, Christian or Parsi. Not quite! This is a negative inaccurate identity. We shall define instead a "Hindustan as a nation of Hindus and those others who proudly acknowledge that their ancestors were Hindus." The Hindu has already defined above by his seven distinctive beliefs.

The sages saw, as analogous with the behavior of beasts, that life cannot be just to hunt for material needs and bodily urges, and decided that the human beings to realize his/her real goal of life, must follow certain discipline and rules of conduct, which the sages formulated in the name of Dharma. They consciously evolved these rules to ensure that the human being gradually and successively carries his journey from body-pleasures towards mental happiness and intellectual satisfaction, finally reaching a state of freedom from all wants and being one with ultimate Reality.

Fully conscious of human nature, they did not demean the importance of body and mind and their pleasures. They assigned due instrumental value to these aspects of material life but did not hesitate to impress on the need to invoke discriminatory and creative intellect (*Vivekbuddhi*) which distinguished the human from animal to realize their impermanence. It is true that desire for pleasure can neither be suppressed nor totally fulfilled but they can be sublimated from individual worldly affairs to the very realization of ultimate Truth, through gradual enlargement of narrow individual consciousness to universal Existence (*Vyashti* to *Samashti* to Srishti to *Parameshti*). This is *adarsh darshan* or enlightened experience. This is the essence of Hinduism, and therefore of Hindutva. Thus, Hindutva is Hinduness in terms of our indigenously (swadeshi) developed value-system which is founded on an *adarsh darshan* derived from our ancestral heritage.

The aim of this value-system is to avoid *cognitive dissonance* that is the mental disorientation that arises from contrasting and conflicting modes of thought. We cannot be noble if we posture to mislead, manipulate without social purpose, and be authoritarian.

The cognitive synchronization takes place when the individual is in a state of steady mind, and remains committed to redeeming society from unrighteous rule without fear or favour.

That means giving up a life style that requires having to change mental gears abruptly, often and completely every day. Thus the Hindutva mindset is focused and is of single pointedness of mind. There is therefore no equivocation but forthrightness, no temporization but steadfastness no procrastination but decisiveness, and no crass self-interest calculation but enlightened personal advancement. This is *Swadharma,* or creative conformism to values. This is the Hindutva mindset that we need to today.

The ultimate highest purpose of human endeavour is founded on sacrifice [tyaga] for the greater good. The Bhagavat Gita outlines seven *sequential* steps [in the seven verses-13-20 of chapter 12] describe how the perfect devotee can evolve on such tyaga:

SEVEN STAGES OF TYAGA IN BHAGAVAT GITA

1. Abstaining from evil and immoral deeds—lying, cheating, eating, drinking forbidden foods, lusting, violence, etc.,
2. Ceasing to perform with a selfish motive.
3. Giving up the thirst for enhancing one's fame, honour, social prestige etc.,
4. Taking service from another with a selfish motive—seeking to use others for self-aggrandisement.

5. Giving up sloth and procrastination in performance of one's duty.
6. Ceasing to entertain all sense of attachment with regard to action performed through the mind, speech, and body.
7. Totally disclaim do-ership to all actions with regard to all actions performed by mind, speech, and body.

The decline of India as a nation from its zenith of prosperity and civilization, began with the separation of spirituality from politics. The Rishi retreated from the world and the kings lost their guiding spirit. The idea gradually arose in India of the classical period that kingship was a worldly pursuit to be shunned by the wise. The example of the Buddha, who renounced his kingship to find *Nirvana,* became the prime influence. The growth of Buddhism with its emphasis on monastic life was partly responsible for this break between politics and spirituality.

This consequent weakening of the Kshatriyas contributed to India becoming prey to foreign invasions. In fact the parts of Akhand Hindustan that included Pakistan, Afghanistan and Iran that were Buddhist, fell quickly to the Islamic assault. Buddhist Central Asia, then also a part of Greater India, from Bukhara and Samarkand to Western China or the Tokharian region, fell to the first armies of Islam. Buddhism vanished almost without a trace. The Muslims easily wiped out Buddhism by destroying its monasteries and killing its monks. The Buddhist portions of India like Sind and East Bengal were the least able to resist Islam on the subcontinent as well.

This is not to say that everywhere Hindu areas of India resisted Islamic onslaught. Some gave up easily, others entered into alliances with the new invaders, sometimes against other Hindus.

However, when a balance of Brahma and Kshatra did occur there was a remarkable resistance to those outside forces. One can cite the great example of Samartha Ramdas, the great Yogi, and Shivaji, the great king, who in the seventeenth century prevented the

Islamic tyrant Aurangzeb from dominating the country. Shivaji followed the Yogi's guidance, who in turn projected his vision into the political sphere. Earlier, Shankaracharya of Sringeri re-converted two Muslim youth Bukka and Hakka, and founded the long lasting (3 centuries) Vijayanagaram Empire.

But after achieving Independence through struggle and fortitious circumstances, the purohit of the new India, Mahatma Gandhi committed two great mistakes (which is not to deny Mahatma's greatness). The first was turning *ahimsa*—a noble idea, into a dogma, a recipe for all situations. The second was anointing Jawaharlal Nehru, who was neither really a Gandhian nor a true Hindu, nor strong as a leader, prone to putting his personal image above national interests, to lead the country. Nehru had no sympathy with Hindu spiritual ideas, nor did he have any true Kshatriya qualities.

Nehru's vision was purely materialistic that had little place for any spirituality. He was motivated by western political ideologies and its audience, not by any dharmic teachings of India. Occasionally he would, as on the Kashmir issue, he act on the advice of Ms. Edwina Mountbatten, at a huge cost to the nation, that we are even today paying. The country became during his tenure dominated by an anti-spiritual Marxist political class, with loyalties to Moscow, Beijing or to Cambridge Leftists, not to India as an ancient civilization or possessed of Hindutva. Politicians and intellectuals thus soon became self-alienated and self-serving, under Nehru's rule, using their influence to promote their own personal and family interests even if destructive to real national unity. In short he was bereft of *Sanatana Dharma*.

Dharma is not an antiquated phenomenon which is unrelated to current practices, but is a living functioning paradigm of human behaviour. This is woven into the ideas of karma and birth and rebirth as also on the concept of ancestry and obligations to ancestors, which survives even death, and the survivor's responsibility links faith in rebirth and 'Pithr Dharma', namely the duty to the ancestor which duty continues even after his death.

This central feature of Hinduism, the idea of Dharma, is common to all Indic Religions (i.e. religions born in India). At the micro level, that is at the individual level, Dharma is a part of the rules of life instituted in what is known as the fourfold disciplines embedded in the concept of 'Purushartha', namely, 'Dharma', 'Artha', 'Kama', and 'Moksha'. At the macro level Dharma is structured on 'Vyakti' Dharma, that is, the individual's duty to the society, and 'Rashtra' Dharma, that is duty to the nation. Thus the human life at the individual and collective levels was defined in terms of the institution of Dharma. This comprehensive edifice founded on the consciousness of Dharma has preserved the integrity and personality of the Indian society for several millenniums thousands of years. Therefore it was regarded the foremost duty of all to protect Dharma at all levels so that Dharma in turn protects all. This is captured in the ancient Hindu concept "Dharmo Rakshati Rakshitaha," meaning, Dharma should be protected by you so that it protects you.

It is only the idea of Dharma, as practised by families irrespective of their Indic religious affiliations that has institutionalised a privatized social security system in India, entirely provided by families and communities. This practice of Dharma has saved the State of India from its failure to undertake the burden of a publicly administered social security. Dharma has prevented atomisation of the families and preserving to-date the noble ideas of 'Gruhastha Dharma' [duty of a householder] and 'Pithr Dharma' [duty to ancestors] which mandate and bind a person to provide for the elders and also look after the younger ones. Globalization and pure materialism is now threatening this social contract.

Thus the concept of dharma is founded on essentiality of character. Character is visualized in two dimensions—an individual's personal character [*vyaktigat charitra*] and his national character [*rashtriya charitra*]. Individual character without national character is of not of much value in nation building.

Character of a person has of course always been the most lofty attribute in Hindu religion. Thus Hindutva's first dimension is character. However, there can be no character in the personality make-up of an individual in Hinduism without a willingness to harmonise personal aspirations with national goals, and even the readiness, if necessary, to sacrifice personal gain for a larger national or social gain. This is the essence in Gita when Krishna Bhagvan keeps reminding Arjuna of his duty, while Arjuna attempts to wallow in self-pity because of his personal character, agonising in not wanting to harm his brothers and elders. This is also brought out when Draupadi was being disrobed; the Pandavas, Bhisma and Drona were standing mute because of their allegiance to a concept of personal character to respect a contract made while playing dice.

In the context of the new research on human intelligence and social behaviour, this fundamental concept of character may be re-stated as follows: Character is the adherence to norms that are founded in spirituality, and represents the intelligence of the person in its application to situations according to these norms.

Modern research on psychology suggests that such intelligence is in five dimensions—*cognitive*, and four other dimensions of collective intelligences—*emotional* [team spirit and rational risk-taking], *moral* [blending personal ambition with national goals], *social* [to resolve to defend civic rights of the weak, respect gender equality, and courage to fight injustice], and *spiritual* [to recognize and invoke the transformative power of the cosmic energy by neural wifi and thus gain extra logical knowledge as also free himself from greed and jealousy]. *A person has a truly and fully developed character if he has all five components of intelligence in his being.* Thus what modern research has now found. Recently, "green" intelligence, of respecting environment, has been added as the sixth intelligence.

Freedom of an individual is based on rights, enshrined in a Constitution, which is a social contract. A collection of people living in freedom is a free nation which nation can be called "Independent" only if the quality of each person's mindset encompasses dharma i.e., in attitudes to values, duties, inter-personal relations, and nationalism. A free nation of predominantly such citizens is only then fit to be called independent. *Today, India is free but not independent.*

This book has been inspired by a comment noted earlier above, of the greatest sage and sanyasi of the 20th century, namely Chandashekharendra Sarasvati, the Shankaracharya of Kanchi Kamakoti Mutt at Kanchipuram, TN, who is reverentially referred to as the *Parmacharya.* The great sage counseled the Indian leadership on August 15, 1947 that "having become free, we must translate that freedom into independence."

It is the content of that independence that should have concerned all thinkers since then, but did not. Prime Minister Nehru disregarded Parmacharya's advice, ignorantly perhaps thinking that freedom and independence were synonymous words. These words are however not synonyms, and moreover, without independence we cannot retain freedom either for long. That is the danger today.

Freedom is a physical attribute of a citizen's rights, such as the right to a livelihood, the freedom of travel etc., while independence of a nation rests on the quality of the citizen's thought such as his or her attitude to duties, morality, inter-personal relations, social commitment, and nationalism. This requires knowledge of the correct history of Hindustan a common language and a healthy mindset to act for the benefit of the nation. Hindutva embodies all these aspects.

Thus, individual and collective dharma provide the code of behaviour for the citizen and the nation-state, and *this code is invariant over time*, save the emphasis and urgency to be placed on its enforcement from time to time. Hence our legacy today is this eternal code or in another form the *Sanatana Dharma.*

THE PARAMETERS OF SANATANA DHARMA

Hinduism, as stated above, is not a theology founded on the revelation of a single prophet or constituted by a single scripture that which all adherents have to blindly believe in. It is instead accumulated wisdom of sages through centuries that has been codified as four Vedas, Upanishad, 18 Puranas, two Ithihasas, etc.. There is in Hinduism, for example, no 'Church' to belong to and to obey its dictums, or to believe in a 'Pope' who is held to be infallible, or to regard a 'Bible' as the sole Holy Book to specify what to believe in and what not to. Nor are there the likes of a Koran, Hadith or a Sura in Hinduism to goad the faithful in the name of submission to God, to commit as His direction violence against unbelievers termed as Kafirs and Dhimmis. Hindu theology instead formally accepts that all religions are paths that can lead to God, the Supreme even as Hinduism claims that its path is superior.

Definition of Fundamentalism

Therefore, structurally, there is no scope for a Hindu to be a fundamentalist. For, fundamentalism by definition requires an unquestioning commitment to a book or scripture in its pristine original version. For Hindus, there is no one scripture to revert to for theological purity since there are many scriptures which raise a plethora of beliefs that sustain faith, debates, and profound speculations on basic questions [e.g., Upanishads], such as on *advaita, dvaita, astika and nastika.* The art of questioning, debating and synthesizing are an integral part of Hindu theology viz., *shashtrathas.*

Nor does Hinduism have just one prophet to revere, or prohibits holding any other view of religious experience. But most of all, true Hindus are committed to the search for truth [including knowing what is truth], for which incessant debate is permitted. Fundamentalists on the other hand unquestioningly are committed to 'the Book'. This again is why Hindutva can never become fundamentalist, while Muslims and Christians can.

In a Supreme Court judgment, a Bench headed by Justice J.S.Verma in 1995 held: "It is a fallacy and an error of law to proceed on the presumption that any reference to *Hindutva* or Hinduism in a speech makes it automatically a speech based on Hindu religion as opposed to other religions or that the use of the word *Hindutva* or Hinduism *per se* depicts an attitude hostile to all persons practicing any religion other than the Hindu religion ... and it may well be that these words are used in a speech to emphasise the way of life of the Indian people and the Indian cultural ethos.... There is no such presumption permissible in law contrary to the several Constitution Bench decisions."

Hindus thus have a vast rainbow spectrum of scriptures and a monumental accumulated wisdom of many sages that is contained in the Vedas, Upanishads, Puranas etc., all of which intellectually hold that the Ultimate Truth is manifested in manifold ways just the colours of the rainbow blend into a single ray of white light or manifestly transparent. Culled from these scriptures are nine basic and liberal beliefs that constitute the Hindu-ness [that is, *Hindutva*] of a believer [see Box 1]. In brief it can be said that parameters of Hindu theology are *Satyam, Shivam, and Sundaram.*

Hinduism also formally acknowledges that that there are many paths to reach God and hence treats other religions with respect on the principle of *Sarva Pantha Sama Bhava* even if these paths are not considered *equally efficacious* for reaching the Divine. *That is why in Hindu civilisational history, there has never been burning of religious books of others, destructing places of these other religions, crucifying of prophets of other religions, holding of inquisitions or even disrespecting other schools of thought.* Jews and Zoroastrians suffering persecution in their own countries and elsewhere found safe refuge only in Hindu India and were assisted by Hindus to practice their religion freely. No other religion has this track record or proud legacy of accommodation.

This approach is now the law of the land. A Supreme Court constitutional Bench headed by Justice P. D. Gajendragadkar, delivered a judgement [(1966) 3 SCR 242] wherein the Bench commented, "*Unlike other religions in the world, the Hindu religion does not claim any one prophet; it does not worship any one God; it does not subscribe to any one dogma; it does not believe in any one philosophic concept; it does not follow any one set of religious rites or performances; in fact, it does not appear to satisfy the narrow traditional features of any religion on creed.*"

Hindus instead have always believed in *shashtrarthas* [debate] to convert others to their point of view. Hence, even when Buddha challenged the ritualistic practices of Hindus or Mahavira and Nanak gave fresh perspectives on Hindu concepts there was never any persecution or denunciation of these great seers. Indeed these visionary seers are considered as having benefitted Hinduism.

In the vast epistemology of Hindu theology, three pillars (triad) of Hindutva are *Satyam, Shivam* and *Sundaram* which has the ultimate goal of seeking oneness with the *Shashwat* (eternal) Cosmos. The concept of Dharma that is in accordance with this oneness can be said to be *Sanatana* (no end). This complexity has been elaborated by the aphoristic words *SATYAM SHIVAM SUNDARAM.* It means Hindus forever seek unity amidst diversity.

These three words compactly define "Hinduness" or Hindutva as completely and correctly as is possible. A rough English translation which is not very accurate of the aphorism, would be: Truth, Universal Welfare, Good Feeling of the Inner Being. This triad of Satyam, Shivam, Sundaram had been adopted in the later Augustinian synthesis of Christ and Plato as the classical triad of virtues—truth, beauty, and goodness—to become later a part of the Christian ethic.

Let us understand each of the concepts of Satyam, Shivam and Sundaram to appreciate the depth of the Hindu mind:

Satyam: The first fundamental condition for Hindu Dharm is Satyam or truth. The cosmos or the world is experienced by us through our senses and we make an image of the world or parts of it on our mind. If the image corresponds to the world as it exists, the image is truth or else it is not truth. Our capacities and abilities to see, observe, experience and understand are however limited. Hence, our ability to create mental images of the world is limited. Blind men feeling an elephant for example describe it in different ways. So do the biologist and poet look at a flower in different ways. We too therefore make different images of the world. Hindu accepts this difference in perspective-and therefore opinions-while at the same time giving utmost importance to Satyam or truth. If any idea or thought is against perceived truth, a Hindu will oppose it. That is why Hindus reject the notion that there is only one path to God.

It is important therefore to compare the commitment of a Hindu towards revealed truth with that of the followers of other religions. For a Christian, every word in Bible is the ultimate truth. During the reign of the Church, any attempt to even collect evidence that might contradict something written in the Bible was considered blasphemy and was punishable by death.

Hinduism, by its premises has never and can never be opposed to Science due to the fundamental belief in the search for truth. It was this belief in truth that led to the development and growth of science and knowledge in ancient India far ahead of any other country.

Ancient Indian behaviour codes state a general rule then it is followed up with exceptions. But untruthfulness was never the preferred mode; it was preferred only in situations of emergency e.g., when someone's life was at stake. Having made canons that favour truthfulness, the code-givers, being pragmatied, recognize that lapses will occur and thus concerned themselves with describing those lapses and prescribing appropriate punishments or penances. There was never a blanket approval or even a conditional one for lies. There were exceptions made but for emergencies. Even then, as in the case of Yudhistra and Aswatthama disinformation, the law of *karma* operated.

Nine Sutras where Lying is not Unequivocally Condemned in Hindu Code

Situation	Gautama	Vasistha	Manu
1. When could a verbal promise be broken?	When a request is made for an Unlawful (adharma) purpose, be should not give, even if he has already promised to do so (5.23)	—	A verbal agreement does not become binding, even when it is well supported, if what is said is outside the bounds of justice and outside customary business practice (8.164).
2. What circumstances extenuate the telling of a lie or invalidate a contract?	Untrue statements made by people who are angry, jubilant, afraid in pain, greedy, young, old, feeble-minded, drunk or mad are not sins causing loss of caste (5.24)	—	A contract is not valid when it is made by an unauthorized person or someone drunk, crazy, in pain, or totally dependent, or a child or an old man (8.163)
3. What types of lies are not criminal or sinful?	According to some, telling a lie at marriage, during sex, in jest, or in grief is not a sin (23.29), but not if it concerns an elder (23.30)	A man may tell a lie at marriage, during a sexual encounter, when his life is at stake, when there is a risk of losing all his property, and for the sake of a brahmin. These five types of lies, they say, do not entail the loss of caste (16.36)	But there is no crime in (false) oath about women one desires, marriages, fodder for cows, fuel, and helping a priest (8.112)
4. When is it not an offence, or even desirable, to give false testimony?	It is not an offence to give false testimony if an man's life depended On it (13.24), but not if it is the life of an evil man (13.25)	—	In a case where the telling the truth would cause the death of a servant, commoner, ruler, or priest, one should tell a lie, for that is better than truth (8.104).

Source: Ahiya, Dilip: "Mendacity in our Midst" Economic and Political Weekly, May 3.

It is this commitment to Satyam that makes Hindu theology unique. Even non-speaking of truth or breach of contract has been truthfully codified in the Shastras, as the Table shows summarises. These are part of *apat dharma* prescribed for extraordinary situations.

As a first step we have to inculcate in our youth the need for truthfulness and honesty. They must understand that no Indic religion, certainly not Hinduism tolerates falsehoods. I have heard many young students with half-baked knowledge tell me how lies are justified by quoting to me either the Aswathama incident in the Mahabharata, or Kautilya's Arthsastra. Neither the Mahabharatha nor the Arthasastra gives sanction to individuals or organizations for the speaking of lies. On the contrary, speaking lies invariably attracts the law of Karma except in situations of righteous war when Apatdharma prevails. In such rare situations, only if one's peers sanction it, those persons who stand not to personally benefit from such utterances, are authorised to make them in the interest of achieving victory of the righteous (in such a war). Even then some retribution accrues in later life. However, in a democratic society, our religious tradition can never ever sanction lies, and yet in the name of the same tradition endless lies are spoken everyday.

In Christianity by contrast, the Holy Book says that a man has more teeth and ribs than a woman. During the medieval period, it was blasphemy and criminal offence to try to gather evidence against this sacred book by counting the teeth or ribs of men and women. For hundreds of years no one in Europe could count teeth or ribs. In single-book-based religions such problems are likely to occur at some time or the other. Both Christianity and Islam have at some points in their history opposed science since it clashed with the truth as provided in their sacred books.

Box 1: Nine Beliefs of Hindutva

These nine beliefs summarize Hindutva, and given below:

1. **Reverence for Our Revealed Scriptures**
Hindus believe in the divinity of the Vedas, the world's most ancient scripture, and venerate the Agamas as equally revealed. These primordial hymns are God's word and the bedrock of Sanatana Dharma, which is the eternal religion (which has neither beginning nor end).

2. **All Pervasive Divinity**
Hindus believe in a one, all-pervasive Supreme Being who is both immanent and transcendent, both Creator and Unmanifest Reality.

3. **Three Worlds and Cycles of Creation**
Hindus believe there are three worlds of existence—physical, astral and causal—and that the universe undergoes endless cycles of creation, preservation and dissolution.

4. **The Law of Karma and Dharma**
Hindus believe in karma—the law of cause and effect by which each individual creates his own destiny by his thoughts, words and deeds—and in dharma, righteous living.

5. **Reincarnation and Liberation**
Hindus believe that the soul reincarnates, evolving through many births until all karmas have been resolved, and moksha—spiritual knowledge and liberation from the cycle of rebirth—is attained. Not a single soul will be eternally deprived of this destiny.

6. **Temples and the Inner Worlds**
Hindus believe that divine beings exist in unseen worlds and that temple worship, rituals sacraments as well as personal devotional create a communion with these devas and Gods.

7. **Yoga Guided by a Satguru**
Hindus believe that a spiritually awakened master, or satguru, is essential to know the Transcendent Absolute, as are personal discipline, good conduct, purification, pilgrimage, self-inquiry and meditation.

8. **Compassion and Noninjury**
Hindus believe that all life is sacred, to be loved and revered, and therefore practice ahimsa, "noninjury."

9. **Genuine Respect for Other Faiths**
Hindus believe that no particular religion teaches the only way to salvation above all others, but that all genuine religious paths are facets of God's Pure Love and Light, deserving tolerance and understanding.

Source: April/May/June, 2009 issue of *Hinduism Today,* published in Kuaivei, Hwaii, USA.

DIFFERENCES AND SIMILARITIES BETWEEN EASTERN AND WESTERN RELIGIONS

SIMILARITIES

Eastern View	Western View
On God and Devas: Belief in a Supreme Deity, maker of all souls and all things, and in lesser Deities and Mahadevas.	**On God and Devas:** Belief in a Supreme Deity, maker of all souls and all things, and in the angels and celestial hosts.
On Salvation and God's Will" Salvation is through strict obedience to God's will and the descent of His grace through the enlightened spiritual preceptor.	**On Salvation and God's Will:** Salvation is through strict obedience to God's will, usually through a messiah, prophet or priest.
On Good Conduct: Moral living is essential to spiritual progress, for unrighteous thoughts, words and deeds keep us from liberation.	**On Good Conduct:** Religion must be based on ethical and moral conduct, for their opposite leads us away from God.
On the Soul's Destiny: The purpose of life is to evolve, through experience, into our spiritual destiny. Things of the world are not the purpose of the world.	**On the Soul's Destiny:** Man's destiny lies beyond this world, which is but an opportunity for earning eternal joy or suffering.
On the Nature of Reality: There is more to reality than we experience with the five senses. The soul is immortal, deathless and eternal, ultimately liberated from rebirth.	**On the Nature of Reality:** There is more to reality than the things of this world. The soul is immortal, deathless and eternal, living forever in God's presence or separated from Him in an eternal Hell.

DIFFERENCES

Eastern View	Western View
On Paths to God: Man is free to choose his form of worship, for all paths lead ultimately to God. Sin is only of the mind, not of the soul, which is pure. There is no Judgment Day for God does not judge or punish.	**On Paths to God:** Only one path leads to God, others are false and futile. Everyone must convert to the one true religion. Failing that, the soul, laden with sin, will be damned on Judgment Day.
On Man's Plight: Man's suffering is but his soul's immaturity. he is ever on a progressive path which leads from ignorance to knowledge, from death to immortality.	**On Man's Plight:** Man's plight is due to disobedience to God's will, to non-belief and non-acceptance of His law.
On Hell: God is Love and is inextricably one with the soul, guiding it through karmas into the dharma and finally to, liberation. Hell is a lower astral realm, not a physical place; nor is it eternal. It exists as a period of karmic intensity or suffering, a state of mind in life or between lives.	**On Hell:** On Judgment Day the physical body of every soul that ever lived is brought to life. God consigns pure souls to heaven and sinners to hell, a physical place where the body burns without being consumed and one suffers the anguish of knowing he will never be with God.
On Evil: There is no intrinsic evil. All is good. All is God. No force in the world or in man opposes God, thought he veiling instinctive-intellectual mind keeps us from knowledge of Him.	**On Evil:** There is indeed genuine evil in the world, a living force which opposes God's will. This evil is embodied in Satan and his demons, and partially in man as one of his tendencies.

Box 2 contd.

Eastern View	Western View
On Virtue and Salvation: Virtuous conduct and right belief are the foundation of religious life, the first step toward higher mystical communion. Liberation requires knowledge and personal attainment, not mere belief.	**On Virtue and Salvation:** If one obeys God's commands for a moral and ethical life and believes in Him and in His Prophet—for example, Moses, Jesus, Mohammed or Zoroaster—salvation is assured.
On Religion's Origin: Religion is cosmic, eternal, transcending human history, which is cyclical. Stress is placed on revelation of God's presence in the here and now.	**On Religion's Origin:** Religion is historical, beginning with a prophet or event. Stress is on the past and on future rewards or punishments. History is linear, never to be repeated.
On Doctrines: Doctrines tend to be subtle, complex and even paradoxical. Freedom to worship and to believe in a variety of ways is predominant. Other paths are accepted as God's divine will at work. Universal and tolerant.	**On Doctrines:** Doctrines tend to be simple, clear and rational. Worship and belief are formalized, exacting and required. Other paths are endured, but not honored. Exclusivist and dogmatic.
On Enlightenment: The goals of enlightenment and liberation are to be found in this life, within the context of time, within man himself. Schools may be dual or non-dual.	**On Enlightenment:** Salvation comes at the end of the world, the end of time, and has nothing to do with enlightenment. Strictly dualistic. Minor mystical sects, provide exceptions.
On Sainthood: The path to saintliness is through self-discipline, purification, concentration and contemplation. Value is placed on ascetic ideals, individual sadhana, yoga and superconscious awakening.	**On Sainthood:** Path to saintliness is through self-sacrifice, submission to God and concern for others' others. Value is placed on good works, social concerns and scriptural study, with little emphasis on yoga.
On Worship: Worship is individual, highly ritualistic and meditative, centering around the temple and home shrine all days of the week.	**On worship:** Worship is congregational, simple in its rituals, centering around the church, Synagogue or mosque, mostly on a Sabbath day.
On Creation: The universe exists in endless cycles of creation, preservation and destruction. There is no absolute end to the world, neither is there a duality of God and world, but a unity.	**On Creation:** The world was created by God and at some point in the future will be forever destroyed by Him. He is distinct from it, and rules it from above. Stresses a dualistic nature of the world.
On the True God: There is but one true and absolute Self or God. All souls are destined to receive God's grace through experience on many paths according to their understanding, temperament and maturity, God is pure Love and Consciousness.	**On the True God:** There is but one true God and one true religion. Those who accept it will enjoy God's grace; all others, unless they repent and come to my God, will suffer eternally in hell. God is loving as well as wrathful.
On Proof of God: Proof of God's existence and love leis in direct communion, and indirectly through enlightened gurus, the God-Realized men of all ages, and the revealed scriptures they bring forth in every age.	**On Proof of God:** Proof of God's love and promise for man is in the person of His Prophet and in His unchanging and unique revealed scripture.

Box 2 contd.

Eastern View	Western View
On Knowing God: Personal, inner and often mystical experience of God is the crux of religion. Man can and ultimately must know God during earthly life. Individually oriented and introspective.	**On Knowing God:** It is presumptuous for man to seek personal knowledge of God. The linch-pin of religion is not experience but belief and faith, coupled with a virtuous life. Socially oriented and extroverted.

SHIVAM—After accepting Truth, it is necessary to go a step further and look at the welfare of the world. Every act, belief and thought of a human being must be evaluated on the basis of the criterion of welfare of the world. An act or belief or thought is not proper or acceptable if it does not promote the welfare of the world even though it may be based on Truth. For example, a person's strong desire may be a reality or a truth but if that satisfaction of the desire does not lead to universal welfare, it is not proper to permit the person to satisfy his desire. In the Vedas, a sloka summarises this idea of Shivam:

अयं निजः परो वेति गणना लघुचेतसाम्।
उदारचरितानां तु वसुधैव कुटुम्बकम्।।

"What is one's own or not is the calculation of those with small minds. Of those who are noble minded, indeed the world itself one family." Or alternatively, do not be petty about 'this is mine and this not yours', but have as your thought the welfare of the whole world as your family.

Just as there can be differences of opinion and perception in matters related to truth, there may be differences of opinion regarding the concept of universal welfare, which may change from time to time and from region to region and also based on the nature and aptitude of various individuals. Such differences of opinion are well accepted and hence there would be debate or discussion to resolve the differences [Shashtrathas]. The acceptance of differences based on the needs of place, time, and of individuals, has led to Hindu religious practices becoming different for each person, for every region and from time to time.

The concept of SHIVAM as universal welfare is based on the realities of time and place which is deeply embedded in the Hindu psyche. *That is* why India accepted abortion and legalized it without much protest. Or in matters such as equal electoral rights for women, there has been no dispute since the issues are examined on current merits rather than on the basis of books written a few centuries ago.

Thus, examples of contradictory behaviour and beliefs of Hindus that arises from different ground realities are too numerous to cite. There are Hindus who are strictly vegetarians while there are others who are permitted to eat meat. There are Hindus who fast on some days during the year while on the same days there are Hindus who would eat meat and offer meat to their family deities. The opposites are always justified by logic of welfare or Shivam as might be existing at that time and place.

SUNDARAM: The triad's third fundamental concept of Hindutva is *Sundaram*. Anything that leads to nice (or "Su") feelings in the inner being of a person can be called as Sundaram or aesthetic. It is very difficult to define the nice feelings in the inner being and each person may have his own opinion in the matter. The purpose of all arts is to give pleasure by creating nice aesthetic feelings. A Hindu accepts all arts and accepts each person's version of Sundaram. The Hindu thus accepts the asthetic freedom of the individual subject, of course, to Satyam and Shivam.

It may seem strange that something as obvious as aesthetics needs to be defined as a key fundamental block of human quality. Yet if we look at the treatment of the subject by other religions, the distinction is too glaring. Islam treats all visual arts like painting and sculpture as forbidden and even puts strictures on music. Christian churches have also from time to time made attempts to prescribe what *is* right and what is wrong in arts. In more than ten thousand years of history of Hinduism there have never been any such attempt of similar nature.

The triad SATYAM SHIVAM SUNDARAM thus expresses completely and comprehensively the essence of Hindu Dharma. It may well be asked that which of the three is more important and in case of conflict, which one should be given priority. There have been different opinions in this regard, yet a prominent view has been that the conflicts among the three are only apparent. Deep within there is a unity in the three elements of the triad. So, a fundamental conflict is not possible.

A Hindu is expected to follow all three elements of the triad and give due importance to each in his life. However, even while giving due importance to all three, it is likely that an individual may emphasize one or the other element depending on one's own nature and aptitude. For example, truth may be more important for a scientist while aesthetics may be the central concern for an artist. Both are members of one unified society and many such different persons combine together to form a balanced society which has the correct combination of Satyam, Shivam and Sundaram.

Thus holy triad can also be expressed as Science, Ethics and Art. Any one who accepts the triad as the fundamental basis of his belief system is a Hindu, irrespective of his/her geographic location, race, national loyalties, system of worship, deity of worship, food habits, language, etc. Defined in this manner, Hindu Dharma becomes a truly global religion of the modern world. Acquiring strengths from its ancient roots Hindu Dharma becomes the human-values-based religion of the modern scientific age. The ability to constantly transform itself enables Hindu Dharma to rejuvenate and always be fresh and new. Hindu Dharma is neither "opium for the masses" nor does it bind anyone in perennial chains. It is the liberator of mankind and is an engine of growth, prosperity and fulfillment for the individuals as well as for the society on a long term sustainable basis.

From this it is also clear why Prophet-based revealed religions always claim to be monotheistic; one God allows only one Intermediary. So every monotheistic religion also tends to be monopolistic. It also requires a thought police to enforce this belief system, just as every earthly dictator does. So they invariably become theocratic political systems. In contrast, in Hinduism, God is internal to the seeker. Each seeker can have his or her own version of God. Different traditions like Dvaita, Advaita and others represent different pathways. They exercise no authority and there is no clergy to enforce. This is why too Hindutva induces a democratic temper.

So the single most important theme of Hinduism is the freedom of the spirit to question, assimilated, synthesis and then re-question is the process of inquiry in Hindu theology search and Just as science insists on freedom in exploring the physical world, *Sanatana Dharma* embodies freedom in the exploration of the spiritual realm. Hindutva is spiritual scientific quality. This quality of inquiry has led Lisa Miller of *Newsweek* magazine to write as we saw above, that modern American is "conceptually, at least, are slowly becoming more like Hindus and less like traditional Christians in the ways we think about God, ourselves, each other and eternity." That is Hindutva is permeating USA by logical deduction and by osmosis.

THE IDENTITY OF AN INDIAN

Every nation must have an identity to be regarded distinct. Even in United States of America, a relatively young nation created by an influx of immigration from diverse countries, scholars have felt the need to define the identity of an American. Harvard Professor Samuel Huntington has penned a book titled *Who Are We?* [Penguin Books, India 2004] to define the American's identity as a "White Anglo-Saxon Christian who speaks English." It seems contrived since majority of Americans are not 'White', but Huntington is emphatic.

However, Huntington's contribution is in seeing the two components of this identity that define it: *Salience,* which is the importance that the citizen attributes to national identity over the other many sub-identities. Second, *Substance,* which is what the citizens think they have in common, and which distinguishes them from others of other countries.

We in India today do not have to conjure up a contrived identity as Huntington valiantly had to do, because for us *Salience* is imbedded in the concept of *Chakravartin,* which Chanakya had spelt out with great clarity, while *Substance* is what Hindus have always searched for and found unity in all our diversities in, thanks our spiritual and religious leaders. And that invariably is the Hinduness of our people, which we now call as *Hindutva.*

The whole world has known our vast territory and millions of the inhabitants for centuries and called us as 'India' and 'Indians' or 'Hind and Hindi' or as the Chinese know us even today both as nation and people as 'Yindu'. The root word in all these terms is 'Hindu', which word for the Persians, Arabs and Europeans meant a people living beyond the Sindhu river, and for the Chinese a people living beyond the Himalayas and bounded by the Indu Sagar [Indian Ocean].

Is today's India as a nation state a British imperialist by-product, or is an ancient nation of continuing unbroken civilization? In other words, in the past was the word 'India' used the way we today use 'Africa' or 'Europe' to denote a region of separate nations and cultures or was India always a nation of one culture of a people with a common history? The battle to settle the answer to this question is on today between the Indian nationalist and the internationalist liberal.

I can do no better than refer again [Chapter I, p. 30] to Dr. Ambedkar's paper presented in a seminar at Columbia University (in 1916!) and titled "Castes in India, Their Mechanism, Genesis and Development" wherein he stated:

"Ethnically all people [may] be heterogeneous. [But] it is the unity of culture that is the basis of homogeneity. Taking this for granted, I venture to say that there is no country that can rival the

Indian peninsula with respect to the unity of its culture. It has not only a geographic unity, but it has over and above all a deeper and much more fundamental unity—the indubitable cultural unity that covers the land from end to end." [p. 84]

Ambedkar wrote in this vein several such brilliant books, but alas, Nehru and his cohorts so thoroughly frustrated him and electorally humiliated him that in the end bitterness drove him to his sad end. We must honour him now as a great Maharshi and co-opt his writings as part of the Hindutva literature. Ambedkar never in substance disowned his views, in fact when he agreed to sign the Poona Pact in 1932, he reiterated it. Again re-iterated it when he refused to convert to Islam or Christianity (but did to Buddhism).

But despite Ambedkar's writings, British imperialist inspired historians and their tutees, and the Communists in tandem, have propounded India as a multi-nation artificial construct and as an administrative by-product of colonialism. These British Imperialists were clear about their design. Thus the Aryan-Dravidian theory, the racial basis of *varna*, the artificial construction of linguistic differences, and the Hindu-Muslim cultural divide, have all been fostered by them.

The Aryan Dravidian theory is centered on the thesis that the Rg Veda was written *no earlier* than 1500 BC, and that carbon-dating of Indus Valley's Mohendajaro/Harappa excavations place it as ending in 1500 BC. A pastoral society described in Vedas and a city civilization in the latter, could not be of the same people it is inferred.

'Arya', 'Dravida' were falsely given racial meaning. In the face of DNA evidence of all Indians, plus the reality of Sarasvati River held earlier as "mythical" to debunk the Vedas, most independent scholars now have disowned the racial/migration theory of Aryans & Dravidians.

The next division is varna's colour/caste basis. Hinduism nowhere in its Sruti scriptures states varna is skin colour-based. Although varna means "colour," it is used by the founding rishis,

Bhrigu and Baradwaja, as an insignia colour. Thus Brahmin is 'white', Shudra is 'black', *but Kshatriya is 'saffron' and Vaishya is 'Green'*!

Nor our languages are fundamentally different—Sanskrit vocabulary is common to all languages. Even Tamil has 40% or more words in common with Sanskrit. That is, Hindus are one indigenous people. Hindu culture and religion gives the geographical area its distinctiveness. The make this issue as a settled issue, we need a definition of who is an Hindu, and thereby Hindutva.

DEFINITION

I define therefore an Indian as one who is a Hindu, or one who acknowledges that his ancestors are Hindus. This concept would include willing Muslims, Christians, Parsis and Jews. Religion of any Indian can charge, but not his or her Hindu civilization culture. Thus Hinduism provides the foundation or the defining characteristic of an Indian.

The world knew us in these millenniums not as nomads but as a highly civilized people who produced exotic goods the world had never seen before and who were hospitable to visitors from abroad. Many travelers such as Fa Hsien, Yuan Chuang, Marco Polo, Vasco d'Gama, and Mark Twain wrote glowingly about the behaviourial quality of the Hindus, which can be summarized as the Hindu-ness [i.e., *Hindutva*] of the Indian people. For examples:

> "India was the cradle of the Human race, birth place of human speech, mother of history, grandmother of legend, great grandmother of traditions; the one land all men desire to see, and having once seen by even a glimpse, would not give that glimpse for all the shows of all the rest of globe combined."
>
> —*Mark Twain 1806.*

> "Whenever I have read any part of the Vedas, I have felt that some unearthly unknown light illuminated me. In the great teaching of the Vedas, there is no touch of the sectarianism. It is of ages, climes, and nationalities and is the royal road for the attainment of Great Knowledge. When I am at it, I feel that I am under the sprangled heavens of a summer night."
>
> —*Henry David Thoreau (Eminent author and Philosopher)*

> "India conquered and dominated China culturally for twenty centuries without having to send a single soldier across her border. This cultural quest was never imposed by India on her neighbours. It was the result of voluntary searching, voluntary learning, voluntary pilgrimage and voluntary acceptance on the part of China."
>
> —*Dr. Hu Shih, Ambassador of China to USA (1939-42) and President, Peking University (1936-39)*

More recently, Mr. Jonah Blank, an American journalist curious about this *Hindutva,* took a journey in 1991-92 from Ayodhya to Sri Lanka on the route taken by Lord Rama. He then wrote a book about titled: *Arrow of the Blue-Skinned God—Retracing the Ramayana Through India* [published by the well known Houghton Mifflin of Boston USA]. He writes:

> "India's land may be ruled by aliens from time to time, but never her mind, never her soul..... In the end, it is always India that does the digesting" [p.217]. He concludes: "But somehow a nebulous sense of "Indianness" does exist, and it binds together Gujaratis, Orissans, to Nagas who might seem to have nothing at all in common. Perhaps it is this elusive, undefinable [yet very real] link that has allowed the sub-continent's multitude of races to live in some rough semblance of harmony for four thousand years"[p.218].

Despite Blank's unthinking adherence to "facts" of Indian history as written out by British colonialists, the reality of his direct experiences from his travels in India makes him come to the opposite conclusion to the British colonialists viz., India has always existed because of the Indian-ness [read: Hindutva as *Substance*] of the people.

"In all the fleeting centuries of history" holds Dr. Radhakrishnan in his work on Indian Philosophy, "in all the vicissitudes, through which India has passed, a certain marked identity is visible. It has held fast to certain psychological traits which constitute its special heritage, and they will be the characteristic marks of the Indian people so long as they are privileged to have a separate existence."

"If we can abstract from the variety of opinion Dr. Radhakrishnan adds: and observe the general spirit of Indian thought, we shall find that it has a disposition to interpret life and nature in the way of *monistic* idealism, though this tendency is so plastic, living and manifold that it takes many forms and expresses itself in even mutually hostile teachings."

This Hindu-ness or *Hindutva* has been our identifying characteristic, by which we have been recognized world-wide. *The territory in which Hindus lived was known as Hindustan, i.e., a* specific area of a collective of persons who are bonded together by this Hindu-ness. The *Salience* thus was given religious and spiritual significance by *tirth yatra, kumbh mela,* common festivals, and in the celebration of events in the *Ithihasa,* viz., Ramayana and Mahabharata.

Hindu Rashtra thus defined, is our nation which is a modern Hindustan Republic today, whose foundation of which is also in the long unbroken Hindu civilisational history. Throughout this history we were a Hindu Republic and not a monarchy [a possible but weak exception being Asoka's reign]. In this ancient Republican concept, the king did not make policy or proclaim the law. The intellectually accomplished (but not birth-based or determined) elite in the society, known as Brahmans, framed the laws and state policy and the King (known as Kshatriya) implemented it. Thus it was ordained.

"I deem that country as the most virtuous land which promotes the healthy and friendly combination of *Brahma* and *Kshattra* powers for an integrated upliftment of the society along with the divine powers of the Gods of mundane power of the material resources" [Yajurveda XX-25].

Hindutva hence, is our innate nature, while Hindustan is our territorial body, but Hindu Rashtra is our republican soul. Hindu *panth* [religion] is however a theology of faith. Even if an Indian has a different faith from a Hindu, he or she can still be possessed of Hindutva. Since India was 100 percent Hindu a millennium ago, the only way any significant group could have a different faith in today's India is if they were converted from Hindu faith, or are of those one of whose ancestors were Hindus. Conversion of faith does not have to imply conversion to another culture or nature. Therefore, Hindutva can remain to be interred in a non-Hindu in India.

Hence, we can say that Hindustan is a country of Hindus and those others whose ancestors were Hindus. Acceptance with pride this reality by non-Hindus is to accept Hindutva. Hindu Rashtra is therefore a republican nation of Hindus and of those of other faiths who have Hindutva in them. *This formulation settles the question of identity of the Hindustani or Indian.*

We Indians have been waffling on the question of identity now for over six decades. Time is at hand to rectify that waffle by adopting an *Agenda for Action* to inculcate Hindutva as the core of our identity. Its implementation requires political action. *This is the goal of this book: to chart a road map for India that is Hindustan to become a Hindu Rashtra based on Hindutva.*

Hindutva however has to be inculcated in our people from values and norms that emerge out of Hindu renaissance, that is, a

Hindu theology which is shorn of the accumulated but unacceptable baggage of the past as also by co-opting new scientific discoveries, perceptions and by synergizing with modernity. This is the only way that Hindustan can become a modern Hindu Rashtra, thus achieving independence after having recovered our freedom [in 1947]—as *Parmacharya had wanted.*

Hindu-ness of outlook on life had been called *Hindutva* by Swami Vivekananda also and Hindutva's political perspective was subsequently developed by Veer Savarkar. Deendayal Upadhaya briefly dealt with the concept of Hindutva when he wrote about *chiti* in his seminal work: *Integral Humanism* [see Chapter VI]. The focus of all three profound thinkers is the multi-dimensional development of the Hindus as an individuals harmonizing material needs with spiritual advancement and which needs then have to be aggregated and synchronized to foster a united community on the collective concept of Hindutva.

I shall therefore rely on the works of all three visionaries to formulate the Agenda of Hindutva herein. Thus, I shall address the question of agenda of Hindutva for political action in later Chapters within the parameters set by Swami Vivekananda, Veer Savarkar and Deendayal Upadhyaya.

Swami Vivekananda defined Hindutva, upon returning from Chicago in 1896 in an address in Lahore as follows:

> "Mark me, then and then alone you are a Hindu when the very name Hindu sends through you a galvanic shock of strength. Then and then alone you are a Hindu when every man and woman who bears the name Hindu, from any country, speaking our language or any other language, becomes at once the nearest and dearest to you. Then and then alone you are a Hindu when the distress of anyone bearing the name Hindu comes to your heart and makes you fell as if your own son or daughter were in distress" [*Collected Works,* vol 3, page 379].

Paraphrasing what Veer Savarkar had said, the following is what he said enlightened Hindus need to tell India's minorities and others:

> "If you come along with us, *then with you.* If you do not, *then without you.*
> If you oppose us, *then inspite of you.* Hindutva shall prevail."

And Deendayal Upadhyaya outlined how to modernize the concepts of Hindutva as follows:

> "We have to discard the *status quo* mentality and usher in a new era. Indeed our efforts at reconstruction need not be clouded by prejudice or disregard for all that is inherited from our past. On the other hand, there is no need to cling to past institutions and traditions which have outlived their utility." *This is the essence of renaissance.*

Thus, we should invite Muslims and Christians to join us Hindus on the basis of common ancestry or even their return if they wish to our fold as Hindus, in this grand endeavour as Hindustanis, on the *substance* of our shared and common ancestry.

However, to defend this Hindutva it is essential to resolve an intrinsic paradox of Hindutva arising out of the individual freedom afforded by Hindu theology. The individual-centric distinctiveness of Hinduism, makes it possible to see millions of Hindus, for example, to come to Kumbh Mela on their own, without a *fatwa* or invitation, or travel subsidy, or even any publicity about date and place of the Mela, and peacefully and without guidance or dictation, perform their pujas and then depart. It is purely voluntary even as the state does not provide any organization. This is individualism *par excellence.*

With this kind of widespread voluntary commitment of Hindus, seen not only in Kumbh Mela, but in other pilgrimage occasions such as in Sabarimalai, Vaishno Devi, etc., and the reality of our tolerant civilisational history, can we feel secure that we Hindus can and will unite with a collective mindset when it becomes necessary to defend against sinister, sophisticated, and violent threats that the religion faces today from within and from abroad ?

We cannot be sure, because the Kumbh Mela spirit not only represents the innate strength of Hinduism, *but paradoxically also its main weakness.* That is, those who assemble at Kumbh Mela do it as an act of individual piety. Hindus do not go to Kumbh Mela to be with other Hindus in a religious congregation, but because they believe that their individual salvation lies in going there. But the current threats to Hindu religion requires a coordinated collective response. Therein lies the paradox to be resolved.

Hindus therefore lack the necessary modem mindset that can collectively bond the community in an inclusive virile wholesome unity, which is necessary today to meet the threats that religion faces from terrorism, conversions, religious minority appeasement, and distortions in the history textbooks. We can meet these threats if we define it, elaborate it by example, and organize for it.

Patriotic Hindus should understand this structural limitation in the theology of Hinduism, that is individualism, is mistakenly taken as apathy, but it requires us to find ways to rectify it for the national good. In the Ramjanmabhoomi Mandir campaign, and the Rama Setu Raksha Abhiyan, the VHP had demonstrated that this individualism is not apathy and that this limitation can be overcome by mass action.

This limitation must not only be overcome but we must try rectify it not on an *ad hoc basis* but on a durable foundation that is sustainable, because Hinduism is being targeted today as never before by terrorism, religious conversion, minority appeasement, debasement in history textbooks, and distortions in the mass media.

It is worthy of notice that, recognizing this limitation, Hindu spiritual leaders in the past have from time to time come forward to rectify it, whenever the need arose e.g., as the Sringeri

Shankaracharya did by founding the Vijayanagaram dynasty or Swami Ramdas did with Shivaji and the Mahratta campaign.

Such involvement of *sanyasis* is required even more urgently today. Following the lead taken in 1964 by Guru Golwalkar, the Sarsanghachalak of RSS, to bring the Sadhus and sanyasis, into a forum for which the VHP was founded. The VHP has since engaged in mobilization of the sants and sadhus through the Dharma Sansad, and now in the Dharma Raksha Manch for social action, which has become crucial for our spiritual consolidation. In fact, this is the real substance of India as Swami Vivekananda had aptly put it when he stated that: "National union of India must be a gathering up of its scattered spiritual forces. A Nation in India must be a union of those whose hearts beat to the same spiritual tune.... The common ground that we have is our sacred traditions, our religion. That is the only common ground ... upon that we shall have to build." For this purpose, Swami Dayananda Sarasvati has performed the miracle of setting up the Hindu Dharma Acharya Sabha [HDAS] of Shankaracharyas, Mahamandelshwars, Muttadeeshs, and Akharas, institutions of more than 100 years standing. Hence the HDAS is the first apex bodies of all major spiritual leaders of Hinduism. I have been privileged to be invited to all their meetings and address the congregation on specific topics of Hindutva.

Let us recall here that well before the birth of Christianity and Islam, Hindu religion had been intellectually dethroned by Hinayana Buddhism. But Adi Shankaracharya rethroned Hinduism through his famous *shastrarthas* [religious debate] and caused a renaissance in Buddhism itself, which later came to be known as Mahayana Buddhism, conceptually in complete harmony with, if not indistinguishable from Hindu theology. It is Mahayana Buddhism that spread to China, Cambodia and Vietnam.

In Tamil Nadu, the Azhwars and Nayanmars, also through *shastrarthas,* repositioned Hinduism after dethroning Jainism and Buddhism. Since then the Hindu dharmacharyas have always been looked up to whenever Hindu society faced a threat or crisis, for guidance to meet these dangers.

Religious persecution however later came to India with Islam and Christianity and through their instrumentalities, in which the Hindus became their targets thereafter. Even today in a 83% Hindu nation, that reality of targeting of Hindus exists in new and more camouflaged forms.

Hence, the essentiality of Hinduism, or alternatively the core quality of being a Hindu, which we may call as our Hindu-ness [i.e., *Hindutva*], is that theologically there is no danger of Hindutva, or the advocacy of the same, of ever degenerating into fundamentalism. In fact, so liberal, sophisticated, and focused on inward evolution is Hindu theology, that in a series of Supreme Court judgments, various Constitutional Benches found it hard even to define Hinduism and Hindutva as anything but a way of life, as we discover from an useful review of these judgments by Bal Apte MP [in *Supreme Court on Hindutva*, India First Foundation, 2005].

The danger lies therefore in not blending Hindutva individuality with the collective determination to defend Hinduism against the multi-faceted threats its faces today. Not only we must harmonise and blend Hindutva individuality with a collective but virat determination to defend it, but we Hindus must also invite Muslims and Christians to join in this grand endeavour of forging a virile identity on the basis of our shared and common ancestors, and repeat what Veer Savarkar had said: "If you come along, *then with you.* If you do not, *then without you. If* you oppose, *then inspite of you we shall prevail.*" Buddhists, Jains, Sikhs and Parsis are already with *us,* and we are with them. On this principle of Hindutva, we can shape events and form a new *Brihad Virat Akhand Hindustan.*

The identity of Indian is thus Hindustani; our nation a Hindu Rashtra i.e., a republican nation of Hindus and those others [non-Hindus] who proudly acknowledge that their ancestors were Hindus. *It is this acknowledgement that remains pending today.* We can accept Muslims and Christians as part of our Hindustani family when they proudly acknowledge this fact of common ancestry and accept furthermore that change religion does not require change of culture. Thus the cultural identity of India is undeniably, immutably, and obviously its Hindu-ness, that is *Hindutva.* A de-falsified Indian history would leave no one in doubt about it.

In history as is being currently taught in our educational institutions however, it is being clandestinely propagated that India has belonged culturally to those who forcibly occupied it. This is the theme around which the Islamic fundamentalists and fraud Christian crusaders are again at work, much as they were a thousand years ago, but of course in new dispensations, sophistication, and media forms.

The Hindu consciousness that is needed today therefore is that which encompasses the willingness and determination to collectively defend the faith from the erosion that is being induced by the disconnect with our glorious past through history books.

Thus the concept of intrinsic Hindu unity based on Hindutva, and India's Hindu foundation are dangerously under challenge by these forces. Tragically most Hindus today are not even cognizant of it because of the History being taught. That is why we need today to campaign today for inculcation of Hindutva, to wake up our people, for which we need a clear commitment an Agenda for change.

By a failure to usher in a renaissance after 1947 India has lost her opportunity to cleanse the accumulated dirt and unwanted baggage of the past. The nation missed a chance to demolish the birth-based caste theory as Ambedkar had wanted to do. The battering that the concept of Hindu unity and Indian identity has taken at the hands of Nehruvian secularists since 1947 has led to the present social malaise. Thus, even though Hindus are above 80 percent of the population in India, they have not been able to understand their roots in, and obligations to, the Hindu society in a pluralistic democracy. As a consequence the Hindu is under a siege today.

Today the sacrilege of Hindu concepts and hoary institutions is being carried out *not with* the crude brutality of past invasions, but with the sophistication of the constitutional instruments of law. The desecration of Hindu icons, for example the Kanchi Kamakoti Mutt, is being made to look legal, thereby completely confusing the Hindu people, and thus making them unable to recognize the danger, or to realize that Hindus have to unite to defend against the threats to their legacy. *We Hindus are not only under siege today; and we do no realize it!!* That is, what is truly alarming is that Hindu society could be dissembled today without much protest since we have been lulled into loss of self-esteem about our past or that the capacity to think collectively as Hindus has been grossly weakened.

Hindus are thus being today systematically prepared for psychological enslavement and conceptual capture by subtle brain-washing. Hindus are being lulled, while Muslims and Christians are being subject to relentless propaganda that they are different, and are citizens of India as would be a shareholder in a company that is run for profit, and not as those who are descendents of Hindus, and a product of conversion and force, and that they too have a duty to perform in protecting Hindu culture.

But, if this degeneration and disconnect are not rectified and repaired by a resolve to unite the people, the Indian nation may go into a tail spin and ultimately fade away like other civilizations, like Greece and Egypt, have for much the same reason.

To resist this siege, we need Hindutva. Numbers [of those claiming to be adherents to Hinduism] do not matter in today's information society. It is the durability and clarity of the Hindu mindset and quality of commitment to Hinduness of those who unite that matters in the forging of an instrument to fight this creeping danger.

However, today the Hindu mind suffers from a *cognitive dissonance,* that is, a mental disorientation that arises from conflicting modes of thought because it lacks a framework of consistent beliefs. Today's Hindu suffers from equivocation and temporization in his mindset in his craze to appear to be impartial and sound secular. We cannot be impartial or equivocate for example between the fire brigade and the fire. We are under a siege and we have to break through it and get it lifted. Equivocation and nonchalance at this juncture will destroy us.

Nor we Hindus can fight this existential threat *unless we first identify what we have to fight.* We cannot effectively respond unless we understand the nature and complexity of the challenge. What makes the task of defending Hinduism much more difficult today is that the oppressors are not obvious murderous entities as were Ghazni, Ghori, or Clive. The means of communication and the supply of funds in the hands of our enemies are multiples of that available in the past, for camouflaging their evil purposes.

That basic strategy of those who want to see a weak and pliant India remains the same as before: Making Hindus to lose their self esteem by disparaging their tradition, the strategy of British imperialists for the conquest of India. Only the tactics have changed. Now the target is the Hindu institutions and Hindu icons, and the route is not the creation of a comprador class of civil servants and Zamindar-revenue collectors as the British did to subdue the nation, but fostering a psychological milieu to denigrate the heritage and to delink the Hindu from his past legacy thereby causing a loss of self esteem and a pride in the nation's past, as had been attempted in the Rama Setu issue. This anti-Hindu charge is being led by pro-Marxist super secular state patronized intellectuals today.

This is understandable since Vedantic Hindutva is antithetical to Marxism. Marx had advocated that human history is capable of economic interpretation only and in this one-dimensional society, violent class struggle between the haves and have-nots is the only method of change. It must lead to the annihilation of the haves by the have-nots, which Marx termed as "revolutionary violence." He thought of religion as the "opium of the masses."

But the, challenge today confronting Hindus is much more difficult to meet than it was ever earlier in history, because the forces at work to erode and undermine Hindu faith, unlike before, are unseen, clandestine, pernicious, deceptive but most of all sophisticated and media-savvy.

Tragically therefore, a much larger numbers and more educated of Hindus have been unwittingly co-opted in this sinister conspiracy directed by foreigners who have no love for India and who also see much as Lord Macaulay did in the nineteenth century, that the hoary Hindu foundation of India is a stumbling block for the furtherance of their nefarious perfidious game.

The concept of a collective Hindu mindset is being ridiculed as chauvinist and retrograde, even fundamentalist. The BJP is regularly advised by its enemies to purge out Hindutva from its poll plank to become more "acceptable." This fatuous advice from enemies deserves to thrown into the dustbin where it belongs, but surprisingly voices are heard from the BJP leaders today that Hindutva is a cashed cheque that cannot be re-issued! There is nothing to debate on the relevance of Hindutva because such a debate would only be dysfunctional and will disrupt the synergy between voter appeal and cadre morale that is necessary for electoral success of the Hindutva forces.

It should always be remembered that despite all the wooing of Muslim vote by diluting the Hindutva agenda, even by eschewing any reference to it, the share of total Muslim vote received by the BJP never exceeded 5%, while the Congress' Party received a steady 36%. The future political action for electoral success for Hindutva forces therefore lies in acquiring a USP, which can be achieved only through Hindu ideological consolidation of the voters.

Hindu civilization, I argue, cannot be defended or protected merely by individual or personal piety or by performing of pujas. Hindus to survive collectively *require a new mindset today* to meet the growing challenge from this highly sophisticated multi-dimensional siege that is international in character, or risk over the next millennium perishing like the ancient Greeks, Egyptians, or Babylonians. It was a new mindset of the Jews after World War II that has kept Judaism alive and vibrant today.

Hindutva or Hinduness envisages a collective mindset that identifies India as the motherland from the Himalayas to the Indian Ocean and with it's glorious past. However pious a Hindu is, however prosperous Hindu temples become from doting devotees' offerings, *it is this collective mindset of the people that matters,* and not the piety of the individual alone in that collective.

It is suggested that in this Hindutva, the religious minorities can join in if they are proud of the truth that they are descendants of Hindus. Then our nation may be defined as Hindustan i.e., a land of Hindus and those others who proudly acknowledge that their ancestors are Hindus.

Eight Components of Hindutva

There are eight components of the Hindutva induced mindset that the nation needs today:

First, India's Hindus and others must regard and foster the concept of the nation as the unbroken civilization of Hindustan; and their common history of endeavours, struggles, defeats and victories. Ancient Hindus and their descendents have always lived in this area from the Himalayas to the Indian Ocean an area called Akhand Hindustan, and did not come from outside.

Second, Hindutva requires that national policies for development should synchronize and harmonize material goals with spiritual advancement, which is Deendayal Upadhyaya's Integral Humanism philosophy.

Third, Modern India is a Spiritual State that adopts the concept: *sarva pantha sama bhaava.* Hence the declaration in the Preamble of the Constitution that India is a Secular State should be replaced by that of a Spiritual State.

Fourth, a national law requiring prohibition of induced and collective religious conversion. Such a law will however not bar re-conversion to Hindu religion, or the return of any Indian to his or her ancestor's faith.

Fifth, that there is no theologically sanctioned concept of birth based social hierarchy. Varna never was conceived as birth-based in Hindu scriptures, but a choice that was subject to each abiding by the prescribed disciplines of that Varna. The present practice of birth-determined Varna is un-Hindu, and is excess baggage to be off-loaded and purged from the body-politic of the nation is the interest of a *virat* Hindu unity.

Sixth, all Hindus to qualify as true Hindus must make effort to learn Sanskrit and the Devanagari script, in addition to mother tongue, and pledge that one day in the future, Sanskrit will evolve to become India's link language since all the main Indian languages already have a large percentage of their vocabulary derived from or in common with Sanskrit. To re-throne Sanskrit, Hindi, vocabulary should keep Sanskritising Hindi itself becomes indistinguishable from Sanskrit, just as Pali became two thousand years ago.

Seventh, Hindus must prefer to lose everything they possess rather than submit to tyranny or to terrorism.

Eighth, the Hindutva art of governance would be structured on the principles of Ramrajya and the tenets Arthsastra of Chanakya the Hindu must have a mindset to retaliate when attacked. The retaliation must be massive enough to deter future attacks.

These eight attributes constitute a mindset that a modern Hindu must have to be in a position to confront the challenge that Hindu civilization is facing from Islamic terrorists and from fraud foreign

Christian missionaries, who unfortunately are also aided and abetted from within the country by confused Hindus.

Without such a virile mindset *which is virat Hindutva,* Hindus will be unable to confront the subversion and erosion that today undermine the Hindu foundation of India. This foundation is what makes India distinctive, and hence we must safeguard it with all the might and moral fibre that we have. National renaissance flows out from that.

Chapter III

HINDUTVA AND CONSTITUTION

India became free of colonial control in 1947. The Indian state power usurped by the Imperialists over a period of two centuries, was transferred to the Constituent Assembly of free India "legally" by the Indian Independence Act which was enacted in June 1947 by the British Parliament.

Guided by the President of the Constituent Assembly (CA) Dr. Rajendra Prasad, and steered by the Chairman of the Drafting Committee Dr. B. R. Ambedkar, the CA thereafter adopted a quasi-federal or quasi-unitary Constitution, i.e., unitary in substance with subsidiary federal principles, on the 26th of November, 1949. One of the most voluminous Constitutions of the world, it is also one of the most amended [over 90 amendments] since its adoption.

India is, according to the Constitution, a Union of States not a Federation of Provinces. Hence no state can secede from the Union, and no territory however small can be amputated out of India henceforth. States can be temporarily or partly administered by the Centre. Article 356 of the Constitution allows the Centre to take over the administration of any State for a temporary period. Articles 247 to 253 empower Parliament to enact laws and establish courts to enable the central Executive to supersede the state's Executive in administering law and order. There is a central civil service and a central police force positioned in the states. Thus, the essence or quality of the modern Indian Constitution is unitary. We must safeguard this quality for our national integrity.

The Constitution of a nation is the framework of principles, values, and canons on which the society's governance is rooted. It is either codified as a written document as in India and US, or unwritten and based on precedents as in UK. From the Constitution flow the criminal and civil statutes which lay down the laws which the citizen have to obey, and the failure to do so invites sanctions and punishments that include imprisonment and/or penalties such as a fine. Enforcement of these statutes is the Rule of Law.

In our Constitution, the Supreme Court of India has perhaps a wider jurisdiction than' the highest court in any other Constitution. That is, while citizen rights are defined by the Constitution, it is to be enforced and given content by the judiciary. The judiciary is neither subservient to the Government on the one hand nor to the people on the other. The judiciary therefore stands above the popular frenzy and the Government might.

As Parliament and Legislatures represent the Will of the sovereign people, the judiciary must represent the conscience of the sovereign people. One is secured by periodical elections, while the other is ensured by life-long training, character, and experience. These two uphold the constitutionality in the rule of law.

In order that the spirit of justice may prevail in the society, therefore a well defined Constitution and independent minded judges are as essential as the structure of Institutions, so that laws are understood and well-administered. Strong, impartial and capable judiciary is the greatest need of the hour today as we are passing through testing times globally.

The concept of Fundamental Rights {Part III of the Indian Constitution} was not a legacy of allegedly 'humane' British Colonial legacy, as British historians claim. The demand for constitutional guarantees of human rights by Indians was made as far back as in 1895 in the Constitution of India Bill, popularly called the Swaraj Bill, which was inspired by Lokmanya Tilak, one of the great freedom fighters and architects of India's independence. This Bill envisaged for India a Constitution guaranteeing to every one of its citizens freedom of expression, inviolability of one's house, right to property, equality before the law, equal opportunity of admission to public offices, right to present claims, petitions and complaints and right to personal liberty. This the British rejected.

In the Madras Session of the Indian National Congress in 1927 it was laid down that the basis of a future Constitution must be a declaration of fundamental rights. But the British Government's Simon Commission in 1930 turned down the demand for fundamental rights on the ground that "abstract declarations are useless, unless there exist the will and the means to make them effective." So much for the British claim of the legacy left behind by them!

In 1952, the Supreme Court held that fundamental rights were within the power of amendment granted under Article 368 of the Constitution. In 1965, though the question did not directly arise, the Supreme Court by a majority of three to two *reaffirmed* the view that the amending power could reach fundamental rights. Strong doubts were however expressed by two Judges, namely, Mr. Justice Hidayatullah and Mr. Justice Mudholkar about the amendability of fundamental rights.

But in 1967, the Supreme Court in the Goraknath case, by a thin majority of six to five reversed their earlier two rulings and held that Parliament had *no power* to amend any of the provisions of Part III of the Constitution so as to take away or abridge fundamental right {AIR 1967 SC 1641}. The Supreme Court held that a constitutional amendment had to conform to the provisions of fundamental rights just like any other ordinary law. Accordingly, if the constitutional amendment violated any fundamental right, it was unconstitutional.

A full Bench of thirteen Judges of the Supreme Court was constituted to consider the question of the validity of the Constitution (Twenty-fourth Amendment) Act. The case directly raised the issue of amendability of fundamental rights.

On April 24, 1973, the Supreme Court delivered its historic judgment in Kesavananda Bharati v. State of Kerala {AIR 1973 SC

1461}case. Six judges held that the power of amendment was plenary and was not subject to any implied and inherent limitations in respect of any matter, including fundamental rights. Six other judges and the CJI held that Parliament could not, in exercise of its amending power, destroy or damage the basic structure of the Constitution by altering the essential features of the Constitution and that fundamental rights were essential features of the Indian Constitution.

Accordingly, a constitutional amendment which merely abridged a fundamental right with 'reasonable restrictions' was not unconstitutional, *but if it abrogated* a fundamental right, the Supreme Court would strike it down as unconstitutional. Hence, by a majority of one, the concept of an *unamendable basic structure* of the Constitution came into vogue. *This is the first pillar of Constitutionality.*

Thus Part III consisting of Fundamental Rights became unamendable and hence beyond any Parliamentary majority. Unless a revolution scraps the Constitution, it is now a permanent given in Indian affairs. The fundamental rights incorporated in Part III of the Indian Constitution have a close similarity to the Universal Declaration of Human Rights, 1948 as can be seen from the table (Appendix I). During the course of the debates in the Constituent Assembly members had also referred to the Universal Declaration of Human Rights.

But in 1975, India experienced a threat to fundamental rights from a new angle-it's suspension. Prime Minister Mrs. Indira Gandhi claimed that the nation was threatened by internal disturbance. Part XVIII of the Indian Constitution deals with Emergency provisions that enable temporary suspension of fundamental rights. Article 352 had empowered the President to issue a Proclamation of Emergency if he was satisfied that a grave emergency existed whereby the security of India was threatened by war or external aggression or internal disturbance. Since this last expression was vague and liable to misuse as was in 1975-77, therefore by the Constitution (Forty-fourth Amendment) Act, 1978 during the Janata Party rule, the expression 'armed rebellion' was substituted for the expression "internal disturbance."

While a Proclamation of Emergency is in operation. Article 359 empowers the President to suspend the right to move any court for the enforcement of fundamental rights. The Supreme Court in its judgment in ADM Jabalpur v. S. Shukia (AIR 1976 SC 1207) held that right to life and personal liberty was suspended during the operation of the Proclamation of Emergency and during that period, the writ of *habeas corpus* is not available.

By reason of the amendment of Article 359 of the Constitution by the Constitution (Forty-fourth Amendment) Act, the provisions of Article 21 cannot now be suspended or derogated from even during an emergency. No court can hereafter rule that habeas corpus is not available during an emergency.

The relationship of fundamental rights with the Directive Principles of State Policy in Part IV of the Constitution has been a subject of considerable and continuing debate. A division of fundamental rights into two categories—justiciable and non-justiciable—was recommended by the Sapru Committee as early as 1945. At the time of framing the Constitution, the Advisory Committee on Fundamental Rights recommended:

"We have come to the conclusion that in addition to these fundamental rights, the Constitution should include certain directives of State Policy which, though not cognizable in any court of law, should be regarded as fundamental in the governance of the country."

Directive principles are not enforceable by any court but the principles laid down are, nevertheless, fundamental to the governance of the country and it is the duty of the State to apply these principles in making laws (Article 37). Part IV prescribes the goals or the ideals to be achieved by India as a Welfare State. Fundamental rights are the means for realizing these goals.

At one stage there was a sharp controversy regarding the role of fundamental rights vis-a-vis directive principles. Early judicial thinking took the view that directive principles were subsidiary or subordinate to fundamental rights.

The Constitution also prescribes the rights and duties of a citizen and it is the responsibility of the State to ensure the citizen gets his rights, as also encouraged to perform his duties as a part of the soft infrastructure *of* good governance.

The structure of our Constitution is consistent with the Hindu tradition, a part of Hindutva. Ancient Bharat or Hindustan was of *janapadas* and monarchs. But it was unitary in the sense that the concept of *chakravartin* [propounded by Chanakya], i.e., of a *sarvocch pramukh or chakravarti* prevailed in emergencies and war, while in normal times the regional kings always deferred to a national class of sages and *sanyasis* for making laws and policies, and acted according to their advice. This is equivalent to article 356 of the Constitution.

In that fundamental sense, while Hindu India may have been a union of kingdoms, it was fundamentally not a monarchy but a Republic. In a monarchy, the King made the laws and rendered justice, as also made policy but in Hindu tradition the king acted much as the President does in today's Indian Republic. The monarch acted always according the wishes and decisions of the court-based advisers, mostly prominent sages or Brahmins. Thus Hindu India was always a Republic, and except for the reign of Ashoka, never a monarchy. Nations thus make Constitutions but Constitutions do not constitute nations.

Because India's Constitution today is unitary with subsidiary federal principles for regional aspirations, and the judiciary and courts are national, therefore the Rajendra Prasad-monitored and Ambedkar-steered Constitution—making, was a continuation of the Hindu tradition. *This is the second pillar ofl constitutionality for us—the Hindutva essence*! These aspects were known to us as our *Smritis*. Therefore, it is appropriate here to explore ways by which Hindutva can be blend into the present Constitution more explicitly.

The framers of the Constitution of India also seemed to be aware of the Hindu heritage of India. A perusal of the final copy of the

Constitution, which was adopted by the Constituent Assembly on November 26, 1949, is most instructive in this regard. The Constitution includes twenty-two illustrations within its main body. These illustrations are listed at the beginning of the Constitution. The illustrations are apparently chosen to represent various periods and eras of Indian history.

These illustrations have been selected to represent the ethos and values of India, which the Constitution seeks to achieve through its written words. The framers of the Constitution appear to have had no doubt in their minds that the Hindu heritage of this country is the ballast on which the spirit of the Constitution sails.

The emphasis of these illustrations is on those symbols that encapsulate the most significant and authentic moments of a nation's history. The personality of Shri Rama, the enunciation of the Gita by Shri Krishna, the valour, humility and service of Shri Hanuman, the teachings of Bhagwan Buddha and Mahavira, the emphasis on academic pursuits symbolized by the Gurukul and the University of Nalanda. These images may not be said to exhaust the Hindu heritage, but they do capture the essential concerns of the Hindu mind: struggle against the evil forces, dedication to duty without passionate attachment, service and humility, compassion and charity, highest importance attached to learning and academic attainments, freedom to hold diverse opinions and view points and an uncompromising spiritual eclecticism. These are the virtues that the Constitution seeks to visually represent and legally enforce without favour and fear. The Constitution, it was intended, to represent Hindu ethos.

The illustrations selected to represent the 'Muslim' period *also* imply this intention: Only two illustrations have been selected: (i) A portrait of Akbar and (ii) portraits of Shivaji and Guru Gobind Singh.

From the whole range of Muslim themes, only Akbar is selected. Akbar come closest in his ideals and practices to what can be called the Hindu spirit: his relatively liberal politics, his reported refusal to make the Mughal state an instrument of exclusive Muslim hegemony, his relatively less hostile attitude towards Hindu religion, his refusal to treat Hindus as degraded dhimmies on account of religious belief. Akbar approximated to a certain extent the Hindu ideal of social and political behaviour and unsurprisingly found a place in the Constitution of India.

The other two men who represent the 'Muslim Period' are Shivaji and Guru Gobind Singh: men who fought the persecution and bigotry of the Mughal rule under the successors of Akbar, especially Aurangzeb. Akbar is chosen because he was liberal: Shivaji and Gobind Singh are chosen because they fought the oppression and cruelty of the Mughal state which was acting as the instrument of Islamic religious supremacy. They refused to recognize a political dispensation that functioned as an instrument for the fulfillment of Islamic religious agendas. They fought for safeguarding the dignity of their culture and religious values from the depredations of a theocratic Muslim state. The three represent the grand spiritual if secular, ethos of Hindutva. *The Constitution of India is cognizant of this fact.*

The pictures chosem from the British period and the era of India's freedom movement are also unique. The former era is represented by Tipu Sultan and Rani Lakshmi Bai, both inveterate warriors against European colonial domination, warriors whose battles were not defined in terms of mere speeches and slogans but enacted within the context of blood and sweat. Another figure chosen from the phase called 'Revolutionary movement for freedom' is Netaji Subhash Chandra Bose. One is compelled to ask the question: Why is Netaji chosen to represent the revolutionary movement for the freedom of India? The fact is that it was Netaji whose gallantry and dedication raised the morale of the freedom fighters and led to wider repercussion in other sections of Indian society. His courage, his sacrifice, his fighting spirit are the true values representative of the final assault of the Indian people on the edifice of colonial rule. The only person chosen to represent the theme 'India's Freedom Movement' is Mahatma Gandhi, whose deep association with Hindu values, Hind Swaraj and Ram Rajya are no hidden facts. The Constitution of India thus seems to have chosen very Hindu icons to represent its ethos.

The 'aroma' of Hinduness or Hindutva also permeates the most important constitutional and administrative units of the Indian state. Nowhere is it more apparent than in the august premises of the Indian Parliament—a house where matters of national concern are discussed and the fate of the nation is decided. The head of the Lok Sabha is the Speaker, and what we find inscribed holdly above the Chair of the speaker is the following: *Dharmachakra Pravartanaya* (for the turning of the wheel of righteousness). It is accepted by all that the notion of 'Dharma' is the most significant cultural signifier of the Hindu world. The rulers of ancient India had accepted the path of dharma as their area of political exertion and the managers of free India's politics accepted that notion by putting the *dharamachakra* on the national flag, and the related motto in the central place of the highest legislative body.

The Parliament of India bears prominent reminders of the Hindu ethos at many places:

(i) At door no. 1 is inscribed –

Lok Devarampatraarnu
Pashyema tvam vayam vera

(Chhandogya)

Open the door for the welfare of the people and show them the path of noble sovereignty.

(ii) At the door of the Central Hall -

Ayam nijah paroveti ganana laghuchetasam
Udarcharitanam tu vasudhaiva kutumbakam

(Panchantantra)

To think in terms of 'me' and 'others' in a narrow say; for the men of liberal character the whole world is one family.

(iii) On the dome near lift no. 1 –

Na sa sabhayata na santi vriddhah
Vriddhah na to ye na vadantidharmam

Dharmah sa no yatra na satyamasti
Satyamna tadyachhalambhyupaiti

(Mahabharat)

No assembly is a sabha which does not comprise elders; he is not an elder who does not speak according to dharma; no dharma survives without truthfulness; and every truth is necessarily devoid of cunning and deceit.

(iv) On the dome near lift no. 2 –

Sabha v na praveshtaya
Vakavyam va samanjasam
Abruvan vibruvan vapi
Naro bluvati kilvishi

(Manusmriti)

"Either do not enter the sabha or speak only according to dharma when you are inside it. Those who do not speak or speak untruthfully and unrighteously are partakers of sin."

These teachings—and there are many more—inscribed on the domes and walls of the Indian Parliament signify the values that the fathers of Indian democracy and parliamentarianism wanted to inculcate. It goes without saying that all the noble virtues included in the above mentioned aphorisms are derived from the Hindu heritage of India. The founding fathers seem to have found a deep consonance between India's Hindu ideals and the ideals of a modern secular democracy.

The impact of Hindu heritage and its value systems on the legal and administrative life of India becomes all the more apparent when one examines the core ideals adopted by various institutions. Some of the examples are as follows:

(i) Government of India—*Satyameva Jayate*
(ii) Lok Sabha—*Dharmachakra Pravartanaya*
(iii) Supreme Court—*Yato Dharmastato Jayah*

(iv) All India Radio—*Bahujanhitaya*
(v) Doordarshan—*Satyam Shivam Sundaram*
(vi) Indian Army—*Seva Asmakam Dharmah*
(vii) Indian Navy—*Shan No Varunah*
(viii) Indian Air Force—*Nabhah Sprisham Diptam*
(ix) Delhi University—*Nistha Dhriti Satyam*
(x) Life Insurance Corporation of India–*Yogakshemam Vahamyaham*

These ideals are ideals of the Hindu world. They do not convey religious dogmas, therefore no rituals or gods are invoked in them; they are civilisational values whose sanction comes from deep humanism and a commitment to a righteous way of life. They are noble virtues whose adoption was deemed to be relevant for the future of modern India's democratic polity. The Indian Constitution and the Indian polity pay their homage to the ancient value systems of the Hindu way of life, and Hindutva.

Thus the interpretations of the higher judiciary of the land, assigning the Hindu way or Hindutva to the centuries old socio-cultural underpinnings of India are not an exercise of mere juristic interpretation. It is more fundamentally the acknowledgement of those social, cultural, ideational and political norms that give the people and territory of India their defining identity.

Inspite of the currently fashionable denial by the purveyors of a warped secularism, the Hindu underpinning of India's milieu have been vested with great significance by the leaders of the freedom movement and has been subtly but insistently stated in the structures of the democratic institutions set up by Independent India. Our Constitution, our Parliament, our highest Judiciary, and other important organs of the state recognize most clearly that the ultimate normative sources of inspiration for shaping free India's destiny would remain the millennia old heritage of Hindu ideals and civilisational concerns.

The founding fathers of India's political regime seem to have no doubt in their minds that India can remain a pluralistic and democratic polity only to the extent that it adheres to the fundamental values of a democratic, poly form and pluralistic Hindutva.

So the question arises: Will Hindutva be a contradiction or violative of the Constitution? In other words, can Hindutva be incorporated by amending the present Constitution subject to the Basic Structure Rule? I find from my research that most major Hindutva goals do meet the test of Constitutionality and hence need to be pursued even under the present Constitution. Of the decisions of the Supreme Court commonly referred to as the "Hindutva decisions," the most important one is in *Manohar Joshi* [(1996)1 SCC 169].

In his election speeches Manohar Joshi, the winning Shiv Sena candidate had said that "[T]he first Hindu State will be established in Maharashtra." The High Court of Bombay set aside his election. But the Supreme Court restored Joshi's election observing that "a mere statement that the first Hindu State will be established in Maharashtra is by itself not an appeal for votes on the ground of his religion but the expression, at best, of such a hope."

The Court went much further and using the words "Hindu," "Hinduism" and "Hindutva" interchangeably observed that those terms were not amenable to any precise definition and no meaning in the abstract *would confine the term "Hindutva" to the narrow limits of religion alone*. The Court further observed, "[T]he term 'Hindutva' is "related more to the way of life of the people in the sub-continent. It is difficult to appreciate how in the face of [prior rulings] the term "Hindutva" or "Hinduism" per se, in the abstract, can be assumed to mean and be equated with narrow fundamentalist Hindu religious bigotry...." (p. 159, para 37).

First, Rule of Law which is governance based on citizens' rights and duties, is structured in the Constitution of a nation while the enforcement mechanisms are based on procedures set out in the Constitution [e.g., Article 226 and 32 on Writs] and statutes consistent with it. The Courts provide as an independent judiciary, the interpretations of and direction to the State of the same by. In Hindu tradition, there is a highly sophisticated body of rules of interpretation and procedures prescribed in Jaimini's *Mimamsa* (in Sanskrit means "investigation") which sums up the general rules of *Nyaya*. Can we blend Mimamsa rules into the Constitution? Yes indeed. Recently, a Supreme Court judge Markandeya Katju in open court suggested the use of Mimamsa rules to fill the gaps in the traditional western Maxwell procedures in our courts.

Thus, Constitutionality consists of the *quality* of the statutes, of enforcement procedures of rights and the performance of duties, in conformity with the provisions and principles of the Constitution. This quality can be imbibed by us from the glorious Hindu texts of Mimamsa and Vedanta. In the name of modernity, defined as by our elite as anything Western, we have shown scant regard for our ancient tradition of legal argumentation. The Supreme Court on December 18, 2007 the UP State Agro Industrial Ltd case observed that the Mimamsa Rules of Interpretation (MRI) were still relevant and ought to be used in Courts alongside the traditional Maxwell Rules. Mimamsa Rules have been used by our *rishis*, since Jaimini wrote his Sutras, to resolve conflict between various Smritis. The Supreme Court applied these Rules to classify "animal driven vehicles" in their judgment.

A Bench of Justice Markandey Katju and Justice A. K. Ganguly in its order in another case said "It is deeply regrettable that in our Courts of law, lawyers quote Maxwell and Craies but nobody refers to the MRI. Most of today's lawyers would not have even heard of its existence. Today our so-called educated people are largely ignorant about the great intellectual achievements of our ancestors and the intellectual treasury which they have bequeathed us."

The Bench said further: "the Mimansa Principles were our traditional system of interpretation of legal texts. Although originally they were created for interpreting religious texts [pertaining to the Yagya sacrifice], gradually they came to be utilised for interpreting legal texts and also for interpreting texts on philosophy, grammar, etc. i.e. they became of universal application. Thus, Shankaracharya has used the *Mimansa adhikaranas in his bhashya* on the Vedanta sutras. There were hundreds of books [all in Sanskrit] written on the subject, though only a few dozens have survived the ravages of time, but even these show how deep our ancestors went into the subject of interpretation."

The Mimansa or the Purva Mimansa Rules to be exact, were laid down by Jaimini in his *Sutras* written around 600 B.C. That they are very ancient is proved by the fact that they are referred to in many Smritis which themselves are very old. Thus, the Apastamba Sutras copiously refer to Jaimini's principles. Since these Sutras are written in very concise form it became necessary to explain them. Many commentaries were written on them, the main ones being of Sabara, who lived around Second Century A.D., and Kumarila Bhatta and Prabhakara, who lived around the Eighth Century A.D.

Before mentioning some of the Mimansa Principles it is necessary to give a short background. Classical Hindu Philosophy has six schools (shatdarshan) all of which aim at Moksha (liberation). Purva Mimansa is one of these schools, and according to it one can achieve Moksha by performing Yagya (sacrifice) in accordance with the Shastras. The Shastras consist of Shruti and Smriti, the former being superior to the latter. Shruti consists of the four Vedas, the Brahmanas, the Aranyaks and the Upanishads. Brahmanas are treatises written in prose which prescribe methods of performing various Yagyas. To every Veda one or more Brahmanas are attached. Thus, the Aitareya Brahmana is attached to the Rig Veda, the Taitareya Brahmana to the Black Yajur Veda, the Shatapatha Brahmana to the White Yajur Veda, and the Tandya Brahmana to the Sama Veda.

After Shankaracharya's historic victory over Mandana Misra, Purva Mimansa, as a philosophic system, declined in importance. Shankaracharya was a proponent of Uttar Mimansa (also known as Vedanta), according to which Moksha can be achieved by knowledge of Brahma. Shankaracharya preached that Jnanakanda (the Vedantic Path) is superior to Karmakanda (the performance of Yagya). He shifted the emphasis in the Shrutis from the Brahmanas to the

Upanishads, and his view was accepted, and ever since Vedanta became the dominant school of Hindu philosophy.

However, though Purva Mimansa lost prominence to Vedanta in Philosophy, its importance remained as paramount as before in the legal sphere. It must however be clarified that the Mimansaks were not jurists. Their aim was to perform the Yagya properly, for they sincerely believed that this was the means to achieve moksha. For the conduct of Yagyas in accordance with the rules they had to devise a system of interpretation to resolve the conflicts, ambiguities, etc. in the Shrutis, which were aggravated by the archaic, pre-Panini Sanskrit employed in the Vedic texts. No doubt the principles of interpretation were initially evolved to resolve conflicts that arose in connection with the meaning of rules governing performance of the Yagya, but gradually these principles came to be accepted for interpreting legal texts also which were mixed up with religious rules in the Smritis. It was therefore natural that our great commentators like Vijnaneshwara, Jimutvahana, etc. had utilised these Mimansa principles whenever faced with any ambiguity or conflict in the various Shastras. Unfortunately, there has not been much effort to explain these principles. The advent of Anglo-Saxon Law coerced on us must have been responsible for this lack of study.

The Mimansa principles are in two respects superior to Maxwell's principles of interpretation, viz.: (1) They can be utilised not only for interpreting statutes but also judgments, whereas Maxwell's principles can only be used for interpreting statutory law, (2) They are more detailed and systematic.

The Mimansa Principles distinguish between obligatory statements and non-obligatory statements. The main obligatory rule is called a Vidhi (or a Pratishedh, if it is in negative form). Vidhis are of 4 types, (1) Utpatti Vidhi, or a substantive injunction (e.g. 'perform the agnihotra'), (2) Viniyoga Vidhi, or applicatory rules (e.g. 'with curdled milk perform the agnihotra'), (3) Prayog Vidhi, or rules of procedure, and (4) Adhikara Vidhis (rules regarding rights and personal competence). Apart from these Vidhis proper (mentioned above) there are also certain quasi Vidhis called niyamas and parishankhyas, but it is not necessary to go into details here. Vidhis are found in Brahmanas.

The main non-obligatory statement is known as an Arthavada. An Arthavada is a statement of praise or explanation. Most of the Vedas proper consist of Arthavadas as much of the Vedic hymns are in praise of some god, and do not lay down any injunction. Arthavada is like the preamble or statement of objects in a statute. An Arthavada has no legal force by itself, but it is not entirely useless since like a statement of objects or preamble it can help to clarify an ambiguous Vidhi, or give the reason for it. Sometimes a Vidhi is also seen couched in the form of Arthavada. This situation has necessitated the need for evolving a system of interpretation. Six axioms of interpretation have therefore been developed for the interpretation of *shastras.*

Even in the Ramjanmabhoomi temple case currently entangled on the unauthorized demolition by some people taking law into their own hands, it is an IPC offence and has no constitutional significance. Any government can even now take-over the project for public good, and build a Ram Janma bhoomi temple.

Second, Article 370 is peculiar provision. It can be deleted, without a Parliamentary amendment, by a Presidential notification, subject to the concurrence of the J&K Constituent Assembly which however has long ceased to exist. Moreover, the moral basis for it has eroded completely because the Kashmiri majority has already driven out Pandits completely altering the religious composition of the state, to preserve which the Article was incorporated. Hence, there is no fetter now to constitutionally abolish Article 370 by a notification. By way of abundant precaution the President can obtain the concurrence of the J&K Governor who legally can be treated as a proxy for the J&K Constituent Assembly.

Third, since the Article 44 is a Directive Principle for State Policy to have uniform *civil* code and moreover since the Muslims on ground of violation of the Shariat have not objected to a uniform *criminal* code which the Indian Penal Code is, hence it is constitutional to enforce

Article 44 as not violative of Article 15, since the latter is subject to reasonable restrictions of health, morality and public order.

The question whether India should adopt a uniform civil code should be treated as a legal question because it is a mandate addressed to the 'State' by Art.44 under Directive Principles of the Constitution. Unfortunately, in India, legal questions are politicized when it affects the "Muslim vote bank."

Article 44 of the Constitution says –

"The State shall endeavour to secure for the citizens a uniform civil code throughout the territory of India."

A controversy has however arisen as to the formation of a uniform code relating to the family or personal law of the parties relating to matters such as marriage and divorce, succession, adoption.

The framers of the Constitution clearly indicated what they meant by the word 'personal law' in Entry 5 of List III of the 7th Schedule of the same Constitution.

Entry 5 says:

"5. Marriage and divorce; infants and minors; adoption; wills; intestacy and succession; joint family and partition; all matters in respect of which parties in judicial proceedings were immediately before the commencement of this Constitution subject to their personal law."

The fathers of the Constitution had witnessed the baneful effects of a claim for separate identity of the Muslim community on the ground that their religion prescribed a separate Personal Law,— resulting in the lamentable Partition of India on the footing of the theory of 'two Nations', founded on two religions. Hence, in the Constituent Assembly it was made clear that in a secular State personal laws relating to such matters as marriage, succession and inheritance could not depend upon religion, but must rest on the law of the land. A uniform Civil Code was accordingly necessary for achieving the unity and solidarity of the nation. [K. M. Munshi, VII C.A.D., 547-48]. Every time subsequently the question of uniform Civil Code was raised by anyone in Parliament, the Government of India opposed it on the ground that to achieve it would be to hurt Muslim 'sentiments' and that no implementation of this Directive of the fundamental law could be made so long as the Muslims themselves would not come forward to ask for it. [see Prime Minister Mr. Rao [Statesman, 1-6-1995; 28-7-1995], and also at his Independence Day Speech at Red Fort on 15-8-1995; Law Minister, Mr. Bharadwaj [Jugantar, 12-12-1993; Statesman, 22-7-1995]; Gadgil, Secretary General of Congress (I) Party [Vartaman, 21-4-1995]; Mr. Dinesh Goswami, Law Minister [U.N.I., 22-12-1989]. Nevertheless, the Supreme Court has recommended, more than once, to take early steps towards the formation of a uniform Civil Code [Mudgal v. Union of India (1995) 3 S.C.C. 635—Kuldip Singh and Sahai JJ. (10th May, 1995).

That the Shariat is not infallible or immutable is evidenced by the patent fact that it has been discarded on modified in many respects by variorus Muslim States. And this has been achieved in an orthodox Muslim State such as Tunisia, through the process of liberal or progressive interpretation of the scriptures.

Advocates of immutability should be silenced by the following observations of a Muslim Judge of Pakistan, Huq, J., of the Lahore High Court –

> "it would not be correct to lay it down as a positive rule of law that the present-day Courts in this country should have no power or authority to interpret the Quran in a way different from that adopted by the earlier Jurists and Imams. The adoption of such a view is likely to endanger the dynamic and universal character of the religion and laws of Quran."

The ground of immutability of the Shariat was in fact raised by some Muslim members in the Constituent Assembly of India but was rejected on the opposition from Dr. Ambedkar. It would be an eyeopener to many today to recount what Ambedkar said [VII C.A.D. 55] in this context.

> "... up to 1935 the North-West Frontier Province was not subject to Shariat Law; it followed the Hindu Law in the matter of succession and in other matters, so much so that it was in 1939 that the Central Legislature had to come into the field and to abrogate the application of the Hindu Law to Muslims of North-West Frontier Province and to apply Shariat Law to them ... apart from North-West Frontier Province, up till 1937 in the rest of India, in various parts, such as the United Provinces, the Central Provinces and Bombay, the Muslims to a large extent were governed by the Hindu Law in the matter of succession ... that in North-Malabar the Marumakkathayam law applied to all—not only to Hindus but also to Muslims." [*op. cit*]

Even in India the Koranic laws of crimes and evidence have been supplanted as early as the 19th century by enacting the Penal Code and the Evidence Act, e.g., by saving the Muslims from the following mediaeval atrocities which are still prevalent in Muslim countries like Pakistan and Bangladesh.

(a) Chopping off the hands of a criminal as a punishment for theft, or stoning to death as a punishment for adultery.
(b) Adultery and apostasy being punishable by death.
(c) Where the witnesses are women, their value as against the evidence of men is in the ratio of 2:1.

The entire law of criminal procedure has been replaced in India by statute. The Indians laws of crimes and evidence make no distinction between Muslims and non-Muslims. The Judges in a Muslim dispute need not be Muslims.

In this context, one critic has pointed out that in Goa, from the days of Portuguese rule, the people have been governed by a uniform civil code, but for the matter of that, Goanese Muslims have not lost their identity or culture.

If it is contended that personal law, founded on religion, has any special status, the answer is that it is the British Parliament which made the English Crown the head of the Church and altered the law of royal succession; and an Indian Parliament superseded the Hindu law of marriage and succession, in the teeth of opposition from an enlightened section of Hindus. It was opposed by Dr. Rajendra Prasad himself on the grounds that Article 44, being applicable to all persons in the territory of India, should not be imposed on the Hindus alone and that the Government who sponsored the Hindu Code Bill to replace the personal law of the Hindus had no mandate from the Electorate in this behalf.

Above all, the Muslims who remained in India after the Partition did so with the full knowledge that divided India was going to adopt a Parliamentary system of democracy and not any Muslim system of the Middle Ages where Shariat would be the supreme law of the land. They should also have known that a personal law founded on the religion of different communities was incompatible with the very concept of a 'Secular' State which divided India was going to be.

Factually also, the assumption of the Government of India that the entire Muslim community is opposed to the implementation of Art.44 is not correct. The Shah Bano case demonstrated that it was only a section of the Sunni sect amongst the Muslims which was vehemently opposed to the judgment.

The Supreme Court can no more wash its hands off Art. 44 on the ground that it is a Directive Principle which is not directly enforceable. Jordan v. Chopra (1985) 3 S.C.C 62 Besides, some Supreme Court Judges had expressed their views to the same effect out of Court: Gajendragadkar, C.J., and Chairman, Law Commission, in his book – Secularism and the Constitution of India (1971), p.126; Shelat, J., Secularism, Principles & Application (1972); Hegde, J., in the Law Institute, in January, 1972; Tulzapurkar, J.,—article in A.I.R. 1987 Jours. 17; Beg. C.J., in his Motilal Nehru Lecture on 'Impact of Secularism on Life and Law'. Prior to Kuldip Singh, J., in numerous cases, the Supreme Court has remedied the inaction of the Government in other clauses of Directive Principles to implement various Directives, in Arts. 38, 39, 39A, 41, 42, 43, by issuing 'directions' which are mentioned in Art. 32(2) as legitimate instruments in the hands of the Court.

Even in the matter of Art. 44, previous Benches of the Supreme Court had commented upon the inaction of the Government and the need for an early implementation of the Article –

(a) A unanimous Constitution Bench in the Shah Bano case (para. 32).
(b) A Division Bench, speaking through Chinnappa Reddy, J., in Jordan's case.

That the Shariat on personal law is not sacrosanct will appear from the following examples of Muslim majority countries which have superseded or modified polygamy.

Turkey: The Court can declare a second marriage as invalid on the ground that a spouse is living at the time of the second marriage [Turkish Civil Code, Art. 74].

Pakistan: A person cannot contract a second marriage without the permission of the Arbitration Council; and a wife can obtain divorce on the ground that the husband has married another wife.

Iran: A person cannot remarry without permission of the Court.

Egypt, Jordan, Morocco, Syria: Similar restrictions on bigamy as in Iran and Pakistan have been imposed in Egypt, Jordan, Morocco and Syria.

Tunisia: Bigamy is totally prohibited by the Tunisia Law of personal Status (s. 18).

Registration of all marriages, including those contracted in conformity with Shariat formalities, has been made compulsory in Iran, Algeria, Indonesia, Malaysia.

There is no reason why such law cannot be adopted in India.

Fifth, the call for Hindutva has been held by the Supreme Court in Manohar Joshi [1996] case to be within the Constitutional requirements of free speech. Hence, time has arrived for us to openly declare India as an ancient Hindu civilization, which is the only way we can perform the Fundamental Duty under Article 51-A(f), and boldly up revere our sacred symbols. For example, the total ban on cow slaughter in Article 48 has been held by a 1958 Constitution Bench to possess constitutionality in the sense that the total ban is held to be a reasonable restriction on fundamental rights of all Indians.

Sixth, at present the Government has been taking over Hindu temples its resources and land and using it for all kinds of non-religious purposes under the states enacted Hindu Religious Institutions and Charitable Endowment Acts on the pretext of mal-administration of the temple properties. Under Article 31A of the Constitution such a take-over cannot be permanent. If mal-administration charge is true, then the Government should rectify it within a reasonable period such as three years, and then hand it back. At present State governments have taken over tens of thousands of temples for decades. Time is now to get them released.

These six constitutionally valid pillars are what Hindutva is, and it is significant that Hindutva goals can be achieved within the present Constitution.

DHARMA NIRPEKSHTA AND SARVA PANTHA SAMA BHAAVA

Throughout ancient Indian history, Hindu kingdoms, never required any 'subject' to be of Hindu religion in order to be regarded a first class citizen. Only in Asoka's reign and Islamic rule, India was a theocracy. Hindu is naturally 'Secular'. But secularism is a much-bandied-about subject nowadays. Unfortunately, those political parties who have been swearing by it all these years have failed to persuade the masses that secularism is good for country.

In fact, secularism as defined and propagated today has lost its relevance. The concept as understood by the masses of India stands thoroughly discredited. Hence the question is whether we should redefine secularism in keeping our civilization tradition to make it acceptable to the masses or capitulate to the rising fundamentalism in the country with dire consequences for national integrity and security.

When Rev. Martin Luther had defined secularism in Europe, it simply meant that the power of the state would be exercised independently of the directions of the Church. Thus, a secular government would act to safeguard the nation-state, even if such action was without Church sanction. Later, Marx calling religion the 'opium of the masses' defined secularism to completely eschew religion.

In India, Jawaharlal Nehru and his followers subscribed to the later Marxist redefinition of the concept in which even in public functions, cultural symbolism such as lighting a lamp to inaugurate a conference or breaking a coconut to launch a project was regarded as against secularism. This orthodoxy induced a reaction in the Indian masses. Nehru failed to define what historical roots ought to be a part of the modem Indian, and what was to be rejected. In the name of 'scientific temper', he rejected most of our past as 'obscurantism'. His orthodox secularism sought to alienate the Indian from his hoary past. Since nearly 85 percent of Indians *are* pan-Hindu in beliefs, and Hindu religion from its inception *has* been without a 'Church', 'Pope' or 'Book' (in contra- distinction to Christianity), therefore neither Martin Luther nor Marx made any sense to the Indian masses. Since there was little political challenge to Nehru after the untimely death of Gandhiji and Patel, the Marxian secularism concept superficially prevailed till Nehru's demise in 1964. The masses therefore humoured Nehru without accepting his concept of secularism. A Conceptual void however remained to be filled.

But Congress Party continued thereafter to fail to provide a political concept of secularism by which an Indian citizen could comprehend how he should bond "secularly" with another citizen of a different religion or language, or region and feel equally Indian. The Hindu instinctively could not accept the idea that India was what the British had put together, and that the country was just an area incorporated by the imperialists. Such a ridiculous idea, fostered quixotically by Jawaharlal Nehru University historians, found just no takers amongst the Indian people. The void remained thus, but the yearning in the masses to be "Indian" grew over the years with growth of mass media. This void had therefore to be filled and the yearning of national identity required to be articulated for the masses.

The legal perspective on Indian secularism has been brilliantly analysed by Supreme Justice Aftab Alam [in (2009) 10SCC J-60]. While he disapproves of the trends in, and import of the various Supreme Court decisions since 1994, however I welcome them. But I salute his research, which I have used in this Chapter *in fact to prove my point* viz., the Indian Constitution as increasingly interpreted by the Supreme Court is basically becoming 'Hindutva-friendly'.

The Constitution of India recognises twenty-two languages as Indian languages. Indians speaking the same language may belong to different religions. India is home to eight major religions of the world. Conversely, Indians belonging to the same religious group may come from different parts of the national geography and may speak different languages, dress differently, eat different kinds of food in entirely different manners and may have completely different social and economic concerns. In India, religion, a democratic State, and secularism overlap and combine to display a highly interesting and unique society.

India has survived while others with the same concerns have balkanized. But the important fact is that the liberality implicit in the Indian system is owed to the Hindu ethos of our civilization. I elaborate with some specific examples! There are six different ways, sanctioned by law, in which an Indian, depending on his or her religion, can get married. The one mode of solemnisation of marriage that requires formal registration which applies to all Indians irrespective of religion *finds favour with very few.*

As Justice Aftap Alam points out: "The vast body of law dealing with property rights treats two Indians differently, again depending upon their religion. On my death the devolution of my estate upon my heirs will take place in a way completely different than in case of my Hindu friends."

Among Hindus the concept of joint family is quite inseparable from the Hindu way of life. The institution of Hindu Undivided Family or joint family is woven into a number of laws with the result that those laws affect different people quite differently.

For every Muslim going for Haj, the Government of India spends from the taxpayers' money, a substantial amount as airfare subsidy if the pilgrims fly Air India. In the Government of India budget for the year 2009-2010 a sum of Rs. 632 crores (approx.77.53 million pounds) is allocated as Haj subsidy. It is likely to be Rs. 850 crores in 2010-11.

But, Kumbh Mela of Hindus or the Fair of the divine nectar pot, takes place four times every twelve years when millions of Hindu pilgrims congregate to take the holy dip in the river on a single day. In 2010 in Haridwar where the Ganges comes down into the plain the most recent Fair has taken place. The State of Uttarakhand would spend an estimated amount of Rs.500 crores (approx. 62.53 million pounds) for organising the mela.

Besides the Kumbh there would be at least a dozen purely religious festivals where direct government spending would run into thousands of crores of rupees. But unlike for Muslims, no Hindu is paid any subsidy by the State for travel to the Kumbh and for stay there.

The Indian Constitution does not have any provision, unlike the First Amendment of the United States Constitution, proscribing the making of any law respecting an establishment of religion. *It instead recognises religion as a source of law.* With a view to protect minority rights, it confers affirmative social and cultural rights on religious groups. It guarantees the fundamental freedom of religion but enables the State, to regulate religious practices on certain limited grounds of morality, health and public order.

Thus, under the Indian Constitution, secularism of the State involves a plural establishment of religion with the State but maintaining of *equidistance* from all religions. The Court is called upon, in a variety of ways, to oversee and regulate the *distance* that the State ought to keep from religious establishments and the nature of

State intervention permissible in religious affairs. *In that sense it would be more appropriate to designate India as a spiritual state rather than a secular state.* But confusion prevails today in the judiciary on how far to stretch secularism and how cognizant the law should be of the Hindu ethos of the nation.

For instance, keeping a beard by a Muslim student invoked Article 25 of the Constitution that gives to every person (in this case the Muslim student) the freedom of conscience and free profession and practice of religion. A Christian missionary-run school defended its rules not to permit it students with beards and expelled the Muslim student on the basis of Article 30 of the Constitution that gives to all minorities (in this case the Christian) the right to establish and administer educational institutions. The expulsion was challenged unsuccessfully before the High Court and the matter finally came to the Supreme Court. On 30-3-2009 the petition was dismissed *in limine* but in course of the brief hearing, one of the judges made certain observations that were widely reported in the media. The Judge had said: "We don't want to have Talibans in the country. Tomorrow a girl student may come and say that she wants to wear a burqa, can we allow it?" [Times of India, March 31, 2009] He further said: "We should strike a balance between rights and personal beliefs. We cannot overstretch secularism." Hence, the Judge added: "You can join some other institution if you do not want to observe the rules. But you can't ask the school to change the rules for you."

The remarks created an uproar among the Muslims against the remarks calling the beard and the burqa as the mark of the Taliban. Then, on 6-7-2009, on a review petition, the same Bench recalled its order dismissing the petition and requested the Chief Justice to have the case placed before some other Bench. On 11-9-2009 the case came up before another Bench. *And this time the response of the Court was completely different*: "How on earth could a school disentitle a student from pursuing studies just because he has kept a beard? Then there will be no end to such prima facie ridiculous rules."

This exemplifies the difficulties faced by the Court in dealing with two 'competing' constitutional rights in Articles 25 and 30. The first Bench obviously gave precedence to the group right guaranteed by the Constitution (Article 30) to a religious minority, in this case the Christian management of the school. The second Bench, on the other hand, deemed fit, in the context of the case, to uphold the right of the individual (Article 25), the Muslim boy. This deep dilemma, as Justice Alam points out seems to run through the decisions of the Supreme Court on the issue of cultural and educational rights guaranteed by the Constitution to the religious minorities.

In 1957, the Communist Government of Kerala enacted a law bringing the school education in the State under its extensive control. A number of Christian organizations and some Muslim groups threatened to create a political crisis.

The President of India to whom the Bill had come for his assent therefore made a reference to the Supreme Court on the constitutional validity of the Bill. A Constitution Bench of seven Judges, headed by Chief Justice S.R. Das, heard the matter and held [AIR 1958 SC 956] that Article 30 was a *stand-alone* Article and the right guaranteed to the minorities under it was not controlled either by Article 29 or any other Article in the chapter of fundamental rights, or even Article 45 in the chapter of Directive Principles relating to education to children below the age of six years. Speaking for the Court S.R. Das, C.J. said:

> "... So long as the Constitution stands as it is and is not altered, it is, we conceive, the duty of this Court to uphold the fundamental rights and thereby honour our sacred obligation to the minority communities who are our own" (p. 986).

The decision in *Kerala Education Bill, 1957,* however, was not unanimous. There was at least one dissenting voice (of Justice T. L. Venkatarama Aiyar.). He took the view that Article 30 was primarily intended to protect educational institutions established for the conservation and promotion of the *culture, language or religion* of a minority group and thus created a purely negative obligation on the

State and prevented it from interfering with minorities living their own cultural life as regards religion or language. Justice Aiyar observed:

> "... Now, to compel the State to recognise those institutions would conflict with the fundamental concept on which the Constitution is framed *that the State should be secular in character.*" (p. 989)

The two views directly opposing each other and both relying upon the principles of secularism that were manifested in *Kerala Education Bill* appear to run through the decisions of the Supreme Court on all *aspects of* secularism. But with the sole exception in *S. Azeez Basha* v. *Union of India (Aligarh Muslim University case* [AIR 1968 SC 662]) the majority decision in *Kerala Education Bill* was relied upon to expand the scope of the right under Article 30, and five years later in *Sidhrajbhai Sabbai* v. *State of Gujarat* (AIR 1963 SC 540) a six-Judge constitutional Bench went on to hold:

"The right [under] Article 30(1) is a fundamental right declared in terms absolute. Unlike the fundamental freedoms guaranteed by Article 19 *it is not subject to reasonable restrictions.*"(p. 547).

Soon secularism came to be regarded as not only a fundamental right but a part of the basic structure of the Constitution. In the Bommai case [(1994)3 SCC 1] seven out of the nine Judges constituting the Bench reiterated the view that secularism was the basic feature of the Constitution and in case a State Government acted contrary to the constitutional mandate of secularism or, worse still, directly or indirectly, subverted the secular principles, *that would tantamount to failure of the constitutional machinery and the State Government would make itself liable to dismissal under Article 356* (para 434).

But soon enough, the Court started to see the interplay between the community based rights and individual rights in a new light. In *Stephen's College,* a Delhi Christian minority college the Court felt the need to strike a balance between an individual's right based on merits and the right of minorities to set up and administer educational institutions of their choice and directed that *St. Stephen's College* could have no more than fifty per cent seats reserved for Christian students.

Thus, the right under Article 30 was for the first time subject to Article 29 reversing the earlier ominous trend for the better. Article 29 states:

Protection of interests of minorities—(1) Any section of the citizens residing in the territory of India or any part thereof having a distinct language, script or culture of its own shall have the right to conserve the same.

As Justice Alam infers, by 2005, this reversing trend was fortified by several decisions till in the end of Article 30 all but lost its independent identity. The position that emerges from these decisions may be summarised thus:

- The right to set up educational institutions and impart any kind of education at any level is available to every Indian citizen under Article 19(1)(g) of the Constitution as the right "to carry on any occupation, trade or business."
- Article 30 does not give to the religious minorities any additional or separate right. *The religious minority has no special right that the majority does not have under the Constitution.*
- Articles 29 and 30 do not confer any rights but afford certain protections to the minorities. The two articles can be better understood as a protection and/or a privilege of the minority rather than an abstract right. (View of Venkatarama, J. in minority of 1:6 in *Kerala Education Bill*, was thus resurrected!)
- The right under Article 30 is not absolute. It is subject to Article 29(2) and other laws. *It can be restricted in public interest and national interest.*

The Supreme Court's perception of secularism, also underwent change since the Bommai case of 1994 through a catena of judgments since 1995.

In 2002 a public interest litigation [(2002) 7 SCC 368] was filed questioning the curriculum for school education framed by the National Council for Educational Research and Training on the ground that it was heavily loaded with religion and the contents of the Vedas. It was contended that the inclusion of religion, Sanskrit, Vedic Mathematics, Vedic Astrology, etc. in the courses of study for the schools was contrary to secular principles.

Justice Dharmadhikari one of the members of the three-Judge Bench wrote a separate, though concurring judgment in which he discussed in some detail about the true nature of secularism. He observed that the doctrine of the State neutrality towards all religions was a narrow concept of secularism. He further observed that the policy of complete neutrality towards and apathy for all kinds of religious teachings in institutions of the State had not done any good to the country. *The real meaning of secularism is 'sarva dharma samabhav'* meaning equal treatment and respect for all religions, but, we misunderstood the meaning of secularism as negation of all religions." (page 406-407)

In 2005, an organisation representing a section of the Jain community came to the Court seeking a direction to the Central Government to notify "Jains" as a minority community. The Court not only firmly rejected the prayer but also expressed its strong disapproval of the very concept of "minority." Calling it a baggage from India's history, the Court noted *(Bal Patil case, SCC* p. 701, para 25): "Muslims constituted the largest religious minority because the Mughal period of rule was the longest followed by the British Rule during which many Indians had adopted Muslim and Christian religions." It further observed that the concept of "minorities" was the result of the British policy of divide and rule that first led to the formation of separate electorates and reservations of seats on the basis of population of Hindus and Muslims and finally led to the partition of India and formation of a separate Muslim State of Pakistan. The Court pointed out that India was a democratic republic which had adopted the right to equality as its fundamental creed and hence, the constitutional ideal should be the elimination of "minority" and "majority" and the so-called forward and backward classes.

All that remains now is further decisions of the Supreme Court to restrict the meaning of minorities to cover *only ethnic minorities whose DNA is different from majority of Indians.* That would mean only a few tribes of extreme Northeast and Onge tribes in Andamans, but not Muslims and Christians who are not recent converts. Affirmative action of the State however can be extended only to those minorities which have suffered from imposed disabilities, and not those minorities which have been ruling classes. The term 'Secularism' should also be replaced in the Constitution by the alternative more appropriate phrase "spiritual state based on 'Sarva Pantha Sama Bhava'.

The Supreme Court has also tried to regulate the efforts of the State to control religious affairs in the context of Article 26 of the Constitution. Article 26 gives to every religious denomination or any section thereof the freedom to manage its religious affairs, *subject, however to considerations of public order, morality and health.* The extent of the right in evolved from the *essential practices test* according to which immunity from State intervention was available to only such practices that were integral to the faith and not to other practices pertaining to economic and commercial matters though associated with religion [(1954) 1 SCR 1005].

The Court thus preferred to lay down the test, rather than subjecting the law to the test of public order, morality and health (to which Articles 25 and 26 rights are subject). Thus, instead of denying constitutional protection on the ground that a certain practice violated public order, morality or health, the Court preferred simply to hold that a certain practice was not an essential part of a particular religion. The Court also assumed to itself the right to decide whether or not a certain practice was essential to a religion, of course with reference to authoritative sources and texts relating to that religion.

When the Swaminarayana sect took the plea that they did not belong to the Hindu religion and hence their temples were not covered by the Act prohibiting Hindu temples from refusing entry to Harijans, the Court referred to several texts on Hinduism and Indology and concluded that the Swaminarayana sect was indeed a part the Hindu religion, and their temples were fully covered by the provisions of the Act.

In giving itself the power to judge what was an essential practice of a religion—the Court could now hold that those were essential practices *could not avail of the protection of Article 25.* This had enabled the Court to adopt an extremely interventionist approach—even resorting to Scriptural Interpretation. I welcome this.

In Shah Bano case [(1985)2 SCC 556] the statutory provisions of maintenance of divorced wives were held to be applicable to Muslims, in view of the Muslim Personal Law (Shariat) Application Act, 1937. The Court held that there was nothing in the Muslim Personal Law that conflicted with the statutory provisions for maintenance. The decision created resentment against the Court amongst Muslim clerics for arrogating to itself the right and the authority to interpret the Quran, forgetting that the Court had consistently resorted to scriptural interpretation while applying the essential practices test to the Hindu religion.

For political considerations however the Central Government abjectly surrendered and had Parliament pass a legislation. The new Act was challenged in *Danial Latifi case* [(2001)7 SCC 740] *as* violative of the constitutional right of the Muslim woman to obtain statutory maintenance beyond the *iddat* period, which had been upheld in *Shah Bano.* The Court, now while upholding the constitutional validity of the Act, was paradoxically also able to preserve all the rights given to a Muslim divorcee woman in *Shah Bano case,* observing that "it may look ironical that the enactment intended to reverse the decision in *Shah Bano case,* actually codifies the very rationale contained therein."

What, however, is of great significance is that in *Danial Latifi* case the Court reached the same reformist conclusion as in *Shah Bano* but through a different, and more acceptable, route. The Court instead had subjected the Act to the test of Articles 14, 15 and 21 of the Constitution. It effectively held that the Act would be unconstitutional if interpreted to give Muslim women less than other women by way of maintenance.

Thus, if this trend of decisions of the Supreme Court continues, then, it is a matter of time before the issue of minority rights will be addressed afresh, having regard to the concerns and in light of the experience of the past sixty years. By this trend I would hazard a guess: *Hindutva will sooner or later in the future become the basis of Indian jurispudence.*

It is worth a mention here that time has arrived to mount a challenge to the Constitutionality of Government take-over of temples in the name of rectifying the mismanagement of the properties of the temples. While Constitutionally this is not barred under Article 25, the Government keeping these temples for an unlimited period is violative of Article 31 A(1)(b) of the Constitution. I propose to move the Supreme Court to free all temples presently under Government control for a period of 3 years or more. This would free about 500,000 temples.

Chapter IV

HINDUTVA AND MODERNIZATION

Modernization is the process of modernity. Modernity may be defined as a state of mind or mindset that entails a receptive attitude to change, transparency and accountability. The process of reaching and acquiring that mindset is modernization. This is not the same as Westernization.

Hindutva is the quality of being a Hindu, namely the Hinduness of a person. We have already identified (Chapter II) nine beliefs which qualify and distinguishes a Hindu from others as well as the code of good behaviour.

In these nine beliefs include the quality of being receptive to change as immutable law of change, imbedded in the concept of *dharmachakra pravartana.* Hindu theology also extols transparency and accountability in the concepts *of satyam, shivam and sundaram,* and in the concept of *karma* which is nothing but the concept of accountability. The concepts of *yama* and *niyama* define the code for Hindus which is an ingredient of Hindutva.

Hence, there is no conflict or contradiction between Hindutva and Modernization. What needs to be discussed is how to inculcate Hindutva so that we can be acquire a modern mindset and how the modernization process can be structured so that Hindutva can be imbibed in our nature through our educational and family system.

Modernization is embedded in mind development that takes place because of growing stock of knowledge. This knowledge has to be pursued with character that seeks to use knowledge to liberate and empower the human and not to enslave him. Thus religious faith has helped to develop the character necessary for imbibing knowledge.

In ancient India, religion played a great role in education. Ancient Indians believed that education should not be only about acquisition of knowledge but it should also bring about realization of the inner soul. Education and teaching evolved as a result of direct relationship between a Guru and his disciple (Sishya) a well-established teaching format known as the Gurukul system.

It was of course not formalized or institutionalized like the modern Western educational system. But knowledge was passed on for generations through personal attention of a 'Guru'. The primary object of education thus was for preparing the mind in all its facets. This training of the mind and the process of thinking were considered as pre-requisites essential for the acquisition of knowledge. Today, the West has re-invented this concept in the development of the intelligence in five dimensions-cognitive, emotional, social, moral and spiritual intelligence.

India today leads the world in the supply pool of youth, i.e., persons in the age group of 15 to 35 years, and this lead will last for another forty years. This generation is most fertile milieu for promoting knowledge, innovation, and research. It is the prime work force that saves for the future, the corpus for pension funding of the old. We should therefore not squander this "natural vital resource."

Modern economic growth also is powered overwhelming (over 65% of GDP) by new innovation and techniques (e.g., internet). More capital and labour contributes less than 35% of growth in GDP. We must hence by proper policy for the young, realize and harvest the demographic potential. China is the second largest world leader in young population today. But the youth population in that country will start shrinking from 2015, i.e., less than a decade from now because of lagged effect of their ill-thought one-child policy. Japanese and European total populations are fast aging, and will start declining in *absolute* numbers from next year. The US will however hold a steady trend thanks to a liberal policy of immigration, especially from Mexico and Phillipines. But even then the US will have in a decade hence a demographic shortage in skilled personnel. All currently developed countries thus experience a demographic deficit. *India will not.* Our past alleged liability, by a fortuitous turn of fate, has (now become to be globally regarded as our potential asset.

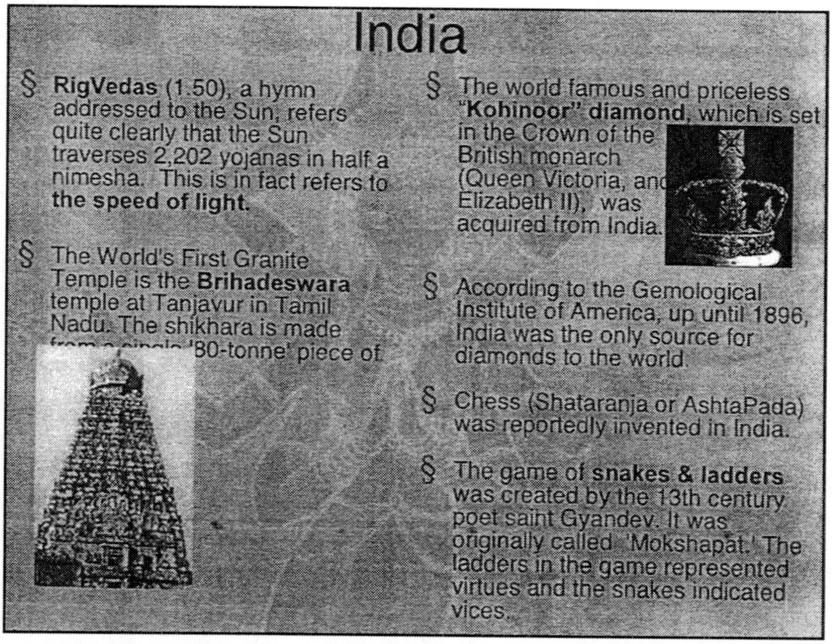

Demographic Dividend

Thus, India has now become, by unintended consequences, gifted with a young population. If we educate this youth to develop and attain a high quotient of *cognitive intelligence* [CQ] to become original thinkers, imbibe *emotional intelligence* [EQ] to have team spirit and rational risk-taking attitude, inculcate *moral intelligence* [MQ] to blend personal ambition with national goals, cultivate *social intelligence* [SoQ] to defend civic rights of the weak, gender equality, and the courage to fight injustice and nurture *spiritual intelligence* [SQ] to innovate the transformative power of vision and intention to access the vast energy the pervades the cosmos to innovate and out of box research, then we can develop a superior species of human being, a modern Indian youth who can be relied on to contribute to make India a global power within two decades.

Computers may have high CQ because they are programmed to understand the rules, and follow them without making mistakes. Many mammals have high EQ. Only humans know to ask why, and can work with re-shaping boundaries instead of just within boundaries. Human can innovate, not animals.

The nation must therefore structure a national policy for the youth of India so that in every young Indian the five dimensional concept of intelligence, viz., *cognitive, emotional, moral, social and spiritual* manifests in his character. Only then, our demographic dividend will not be wasted. These five dimensions of intelligence *constitute the ability of a person* to live a productive life and for national good. Hence, a policy for India's youth has to be structured within the implied parameters of these five dimensions.

The parameters of such a national youth policy are: [1] ability empowerment—that is the development of the five types of intelligence stated above; [2] a collective mindset about the legacy and future of the nation which means knowing the correct de-falsified history of India and learning of Sanskrit; [3] commitment to a social contract of rights and obligations such as a fundamental right to quality primary and secondary education, right to work, an inculcated drive and obligation to compete for positions on merit, practice gender equality, harmonize national interest with personal interests and blend material aspirations with spiritual advancement in one's life span.

A National Youth Policy is therefore a framework for the comprehensive growth of the nation's young population between 15 and 35 years of age, and for enabling this youth to be positioned in life for contented personal advancement as well as for contributing to the nation's greatness.

The Union Government of India has the prime responsibility to formulate, within these three parameters, such a policy for youth. Twice, first in 1988 and again in 2003, a policy for youth was announced by the government. Let us look at these two formulations to see if indeed the announced policy is within the above stated three parameters, and meets the requirements of India's youth of the 21st century, necessary for the nation to maximize the demographic dividend due to India.

The 1988 formulation was seriously flawed and inadequate because it emphasized the listing of needs of the youth and what the government can provide for them. It blandly lists youth needs as education, employment, sports, and participation in decision-making. The policy does not visualize the youth as a raw material for human capital development, but as some disgruntled alienated social group that-has to be co-opted and given some goodies. Hence it made no impact on the youth of India because there was no inspiration in these goals.

The National Youth Policy 2003 was better formulated, but again the focus was to design "an appropriate policy framework to be in place to harness the energies of the youth...." That is, the object of the policy was not for positioning the youth in society within the three parameters, but as a reservoir of energy to be harnessed, much as we would with bullocks and horses—fit and able for traction. The objectives stated in the 2003 policy document are extensive, but do not constitute a *coherent* agenda. For example it talks of the need to "instill in the youth an adherence to secular principles." Now what does that mean? Does the asymmetrical commitment to secularism, e.g., Muslim silence on me arrest, on a bogus case, of the Kanchi Shankaracharya and the Hindus howl against a cartoon published in far away Denmark disparaging Prophet Mohammed, define secularism? That is, is secularism a one way obligation for Hindus? Is it secularism for the nation to have uniform criminal code [the Indian Penal Code] but not uniform civil code? If the *Shariat* is unacceptably violated by the latter why not by the former? Why this double standard? Thus the 2003 policy also floundered because there was no cohesive agenda for the youth.

That is, we lack today a properly structured policy for India's youth. There is however an urgent need for designing such a policy because of the potential that we have to reap the demographic dividend from our large national pool of youth, and more importantly make such youth imbibed with Hindutva.

I would define an appropriate National Youth Policy as "an architecture" that enables the youth to bloom to the maximum feasible human capacity by the time of attaining full adult maturity. In other words, the architecture consists of *objectives* of youth development, *priorities* in the attainment of the objectives, a *strategy* based on a coherent agenda to achieve those objectives in the order of priority determined, and mobilization *of financial and other resources* to implement that strategy. The overall goal of a National Youth Policy has to be to make the nation a secure civilization. All dimensions of development have therefore to be synergized to that goal.

What are the objectives then that the youth should work toward? *These objectives cannot be purely materialistic* because we know from our past history that though India was the world's most economically developed country, our nation was subject to brutal assault and loot by a handful of foreigners, and for a thousand years we Hindustanis could not rule from Delhi. *Materialistic progress alone therefore does not guarantee national security of a nation.* What is hence essential is the character and integrity of its citizens. Thus, besides the objective of acquiring knowledge and getting employment that requires cognitive intelligence, the youth must be motivated in the other dimensions of intelligence: that of emotional, moral, social and spiritual.

These concepts have been developed in the eighteen chapters of Bhagavad Gita that has been interpreted in modern context by Sri Chandrashekharendra Sarasvati of Kanchi Mutt, Swami Chinmayananda, and Swami Dayananda Sarasvati of Arsha Vidyalaya. In the United States, as the *Business Week* magazine reported [in 2007], these concepts have become highly popular in the corporate world, and which have also been incorporated in the best-selling books written by Daniel Goleman, Deepak Chopra, and Anthony Robbins among others.

In brief, the National Youth Policy is defined by measures by which we can create a modern mindset in the youth of India, not only to motivate the youth to acquire techrucal competence, but to develop emotional, moral, social and spiritual values that will make that person a self-reliant individual of high character, patriotic, and possessing a social conscience. Such an army of evolved youth will be the asset of the nation, and then collectively the demographic dividend can be reaped by us to usher National Renaissance for the glory of Bharat Mata. A well structured national youth policy is vital for making India global power two decades hence which should also be our objective and a basis for National Renaissance.

Our modernization goal has to be thus the efficient use of resources, human and physical, hardware and software, by an able and human spiritually guided and ethically in dined leadership in a framework of globally competitive market economy. But this goal cannot be achieved unless there is accountability in governance; such accountability requires transparent ethics.

In the ancient past India achieved the heights of modernization, civilization and prosperity by an educational system that was unique to the Hindus—the Gurukul System based on a sacred bond between the *Guru* and the *Shishya*.

The teachers were paid in the form of housing, food etc by society. The regional language was used as the medium of instruction but Sanskrit was taught compulsorily. The teachers were well trained by the master and revered Guru. In short, the indigenous elementary schools were simple and adaptive to the local environment. For centuries, its existence was due to its simple vital nature in spite of varied economic and political vicissitudes and non-formal process. In a nutshell the Indigenous system of education at the end of eighteenth century compared favorably with if not better than the system of education that existed anywhere else at that time. But Lord Macauley had other ideas. Precisely for this reason, he enforced a totally alien system on India—to change our mindset from an independent inquiring one to a compliant slaving one.

A Spanish traveler Peter Delle Valle who came to India in 1623, observed the boys skill in learning arithmetic in a strange manner. There were four boys who were learning the arithmetic tables under the tree. One of them singing musically with a certain tone, recited part of the lesson and others repeated it. At times all the boys recited in unison. The traveler asked who corrected them if they happened to forget or err, in the absence of assistance from the master. They answered that it was not possible for all the four to forget or make mistakes about the same part of the exercise. The logic impressed traveler who also found it an easy and secure way of effective learning. [*Girija O.V* (2008): "A Critical study of Modern Indian Education" Ph.D Thesis University of Madras].

Sir Thomas Munro in his *Report on Education in Madras Presidency*, observed that it was commendable that the standard maintained in India in the Gurukul system was higher than the standard found in other European countries. Hence, if this was so, then: How did the indigenous system disintegrate or why was it displaced by the British system? This uprooting of the indigenous system is well recorded by Dharampal in his book: *The Beautiful Tree* (1983).

In his 1952 Convocation Address at Gurukul Kangri University, the Hindutva scholar and visionary, founder President of Jana Sangh and former Union Industries Minister in Nehru's first Cabinet (and who resigned over Nehru's neglect of Hindus), Dr. Syama Prasad Mookerjee said: "We are not unhappy with the fact that (during the British rule) the doors of Western education were opened for Indians. What distresses us is the fact that this education was being imparted to us by suppressing India's rich heritage of culture and knowledge.... We should cultivate in the hearts of young Indians such strong pride and such deep awareness about our national heritage that makes them rise above the barriers of caste and community."

We cannot recreate the formal aspects of the Gurukul system in today's times, but its core concept is relevant even today that we should enhance the prestige and social status of a teacher to that of a "Guru," because a teacher cannot, merely be a purveyor of information or book-based knowledge. It should become fashionable again to be a teacher. He or she should be in a position to impart wisdom and develop multiple intelligence teaching students how to live life, inculcating in them a strong sense of right and wrong, and stimulating in them varied interest in the wonders of the world. It goes without saying that teachers' own continuous training and retraining is also to receive priority attention of the Government by creating the necessary facilitation for the same.

The present education system is aimed at developing a very small part of the mental potential of our students. The one-sided emphasis on the fulfillment of the material needs of human beings must be replaced by aiming to develop the hidden powers of their minds and hearts (the five dimensions of intelligence) It warp their mind by a false history of our nation and civilization. It places too much emphasis on learning by rote and makes them risk-averse as a mental attitude. We can indeed obtain a qualitatively superior kind of progress in the future if we adopt and adapt the principles of the Gurukul system for educational renaissance.

Mahatma Gandhi at the meeting at the Royal Institute of International Affairs [in October 1931] pointed out to an elite gathering that the British instead of supporting the indigenous system, and by updating it allow it to continue, disrupted it, and as a consequence made it perish.

This goal of the British was well stated by Macaulay in his Minute on Education debated in the British Parliament in 1835. That was to alienate a select chosen set of Indians and make them culturally English in outlook and thus could become compradors.

The beginning to meddle began with the Charter Act of 1813 which was prepared by the British Government on two main issues arising from Minto's Minute (1811): First, the British educational policy and second the Company's educational responsibility in India and the Christian Missionary cause.

The 43rd section of the Charter Act of 1813 stated, "it shall be lawful for the Governor General-in-Council to direct that out of any surplus—which may remain of the rents, revenues, and profits arising from the said territorial acquisitions.... A sum of not less than one lakh of rupees in each year shall be set apart and applied to the revival and improvement of literature and the encouragement of the learned natives of India and for the introduction and promotion of a knowledge of the sciences among the inhabitants of the British territories in India."

The word "literature" in the Charter Act of 1813 did not explicitly specify whether it referred to classical-oriental literature or English literature. Macaulay seized on this vagueness and submitted that this word "literature" to mean only English literature and not Oriental literature. He also argued that science developed in the West could be imparted only through English medium. He thus made a case for English both as a subject and as a medium. He then added that:

> *"It was possible through English education to bring about a class of persons, Indian in blood and colour, but English in tastes, in opinions,*

in morals and in intellect and that education was to filter down from them to the masses".

That in a nutshell was the British imperialist goal, and sadly the system grafted then for this purpose continues even today thanks to the Nehru tradition and imitation in our politics.

Macaulay's Minute was accepted by the then Governor General Lord Bentinck. He passed the Resolution on the Company's future policy on education on 7th March 1835. Promotion of Western science and literature thus became the avowed policy of the British educational policy in India.

But the curriculum did not promote science education as was professed in the policy. The stress on English as the medium made most students shun schooling itself. The adherence to the downward filtration theory—"educate a few who will educate others"—mass education failed to click. The Charter Act of 1835 made no direct reference to primary education. Its focus was only on higher education. The East India Company started schools for secondary education and institution for higher education. The seeds for the woefull plight of primary schools today were planted in 1835 and re-affirmed by Nehru in 1947. Gandhiji's call for 'Nai Talim' was junked after his assassination.

But ironically Macaulay's dream of making "... a class of persons Indian in blood and colour but English in taste and morals, in opinions, words and intellect" and thus perpetuating the British imperial rule through his scheme of education turned out in the 20th century to be detrimental to that very rule. Almost all the elites pioneering India's freedom struggle were English educated. In fact, most of them had been educated in England and were typically Barristers at Law. Most of them became English in speech, taste and to some extent in morals. They remained Indian at the core of their soul. As Dr. Girija joints out (Ibid p.5), it will be an interesting study to find out why and how Macaulay's scheme of education defeated its own original avowed purpose.

Compulsory English education instead unwittingly facilitated the re-exposure to the ideals of liberty, equality and fraternity after 1000 years of brutal Islamic conquests, among the emerging Indian elite whose mother tongue though was different, yet which unified them by that very English, towards the struggle for independence. In other words, the British colonial system of education laid the foundation for a new political awareness that enabled a transformation of a motley collection of submissive princely states into the world's largest democracy and a subject population in British—ruled India to rise in revolt.

However, although English language may have got a fresh lease of life because USA adopted the language and became a superpower, even as Britain has been declining, it is imperative that we in India restructure our education now to focus on the innovative mindset, and through the additional medium of Sanskrit because of three reasons: First, we in the 21st century have been ushered into the "Knowledge Economy" meaning that innovations applied would mostly propel economic growth, and not so much because of more capital and labour as was possible because of the law of Diminishing Returns before. Second, Sanskrit has already been declared by the NASA at the fittest language for the future science of "Artificial Intelligence," which is a computer based accumulation of knowledge. Third, all Indian languages have a high proportion of Sanskrit words. Even the ancient classical language of Tamil has over 40% of its vocabulary in common with Sanskrit.

Sri Aurobindo criticized the colonial system of education and wanted it replaced by a system that was natural, effective and complete." for Indians. He called it 'Integral Education" [Internet source: http://www.ncte-in.org/pub/aurobin.htm]. By this he meant a complete education of the body and the spirit through a self-learning, self-propelling process and not merely by teaching. To quote him:

"An education, which has accepted the goal, [outlined by Sri Aurobindo] and which takes into account the entire complexity of man's nature can rightly be termed an "Integral education."

The role of the teacher, Sri Aurobindo declared, is to be a facilitator and guide for the learner. The principles of his educational theory are nothing but the principles of integral yoga. Education, he believed, must transform the individual to live for the divine, country, for self and others. This should form the basic goal of national education. Both society and education should help the individual to realize the divinity from within.

By this approach Aurobindo felt that education that included the study of mind would initiate changes both in man and in society. This is the root of how Hindutva can modernize the Indian mind. But how will the teacher and student communicate with each other? How can citizen and citizen of India bond with each other if they cannot communicate with each other when it matters?

In ancient India the intention to discover truth was so consuming, that in the process, they discovered perhaps the most perfect tool for fulfilling such a search that the world has ever known—the Sanskrit language.

Of all the discoveries that have occurred and developed in the course of human history, language is the most significant and probably the most taken for granted. Without language, civilization could obviously not exist. On the other hand, to the degree that language becomes sophisticated and accurate in describing the subtlety and complexity of human life, we gain power and effectiveness in meeting its challenges.

The access to modern technology which has been designed to give case, efficiency and enjoyment in meeting our daily needs did not exist at the beginning of the century. It was made possible by accelerated advancement in the field of mathematics, a "language" which has helped us to discover the interrelationship of energy and matter with a high degree of precision. The resulting technology is evidence of the tremendous power that is unleashed simply by being able to make the finer and finer distinction that a language like mathematics affords.

At the same time humankind has fallen far behind the advancements in technology. The precarious state of political and ecological imbalance that we are now experiencing is an obvious sign of the power of technology far exceeding the power of human beings to be in control of it. It could easily be argued that we have fallen far behind the advancements in technology, simply because the languages we use for daily communication do not help us to make the moral and ethical distinctions required to be in balance with the technology that has taken over our lives.

Modernization of the Indian education system to conform with Hindutva concepts thus requires an acceptable indigenous and Indian language for all Indians to communicate with each other in all forums. And for that modernity, science and research, can be only be through Sanskrit.

A society within a well-defined territory is a nation only if it possesses the sentiment of nationality. Such a sentiment of substance and salience (Huntington) obtains only when a sense of shared historical memories and an intense longing emerges amongst its members to live and die together. Such a sentiment can be fostered only by a factual and comprehensive reading of history. *But what is the medium for communicating these shared memories?* While the authority of the State can provide the cohesion for actualizing the nation, it is only when the people are able to mingle freely and communicate effortlessly that the nation achieves its full bloom. This is not so today in India.

Nothing divides our nation today more than linguistic and caste differences, which over the years since independence have become more accentuated. What is more ridiculous to witness than the struggle for the city of Chandigarh or of Belgaum on the issue of language?

The Indian people are across the regions communicating with one another today in a foreign language, which is English. This has not come to be by accident, but by a deliberate decision of Lord Macaulay, made known in 1835, in his now famous Minute. For this to happen Macaulay wanted the English language be foisted and fostered amongst this class of sycophantic and compliant Indians. Although

English is a language worth knowing today only *because the United States has made it an international language,* especially for scholars, diplomats, businessmen in the export-import trade and on the Internet it still is not a live language for us. The nuances, the idioms, and metaphors are made abroad and then imported. We have to accept these without question. If we improvise these locally, then we are made fun of, and derided. How can we therefore communicate with each other in a language which we have imported from over 10000 kilometers away and forced to keep it essentially in a mummified form here?

During the Freedom Struggle, Hindi was proposed as a replacement of English. There was much merit in the choice because in one form or another, Hindi was understood by nearly three-fourths of India. From Kashmir to Raichur (in Karnataka), from Kutch to the corners of Assam, Hindi is an easily understood language. Only some areas of Andhra and Karnataka, and most parts of the States of Kerala and Tamil Nadu do not follow Hindi. But since Mahatma Gandhi and Rajagopalachari propagated the cause of Hindi as the link language in place of English, even these southern areas had enthusiastically begun to learn Hindi. This lasted till Gandhi's assassination. After that, the cause of Hindi began to suffer.

There are two reasons for the decline in the spread of Hindi. First, Hindi began to be promoted by native Hindi speakers such as Purushottamdas Tandon and Dr. Raghuvira, unlike in the past when Gandhiji and Rajaji, whose mother tongue was not Hindi, were leading the campaign. The native Hindi speakers were so virulent in their campaign for the language that they became purists. They were soon perceived as fanatics. Unfortunately these enthusiasts made the acceptance of Hindi a test of patriotism, and sought to raise knowledge of Hindi immediately as a minimum qualification for jobs. This naturally caused a deep and virulent reaction. Second, Jawaharlal Nehru as Prime Minister did nothing to dispel these negative campaigns. His heart was not in Hindi replacing English. He himself spoke a pedestrian version of Hindi, styled as Hindustani. His grand children Rajiv and Sanjay Gandhi were sent to the English-medium hothouse of Indo-English culture, the Doon School, which produces even today the alienated elite crowd. Nehru had digs at Hindi whenever he was afforded a chance. Since he understood no Sanskrit at all, he rebuked the Sanskritization of the Hindi vocabulary and the Devanagiri script.

Between Raghuvira on one extreme and Nehru's sabotage on the other, Hindi became not only discredited in the eyes of the south but a symbol of imposition of the North on the South. Naturally the South revolted. Southerners also feared losing jobs due to the natural disadvantage of not knowing Hindi from childhood, in competition with those whose mother-tongue was Hindi. Thus, the nation had to witness the language riots of 1965 that threatened national unity. The leadership at the centre which had by then passed into Lal Bahadur Shastri's hands, had naturally to yield, to keep national unity, but with that the prospect of Hindi suffered a tremendous reverse.

Hindi, however, is still practically speaking the best link language today. But it is not the best language as an educational medium and for learned discourse. It can never be accepted as the national language. In the centuries to come, it is Sanskrit that will be the most sensible language for us. As stated earlier, there are reasons for it. The first is that all Indian languages have a high proportion of words taken from Sanskrit. In the case of Bengali and Malayalam it may be 90 per cent, while in the case of Tamil it may be at least 35 per cent (even in the DMK version of "pure" Tamil). Bengali is proudly referred to as the "daughter" of Sanskrit, but Tamil which has a proud history of its own, thanks to the long unbroken reign of the Chola kingdoms can be easily thought of as the "sister" of Sanskrit. For this reason, Sanskritized Hindi is easier to understand for the Southerners (and more difficult for those Northerners like Nehru steeped in Urdu). The late Annadurai used to say that for Sanskritized Hindi, "na vadiyar" (I am teacher). Incidentally, the Tamil word "vadiyar" comes from the Sanskrit word "vadi" (preacher). For this reason of common vocabulary, Sanskrit is ultimately the best national language for India.

Secondly, international research in today's most advanced area of computers, namely, Artificial Intelligence, which is to revolutionize the knowledge systems of the 21st Century, is now increasingly coming to the conclusion that Sanskrit is the best language to store knowledge in a computer.

Writing in the spring 1985 issue of the *Artificial Intelligence*, Dr. Rick Briggs of the US National Aeronautics and Space Agency (NASA), states in an article titled "Knowledge Representation in Sanskrit and Artificial Intelligence" that:

> "In the past twenty years, much time, effort, money has been expended on designing an unambiguous representation of natural languages to make them accessible to computer processing.
>
> Understandably, there is widespread belief that natural languages are unsuitable for the transmission of many ideas that artificial languages can render with great precision and mathematical rigour.
>
> There is at least one language, Sanskrit ... (in which) can be reckoned a method ... that is identical not only in essence but in form with current work in Artificial Intelligence.
>
> This article demonstrates that a natural language (Sanskrit) can serve as an artificial language also, and that much work in Artificial Intelligence has been reinventing a wheel millenia old."

Artificial Intelligence will revolutionize all sciences in another fifty years. According to Dr. Briggs, Sanskrit is the best language for it. It is pity that we, the inventors of Sanskrit, have to learn these facts from foreigners, but it is better late than never.

Three decades after trying to make natural languages compatible to computer programming, scientists have begun to realize that they were beaten to it 10,000 years ago. Though much removed in time, space and culture, a 7th century B.C. Sanskrit grammarian seems to have provided all the answers to today's computer problems. Sanskrit is well suited for encrypting without ambiguity.

Dr. Briggs adds: "There is at least one language, Sanskrit, which for the duration of almost 1000 years was a living spoken language with a considerable literature of its own. Besides works of literary value, there was a long philosophical and grammatical tradition that has continued to exist with undiminished vigor until the present century. Among the accomplishments of the grammarians can be reckoned a method for paraphrasing Sanskrit in a manner that is identical not only in essence but in form with current work in Artificial Intelligence. This article demonstrates that a natural language can serve as an artificial language also, and that much work in AI has been reinventing a wheel millennia old."

This discovery of Briggs is of monumental significance. It is mind-boggling to consider that we have available to us a Indian language which has been spoken for 10,000 years that appears to be in every respect a perfect language designed for enlightened communication. But the most stunning aspect of the discovery is this: NASA, the most advanced research center in the world for cutting edge technology, has discovered that Sanskrit, the world's oldest spiritual language is the only unambiguous spoken language on the planet.

Considering Sanskrit's status as a spiritual language, a further implication of this discovery is that the dichotomy of secularists between religion and science is now irretrievably breaking down.

The very name "Sanskrit" means "language brought to formal perfection" in contrast to the common languages, Prakrits or "natural" languages. The form of Sanskrit which has been used for the last 2500 years is known today as Classical Sanskrit. The norms of classical Sanskrit were established by the ancient grammarians. Although no records are available of their work, their efforts reached a climax in the 5th century B.C. in the great grammatical treatise of Panini, which became the standard for correct speech with much comprehensive authority that it has remained so, with little alteration until present times. To date no one has been able to improve on Panini.

Until 1100 A.D., Sanskrit was without interruption the official language of the whole of India. The dominance of Sanskrit is indicated by a wealth of literature of widely diverse genres including religious and philosophical; fiction (short story, fable, novels, and plays); scientific literature including linguistics, mathematics, astronomy, and medicine; as well as law and politics.

With the Muslims invasions from 1100 A.D. onwards, Sanskrit gradually became displaced by common languages patronized by the Muslim kings as a tactic to suppress Indian cultural and religious tradition and supplant it with their own beliefs. But they could not eliminate the literary and spiritual ritual use of Sanskrit which the Hindus zealously protected.

Even today in India, there is a strong movement to return Sanskrit to the status of "national language of India." Sanskrit being a language derived from simple monosyllabic verbal roots through the addition of appropriate prefixes and suffixes according to precise grammatical laws has an infinite capacity to grow, adapt and expand according to the requirements of change in a rapidly evolving world.

The grammarian—Panini—is now being called the first software man, without the hardware. And the focus is on the roughly 4,000 rules of Sanskrit grammar that the evolved. Rules that are so scientific and logical in manner that they closely resemble structures used by computer scientists throughout the world.

How does Panini's grammar work? Grammar is basically an abstraction of the language. As a rule, grammar is usually written after a language has developed. Sanskrit has other forms of grammar, but Panini's is the only one which with only 4,000 rules successfully covers almost the entire range. And each word under the Panini grammar can be traced back to its root. Quite akin in form and essence to computer languages like say COBOL or FORTRAN.

In a natural language like for instance English—ambiguity is inherent in a large number of utterances. A crude example would be the word "bank"—as in a river bank, or a commercial bank. Another hindrance is syntax is, for all intents and purposes, independent of meaning. So computer scientists would like to eliminate such considerations. Yet, in other sentences, the syntax contributes to the meaning and here one wishes to extract it. Scientists say the degree to which a language sounds ambiguous and cumbersome is the degree to which that language is "natural" and deviates from precise or "artificial."

But Panini has made Sanskrit precise, concise and complete. It is like a set of condensed codes for the entire language with some rules attached. It is a terse, very condensed form of Sanskrit, which paradoxically at times becomes so abstruse that a commentary is necessary to clarify it. But the beauty of it is that it can formulate logical relations in the language with scientific precision. Panini, scientists point out, can be conceived like a computer that generates correct words/sentences with the basic inputs. The computer, taking the inputs, uses the Panini rules and flashes the correct words or sentences in a logical order.

Scientists have gone a step forward. They are trying to develop computer-friendly grammar, like Panini, for other languages. All languages have universal rules like all of them have nouns, pronouns, verbs, adjectives etc. Effort is on to work out a Panini model for many languages. Since Sanskrit is said to be the mother of many modern Indian languages, scientists are trying to develop a mathematical and computational grammar for them. These are "catchy ideas" in artificial intelligence today, with pioneering work now being done in India, US and Germany.

Interestingly, many scientists are tempted to speculate how Panini developed his rules in so concise and precise a manner without a computer in 3995 aphorisms in his *Asbadhayayi*.

Thus, as we look back, it seems that the founding fathers committed a blunder in not according Sanskrit its rightful place.

In India's long history, Sanskrit has been the greatest integrating force, the source of cultural continuum, the medium of literary creativity, the voice of the sages and the language of the most sublime thoughts and the profoundest of the philosophies of life. It was the medium of intellectual and spiritual discourse and made its impact on scholars throughout the length and breadth of the country.

It is not generally known that in the Constituent Assembly, there was a body of opinion that strongly advocated the adoption of Sanskrit as the official language [see Subhash Kashyap "Back to Sanskrit" (The Hindu, Jan. 11, 2000 p.21)]. And, not only in India, Sanskrit had its impact in many countries outside. It became the language of the learned even in South-East Asia and to some extent in parts of Central Asia. Most interestingly, many of the ancient Sanskrit plays that exist were found not in India but in Turfan on the edge of the Great Gobi desert in China.

The highly articulate member of the Constituent Assembly, Prof. Naziruddin Ahmad, regretted that we did not know with what great veneration Sanskrit was regarded in the civilized world outside. He quoted W.C. Taylor who said that Sanskrit was the language of unrivalled richness and purity. Max Mueller had called Sanskrit "the greatest language in the world, the most wonderful and the most perfect." According to Sir William Jones, "Sanskrit is of a wonderful structure, more perfect than Greek, more copious than Latin, more exquisitely refined than either." Prof. Sahibdullah, world-renowned scholar of Sanskrit, had said that Sanskrit was "the language of every man to whatever race he may be long."

Prof. Naziruddin Ahmad told the Constituent Assembly that Sanskrit was the grandest and the greatest language *and was impartially difficult for all.* It should therefore be accepted as India's national language in preference to Hindi which gave undue advantage to Hindi speaking areas. "If the non-Hindi people have to learn a language, they would rather learn Sanskrit than a language which is infinitely below Sanskrit in status, quality and rank."

Lakshmi Kant Maitra moved an amendment to the language clause in the Constituent Assembly. He proposed that Sanskrit should be accorded the status of the national and official language of India. He said, if on the attainment of freedom, India wanted to have anything like an official language which was also to be the national language, it could undoubtedly be only Sanskrit which was a "world language in the sense that its importance, its wealth, its position, its grandeur have made it transcend the frontiers of India and travel far beyond India, and it is because of the Sanskrit language and all the rich heritage of Indian culture that is enshrined in it that outside India we are held in deep esteem by all countries."

Maitra made a forceful plea in favour of Sanskrit as he felt that Sanskrit had "the oldest and the most respectable pedigree of all the languages in the world.

The adoption of Sanskrit, Maitra argued, would also avoid the acrimonious feelings and jealousies and accusations that would arise when a provincial language was sought to be raised to the status of a national language. He referred to the adoption of Hebrew as the official language by Israel to "show respect to their ancient language, culture and civilization and their heritage." By adoption of Sanskrit, India also could revive its ancient glories and give her message to the West—the message of the Vedas, Upanishads, Gita Varahamihira, Charaka and Susruta. It is through the message of spiritual life alone that India could regain its position of glory. Adoption of Sanskrit would give India great chance of shaping our future generations and of letting the world know that we also know to respect the rich heritage of our spiritual culture.

However, what came out of all that discussion in the Constituent Assembly was that Sanskrit was included in the 8th Schedule of the Constitution as one of the Indian languages (the number of these languages has now gone up to 18). Also, it was provided that Hindu, which was to the official language, would be developed by drawing wherever necessary for its vocabulary primarily on Sanskrit. This was hardly a fair deal to Sanskrit.

Nehru himself continued to pretend reverence for Sanskrit. While speaking on a Private Member's Bill in 1959, Nehru *inter alia* said that people grew from their roots. India had a history of 5,000 to 10,000 years. Language was a symbol of continuity. The language to which most Indian languages were connected was Sanskrit. But it was lip service. In reality Nehru sabotaged the cause of Sanskrit.

In fact, Sanskrit made a significant contribution to the development of all the Indian languages. With the exception of four languages of the South, almost all the major Indian languages had their source and derived their sustenance from Sanskrit. The languages of the South also had a large part of their vocabulary derived from Sanskrit.

The greatest resistance to Hindi being made the official language of the Union of India was based on the ground that it would mean an inbuilt advantage to those having Hindi as their mother tongue and put the others at a disadvantage. If Sanskrit is made the official language, it will have several advantages:

1. Since Sanskrit is not the mother tongue in any State or for any group of people, it will provide an even playing field to everyone with equal advantages or disadvantages. If anything, it could have been more welcome in the South where there were many more Sanskrit scholars than elsewhere.
2. Sanskrit is a more scientific and phonetic language. As recent studies have shown, it is also most computer-friendly.
3. Sanskrit literature is one of the richest in the world.
4. As the official language, Sanskrit will become the greatest cementing force for national unity and integration and conservation, promotion and renaissance of Indian culture and values.
5. Sanskrit was accepted as the mother of all the languages in what philology refers to as the Indo-European Group of Languages. A large number of words in the modern European languages are derived from Sanskrit.

Also nearer home in south and South-east Asia, Bhasha Indonesia, Bhasha Malaysia, Khmer Rouge and Sinhalese are close to Sanskrit in many ways and have a large common vocabulary. The close links between the languages of Central Asia like that of Uzbekistan and Sanskrit are well known. Recent excavations in Uzbekistan have brought to light old Sanskrit inscriptions and manuscripts dating back to the beginning of the Christian era. If we want a renaissance of values and a revival of culture in our land, we should return to Sanskrit.

Not only is Sanskrit the most efficient language of the 21st Century, but its script, Devanagiri is also the most scientific in reproducing exact sounds. Write any sentence in English, then re-write the Hindi or Sanskrit translation in Devanagiri script, and you will find that in general the latter will take up about 25 per cent less space. It is, therefore surprising to listen to the persistent demand to write Hindi in Roman (i.e. English) script. On the contrary there should be an international campaign, (even if it may take half a century to fructify) to make Devanagiri the international script as well. And why not? After all numerals and decimals were accepted from Hindustan by the whole world.

Anti-Hindi zealots confuse Devanagiri with Hindi. The truth is that Hindi is just one of the languages using this script. Sanskrit, Marathi, Sindhi and some of the hill tract languages also use Devanagiri. This script thus can be used by any language. In fact, the scripts of all Indian languages even including Tamil and *Devanagiri* [considered as "sisters"] are direct descendants of the original *Brahmi* script. Any competent linguist would tell you that [see I. Mahadevan: *Corpus of the Tamil-Brahmi script*].

However, fanaticism blinds logic. The Punjabi (non-Sikh) Hindu under the leadership of Lala Jagat Narain had two decades ago launched a bitter campaign against the *Gurumukhi* script. To avoid being forced to use Gurumukhi they even declared that their language is Hindi and not Punjabi although they spoke the latter. This was out of misguided exuberance because the *Gurumukhi* script is very similar to the *Devanagiri* script, just as the Gujarati script is. Anyone who knows *Devanagiri* can master Gurumukhi in 24 hours. Yet a senseless agitation took place, followed by an unhealthy polarization process that culminated in Operation Bluestar in 1984, the tragic after-affects of which we feel even today.

The point is that even if *Devanagiri* is the most scientific phonetic script ever invented, for practical reasons there is every reason to respect the scripts of other Indian languages. In a calm dispassionate atmosphere which may take decades to attain, young people, especially those entering primary and secondary schools, will learn at least two languages and two scripts: (1) mother tongue and Sanskrit and (2) own script and Devanagiri. In the meantime, Hindi should continue to Sanskritize iteself to the point where it becomes almost indistinguishable from Sanskrit. It will then merge into Sanskrit, disappearing excepting in local dialects. Sanskrit was once long ago uprooted from India by Pali.

But after some centuries, this versatile language was rethroned by the same process via Mahayana Buddhism. A second rethroning of Sanskrit can now be achieved through Hindi. Till that day, if the three languages formula, which requires northerners to learn one southern language, is sincerely implemented, we can make a steady progress towards the goal of making Sanskrit once again the national language of India. Already 70 lakh students are currently studying Sanskrit, more than 200 universities in 35 countries after courses. It may take years to accomplish that but we must commit ourselves to that goal now. We should also commit ourselves to see that no language, especially Urdu, suffers because of the dominance of Sanskrit. In day-to-day conversations, such languages will continue to flourish.

Sanskrit is moreover the language of recitation of mantras – words of power that are attuned to the unseen. The possibility of such a finely attuned language is only conceivable by drawing upon sounds so inherently pure in combinations so harmoniously blended that the result is an refreshing and pure as the energy of creation forming into mountain streams and likes and the flawless crystal structures of natural gems, while at the same time wielding the power of nebulae and galaxies expanding into the infinitude of space.

The attitude towards learning Sanskrit in India today is, "It's too difficult." Actually Sanskrit is not difficult. On the contrary. The first stage, experiencing the individual power of each of the 49 basic sounds of the Sanskrit alphabet must have been worked out by learned grammarians on phonetic principles by long before it was codified by Panini around 500 B.C.

The script used to depict written Sanskrit is known as Devanagari or that "spoken by the Gods." Suitably for Sanskrit, it is a perfect system of phonetic representation. According to linguists, the phonetic accuracy of the Devanagari compares as well with that of the modern phonetic transcription as any fit for the computer.

Because of its inherent logic, systematic presentation and adherence to only the most clear and most pure sounds, the Sanskrit alphabet in its spoken form, is in fact the easiest in the world to learn and recall. Once the alphabet is learned, there is just one major step to take in gaining access to the Sanskrit language: learning the case and tense endings. The endings are what make Sanskrit a language of math-like precision. By the endings added onto nouns or verbs, there is an obvious determination of the precise interrelationship; of words describing activity of persons and things in time and space, regardless of word order. Essentially, the endings constitute the software or basic program of the Sanskrit language.

The rigour of learning the case endings is precisely the reason why many stop in their pursuit of Sanskrit. Yet by effective methods, fluent reading of the Devanagari script, accurate pronunciation, and the locating the ease and tense endings, we can easily learn the language. Such a method must take advantage of the fact that Sanskrit grammar is structured by precise patterns.

Learning of Sanskrit today requires understanding the case endings through the chanting of basic pure sound combinations in musical and rhythmic sequences is a way to overcome learning inhibitions, attune to the root power of the Sanskrit language and access the natural computer efficiency, speed and clarity of the mind.

Although learning Sanskrit in some ways presents challenges similar to those of learning calculus or music, it also induces a lubrication and acceleration of mental function that actually makes such a process exciting and enjoyable. Perhaps the greatest immediate benefit of learning Sanskrit by this method is that it requires participants to relinquish control, abandon prior learning structures and come into a direct experience of the language.

Another reason for the return of Sanskrit lies in computers. Sanskrit and computers are a perfect fit. The precision play of Sanskrit with computer tools will awaken the capacity in human beings to utilize their innate higher mental faculty with a momentum that would invariably transform the world. In fact the mere learning of Sanskrit by large numbers of people in itself represents a quantum leap in consciousness, not to mention the rich endowment it will provide in the arena of future communication.

Thus, for National Renaissance, we must unite the nation by propagating for adoption of Sanskrit as the ultimate national language of India. For the time being Hindi vocabulary should be continually sanskritized till Hindi itself merges with Sanskrit. Modernisation can never be achieved without the re-throning of Sanskrit as Hindustan's national language.

Chapter V

DE-FALSIFICATION OF INDIAN HISTORY

The defining events in our history have to be well understood so that we are not condemned to re-live it. Our national identity has been deliberately distorted by a history written about us by invading aggressors. Hence, today our youth tend to be defensive or ashamed by the 1000 year 'history' of India, of being ruled by foreigners, who came as marauders, looters and rapists.

But in reality, we Hindus and those others who acknowledge that their ancestors were Hindus, instead should be proud of our history even of what happened during the miserable 1000 years. This is because the onslaught of Islam and Christianity on rampage in West Asia, Africa and Europe was deflated and stopped in only India. Persia [Iran], Babylon [Iraq], Byzantine [Turkey] and Egypt, all great civilization capitulated to Islamic jehad within decades and converted 100% to Islam religion, while Europe crumbled to Christianity in just half a century each thereby wiping out their identities.

Even though India was looted, pirated, ravaged, ruled and raped for a 1000 years, however unlike the other peoples, Hindus as a collective did not capitulate. Thus India (in 1947) was still of 75% Hindus in the un-Partitoned Hindustan, 83% of the truncated India, and more significantly a continuing Hindu civilization.

It must be said at this juncture that barring a small exception, Hindus despite being duped, and despite the perfidy of the aggressors for the last thousand years, even while in defeat, remained steadfast in their individual commitment to the Hindu religion. Thus, despite state patronage to the ensuing onslaught, plunder, impoverishment, victimization and forced religious conversion spread over a thousand years, those of Hindu faith could not be decimated, and today, Hinduism remains thus the theology of the vast and overwhelming majority of Indians in the length and breadth of the terrain of India.

Defiant Hindus chose to suffer persecution and economic deprivation during Islamic and Christian reigns, such as through differential taxation {e.g., jezia} and zamindari land revenue appropriation and plain brutality, but by and large refused to capitulate and convert their religion.

This is an unprecedented but impressive achievement of any civilisational history of any nation. Compare this with the historical fact that Saudi Arabia, Iran, Iraq, Egypt, Turkey crumbled to become 100% Islamic within three decades of Islamic aggression, and so did Europe become 100% Christian within five decades of the Crusades.

Thus, even after almost a thousand years of such targeting by Muslims and Christian rulers, India of today still is predominantly Hindu. This was partly because of the victorious Vijayanagaram [which lasted twice as long and reigned over a larger area than Mughal rule from Akbar to Aurangzeb], the Sikh reign, and Mahratta kingdoms, and later the Freedom Movement, each inspired by sanyasis such as Sringeri Shankaracharya, Swami Ramdas, Guru Nank, Swami Vivkananda, Swami Dayanand Sarasvati of Arya Samaj, and Sri Aurobindo, besides patriots like Bankim Chatterjee and Subramania Bharati, who by their preaching and stirring poems about the Hindu identity ensured that the flame of Hindu defiance never dimmed.

It was also due to individual defiance of Hindus such as of Rana Pratap, Rani Jhansi, Rani Chennamma, Kattaboman and Netaji Subhas Bose. These icons are admired not because they led us to victory {in fact they were defeated or killed}, or had worked out for the Hindus a safe compromise with the aggressors {they did not!}, but because of their courage of conviction in the face of huge odds not to submit to tyranny, even if it meant death and/or impoverishment.

That courageous defiance is also part of our glorious legacy of Hindutva. But those who like Raja Man Singh or Jai Chand or Pudukottai Raja in order to live in pomp and grandeur, capitulated before the invader for selfish motives and betraying our heroes in war with the aggressor, are despised today by the people. Thus, Hindus safeguarded the nation remembering their heroes even those who lost, and rejecting those who had capitulated to the invader even if they had prospered. This is also an essence of Hindutva … the primacy of integrity over easy compromise.

But such passive defiance or intermittent victories in the battlefield to safeguard Hindu Rashtra—as Shivaji had called the motherland—is not sufficient for the future survival of the Hindu civilization. *Hindus today have won their freedom but it has not been translated into civilisational independence* as Parmacharya the Shankaracharya of Kanchi had wanted the Congress to ensure in 1947.

When the hordes of militant and terrorism-prone *Jehadis* and later the crusading Christianity arrived in India, they had aggressively challenged Hinduism. We had then very civilized rules of warfare in India such as fighting only in open barren fields, between sunrise and sunset, besides forgiving the loser and sending him back with due honour.

But these Muslim and Christian invaders by the changing of the rules of combat, despite being much smaller in number, seized power in sequence and thus established their own state in India, committed plunder lasting centuries. We became poor and weak as a consequence.

Change of rules of combat and war is what Prithviraj Chauhan had not realized while repeatedly defeating Mohammed Ghori and then forgiving him. Islam was established in India because of this error. But Chhatrapati Shivaji had fully understood the perfidy of these aggressors and their progeny, and accordingly improvised new tactics while dealing with the likes of Aurangzeb and Afzal Khan. The difference (in outcomes achieved) between Chauhan and Shivaji speaks for itself on this score.

Today the terrorists and religious missionaries are playing by even more clandestine and deceptive new rules, and by media management. Hindus have to accordingly devise a new strategy for dealing with such perfidious sophistication. Hindu civilization can be successful only after understanding the rules by which these enemy forces will scheme against us as a nation.

For example, modern India was portrayed by foreign rulers through school and college curriculum as a discontinuity in history and as a new entity much as are today's Greece, Egypt or Iraq. That curriculum is largely intact today. On the contrary efforts are afoot to bolster the disparagement of our past in the new dispensation today. A rudderless India, disconnected from her past has, as a consequence, becomes a fertile field for religious poachers and neo-imperialists from abroad who paint India as a mosaic of immigrants, not as a nation, but much like a crowd on a platform in a railway station. Instead the reality is that today's India is connected to her hoary past because this India is a nation of Hindus and those others {such as Muslims and Christians} who acknowledge that their ancestors were Hindus.

HINDU HISTORY

Well before the birth of Christianity and Islam, Hindu religion had been once intellectually dethroned by Buddha who introduced Hinayana Buddhism. But Adi Shankaracharya brought about a renaissance in Hinduism through his famous *shastrathas* {religious debate} on Advaita and caused a renaissance in Buddhism itself, which then came to be known as Mahayana Buddhism, conceptually in complete harmony with, if not indistinguishable from Hindu theology. He also challenged to a debate Mandana Mishra at Varanasi, who was then also an exponent of the Uttara Mimamsa school. The followers of the synthesis that emerged from this debate formed the school of Vedanta. Mishra became the first Shankaracharya of the Sringeri Mutt.

India is the country where Buddhism was born around 800 BC. It was the faith evolved and preached by a Sakya prince, Siddhartha Gautama, in the 10th century BC. He organized the new faith into an order and spread his message through his monk missionaries. During his long ministry, the Buddhist doctrine spread over what then were Magadha and Koshala {modern Bihar and Uttar Pradesh}.

During the reign of Ashoka of the Mauryan dynasty, Buddhism was proclaimed to be the religion of the state and actively promoted by the rulers. Missionary activity sponsored by the state took the religion outside the Mauryan realm. Sri Lanka (Ceylon) and Central Asia converted to Buddhism.

Over the next 1,500 years, Buddhism became the dominant religion in India and much of what is now East Asia, China included. Missionaries traveled out of India and pilgrims came to it from afar.

The Kushanas {identified as the Yueh tribe of western China} ruled North India, including what is now Afghanistan, during the lst century AD. The Kushanas were Buddhist by faith. Their emperor, Kanishaka hosted the third great Buddhist conclave, wherein the split between Mahayana and Hinayana Buddhism was recognized.

Then Buddhism disappeared from India, the country of its origin. Was it a result of Hindus slaughtering non-violent Buddhists, as Islamic Publications allege, toppling the stupas and taking over the monasteries with their fabled wealth? Not at all.

As Akhilesh Mithal (Covert, July 1-14, 2009) writes, this interpretation was also propagated during the British rule as it helped the colonialists justify their intrusion by pronouncing the Indians genetically incapable of living in peace with each other, without British rulers to keep them from being at each other.

Facts, however, do not support the thesis that Buddhism got wiped out of India because of violence. There may have been some cases of violence of course but mass slaughter did not occur.

The decline of Buddhism is mentioned in the travelogues left by devout Chinese pilgrims of the period 5th-8th century AD (Fa Xian,

Xuanzang, I-Ching, Hui-Sheng and Sung Yin). The successful 5th century Hun invasion is mentioned as one of the causes of Buddism's decline. The Brahmins of the time provided these newcomers (Hunas) with a method to enter the caste system at a high level. The ritual involved the tribal chief participated in a yajna. At the culmination of the ceremony, the chief was required to enter a large gold vessel. When he emerged after a few seconds he was proclaimed as being born of a gold womb and henceforth a Rajput or Kshatriya, and took the surname 'Singh'.

As the legitimization of the Hunas and their absorption in the Hindu fold came from the Brahmins, the new rulers gave all their support and offerings of gold, cattle and wealth to the temples. Little, if anything these after trickled to the viharas and the stupas of the Buddhists.

The Central Asians became Muslim in the 8th and 9th centuries, and the new convert's bigotry led to the slaughter of the Buddhist monks and to iconoclasm. Mahmoud of Ghazni, in the 10th century, and Shahabuddin Muhammad of Ghor, in the 12th century, brought this practice to the Indian plains. World famous universities like Nalanda were destroyed and the easily identifiable ochre-robed monks were slaughtered.

Hinduism had started absorbing Buddhist ideas and practice. Buddha himself became an avatar (incarnation) of Vishnu in sculpture as well as poetry. The growing Krishna cult saw him worshipped as such in the poetry of masters like Jayadeva.

Then how did this myth of Hindu slaughter of Buddhists take root? The cry over the violent end of Buddhism was raised in the 19th century by a Sinhalese called Anagarika Dharampal. Born in Colombo on 17 September, 1864, Anagarika Dharmapal took the vow of celibacy when he was eight years old.

In 1891, aged 27 years, Anagarika Dharmapal went on a pilgrimage to Bodh Gaya and found that the site greatly revered by Buddhists was under the control of a Brahmin priest who had supplanted the deity in worship with a Hindu icon and suppressed all traces of Buddhism.

At the time, the Theosophists were taking active interest in Indian political and religious awakening, and they were close to Anagarika who started the Mahabodhi Society in 1892, with the avowed objective of ousting the Brahmin priest and regaining control over the Bodh Gaya site sacred to Buddhists. The result was a long drawn law suit which achieved some success half a century later (in 1949), by which time much of the tension that had been generated between Hindus and Buddhists had dissipated.

In the 20th century, the urge for equality amongst the scheduled caste peoples of India drove reformers like Dr. Bhimrao Ambedkar to seek shelter in Buddhism. In 1959, Tibet militarized by the Chinese, saw its ruler, the Buddhists high priest known as the Dalai Lama, in effect driven out to India for survival and shelter. That formally ended Hindus-Buddhist tension. Today the Indian population (83% Hindu) has no antagonism towards Buddhism and accommodates it as another colour or hue, in a many-splendoured thing that Hindutva is.

Swami Vivekananda, in the nineteenth century, by recognizing that even if God is Absolute reality as in Advaita, one could not totally negate the reality of the world which regarded as a relative reality. As a logical corollary, Swami Vivekananda propounded the concept of Hinduness, which Savarkar gave a political content to, in the term Hindutva. The roots of of Hindutva are in Swami Vivekananda's sermons and writings, and represent a definition of the identity of the moden Hindu.

However, Marxist intellectuals and their Macaulayist fellow travelers have deliberately obfusecated the Vedanta roots of Hindutva and have run a vicious campaign to wrap the concept in Fundamentalism. Hence before I venture further here, I need first to rebut the premises underlying this campaign since the renaissance that had begun in the late nineteenth century to redefine the Hindu identity {in contemporary terms and norms valid in a pluralistic society}, was aborted by the confusion thus created in Hindu minds by a vaguely understood concepts implicit in the Marxist and neo-Marxist verbiage because of which Indian society became gradually and increasingly fragmented in outlook and of confused perspective.

This is understandable since Vedantic Hindutva is antithetical to Marxism. Marx had advocated that human history is only capable of economic interpretation and in this one-dimensional society violent class struggle between the haves and have-nots is the only method of change. It must lead to the annihilation of the haves by the have-nots.

Hindu society thus under Marxian intellectual influence through academia and media became confrontationally divided by caste, even by religion as in Nandigram, hence became increasingly mutually antagonistic.

Further attempts at creating disharmony were made through falsification in history texts. One of the fraudulent ideas of Indian history is the Aryan Invasion theory, originally devised by F. Max Muller in 1848 who was paid by the East India Company trace the history of Hinduism as originating in the alleged invasion of India's indigenous people by "white skinned" Aryans around 1500 BCE. The theory was reinforced by other paid research over the next 120 years of Indian scholars, and became the accepted history of Hinduism, not only in the West but in India. There is now enough evidence to show that Muller, and those who followed him, were completely wrong.

Attempts at Hindu debilitation thus made through falsification in history texts adopted for curriculum in the education system, was to disconnect and disinherit the contemporary Indian from the past glory of Hindu India. The intrinsic Hindu unity has been sought to be undone by legitimizing such bogus concepts as Aryan-Dravidian racial divide theory {AIT}, or that India as a concept never existed till the British imperialists invented it, or that Indians have always been ruled by invaders from abroad.

There is no such word as "aryan' in Sanskrit literature {closest is 'arya' meaning honourable person, and not community}or Dravidian {adi Sankara had in his *shasthrartha* with Mandana Mishra at Varanasi, called himself as a "Dravida shishu' that is a child of where three oceans' coastline meet, i.e. Kaladi in Kerala and Kanyakumari in Tamil Nadu; i.e. south India}.

The theory was deliberate distortion by British imperialists and propagated by their witting and unwitting mental slaves of India. Incidentally, the Aryan-Dravidian myth has now been exploded by modern research on DNA of Indians and Europeans conducted by Professor C. Panse of Newton, Mass. USA, Dr. Ms. Patel of Houston, Texas USA, and other scholalrls. Most recently, Dr. Toomas Kidisild of Cambridge University, U.K., and Dr. Gyaneshwar Chaubey of the University of Tartu in Estonia, have concluded after four years of research on 12,000 samples that all Indians "had common genetic traits irrespective of the regions of India to which they belonged." Thus they rule out the so-called AIT {Aryan Invasion Theory}.

In light of such new research, the British Broadcasting Corporation {BBC} service in it's October 6, 2005 service completely debunked the Aryan-Dravidian race theory stating that: "Theory was not just wrong, it included unacceptably racist ideas" {www.bbc.co.uk; religion&ethics homepage, Thursday, 6/10/05}. Even the tutees of British imperialist historians have begun to sing a different tune on the "Aryan invasion" theory {see my exchange in The Hindu with Dr. Romilla Thapar}.

The Aryan Invasion Theory was claimed to be based on archaeological, linguistic and ethnological evidence. Recent research has discredited this evidence. The changes brought to India by other cultures are not denied by nationalist historians, but they are no longer thought to be a major ingredient in the development of Hindu civilizational theory.

The Aryan Invasion Theory denies the Indian origin of India's mainstream culture but gives credit for it to invaders from abroad. It devalues India's culture by portraying it as less ancient that it actually is. The theory included unacceptable racist ideas, in a nutshell given below:

1. It suggests that Indian culture is a synthesis of cultures; and not intrinsically Hindu.
2. It implies that Hinduism is not an authentically indigenous religion but the result of cultural imperialism of invading Aryans.
3. It suggests that the "dark-skinned" Dravidian people of the South of India had got their present faith and culture after their conquest by the Brahmins who were Aryans.
4. It provided a basis for racism in the Imperial context by suggesting that the peoples of Northern India were descendants from Aryan invaders from Europe and so racially closer to the British, and hence British Imperialism was a continuation of Aryan rule.
5. It sought to justify the status of the British Raj to Dravidians who could argue that they were transforming India for the better in the same way that the Aryans had done thousands of year earlier; and impliedly thereby creating animosity towards Brahmins.

The Journal *Human Genetics* (In January, 2009) published an Indian genetic researchers' report titled, "The Indian origin of Paternal Haplogroup Riai Substantiaties the Autochthonous Origins of Brahmins and the Caste System." This report may deal a final and definite blow to the Aryan Invasion theory. The highly technical, original report is now available at:

[http://www.nature.com/igh/search.]

It shows that Brahmins, Scheduled Castes and Tribals of India all have a common genetic ancestry. The age of this yet-to-be-determined common parentage goes back, in India itself, to at least 9,000 years and possibly 20,000 years, leaving no genetic support for recent migration theories, including the Aryan-Dravidian theory concocted by the British Imperialists.

What however the current history textbooks today teach is still basically the theory of a few nineteenth-century European scholars (including Max Muller): according to them, around 1500 BC hordes of semi-barbarian, pastoral nomads, the so-called "Aryans," poured out of Central Asia into Northwest India, and drove south the ancestors of today's Dravidians; then, over a few centuries, they composed the Vedas, gradually got their "Aryan" culture (with its language, Sanskrit) to spread all over India, and eventually built the mighty Ganges civilization. This is so estimated because the Indus Valley layers so far excavated show destruction from unnatural causes of a city civilization, by carbondating, to be around 1500 BC, while the Rg Veda dated around the same period talks of a pastoral society. Thus pasting together, it means Vedic people destroyed the Indus Valley civilization. This, with some variations, is still today what the school-going child is taught. Not only textbooks, even respectable dictionaries and encyclopaedias will tell you more or less the same thing.

However, a debate now rages not only in India but in Western universities and among eminent scholars and archaeologists. Many of them have in recent years called for a new look at this Aryan Invasion Theory (AIT). In India that includes reputed scholars such as B.B. Lal, Dilip Chakrabarti, S.R. Rao, K.D. Sethna, V.N. Misra, J.P. Joshi, S.P. Gupta, R.S. Bisht, K.M. Srivastava, Madhav Acharya, N.S. Rajaram and others; in the West, Jim Shaffer, J.M. Keyoner, G.F. Dales, Colin Renfrew, J.F. Jarriage, K.A.R. Kennedy, Michel Danino, David Frawley, Koenraad Elst, Subhash Kak, Klaus Klostermaier, A.K. Biswas, Shrikant Talageri, Bhagwan Singh.

All of them agree that archaeological evidence entirely fails to support the Aryan invasion theory and actually goes against it; many of them also find the linguistic evidence that was used to buttress it quite shaky. But this debate, as we shall see, is by no means limited to the academic world; it is not a dry scholarly matter, and it has far-reaching repercussions on today's India, especially where her unity is concerned. In fact, Romilla Thapar, a tutee of the Imperialist West's historians, long the principal campaigner for AIT is now beginning to wobble.

I rely here on the works of N.S. Rajaram and Michel Danino, and have argued herein on their researches since I am no historian. But on chronology my own researches in 1968 at Harvard show that it was deliberately falsified by the British Imperialists to suit their nefarious aims in India.

Such a "history" has been deliberately created by the British as a policy. Sir George Hamilton, Secretary of State for India, wrote on March 26, 1888 that "I think the real danger to our rule is not now but say 50 years hence .... We shall (therefore) break Indians into two sections holding widely different views.... We should so plan the educational text books that the differences between community and community are further strengthened."

After achieving independence, under the leadership of Jawaharlal Nehru and the implementing authority of the ICS, revision of our history was never done, in fact the very idea was condemned as "obscurantist" and Hindu chauvinist. For a brief period, when Murli Manohar Joshi was in charge of Education portfolio at the Centre, an attempt was made to de-falsify history. But again it was done the same way, not by scholarly debate, but by changing textbooks, putting the 'cart before the horse'. The effort became discredited as saffronisation. But Joshi had got it right conceptually.

The fabrication and falsification of our History begins with chronology. The customary dates quoted for composition of the Rig Veda are: circa 1300 B.C., Mahabharat: 600 B.C., Buddha's *Nirvana:* 483 B.C., Maurya Chandragupta's coronation 324 B.C., and Ashoka: 268 B.C., These dates are entirely wrong. Those dates are directly or indirectly based on a selected reading of Megasthenes' account of India: 'Indika'. In fact, so much so that eminent British trained historians have called it the "sheet anchor of Indian chronology." The account of Megasthenes has also an important bearing on distant questions such as the two-race (Aryan-Dravidian) theory, and on the pre-Vedic character of the so-called Indus Valley Civilization.

Megasthenes was the Greek ambassador sent by Seleucus Nicator in c.302 B.C. to the court of the Indian king whom he and the Greeks called "Sandrocottus" stationed in "Palimbothra," the capital city of the kingdom. His son was called Sandrocryptus by Megasthanes. It is not clear how many years Megasthenes stayed in India, but he did write an account of his stay, titled *Indika.* The manuscript *Indika* is lost, and there is no copy of it available. However, during the time it was available, many other Greek writers quoted passages from it in their own works. These quotations were meticulously collected by Dr. Schwanbeck in the nineteenth century, and the compilation is also available to us in English (J.M. McCrindle: *Ancient India as Described by Megasthenes and Arrian*).

When European indologists were groping to date Indian history during the nineteenth century (after having arbitrarily rejected the various *Puranas),* the Megasthenes account came in very useful. These scholars simply identified "Sandrocottus" with Chandragupta, and "Palimbothra" with Pataliputra. Since Megasthenes talks of Sandrocottus as being a man not of "noble" birth who essentially usurped the throne from Xandrames and founded a new dynasty, the western writers took it as enough evidence to suggest that Sandrocottus was Maurya Chandragupta, who deposed the Nanda (=Xandrames) dynasty, and founded the Maurya dynasty. This identification, thus places Maurya Chandragupta circa 302 B.C.

Megasthenes also notes that Sandrocottus was a contemporary of Alexander, and came to the throne soon after Alexander's departure. With a little arithmetic on how many days it would have taken Alexander to cross the Indus, etc., the scholars arrive at c.324 B.C. as the date of Chadragupta Maurya's coronation. *It is on this date that every other date of Indian history has been founded and re-constructed.* The western writers constructed other dates of Indian history by using the date on the number of years between kings given in the *Puranas,* even though they have generally discredited this source. For instance, the Puranas give the number of years for the reign of Chandragupta and Bindusara as 62 years. Using this period, Asoka's coronation year is calculated by them as 324-62=c. 262 B.C. This estimated year is then cross-checked and adjusted with other indicators, such as from the Ceylonese Pali tradition. The point that is being made here is that some of the important dates of Indian history have been directly determined by the identification of Megasthenes' Sandrocottus with Maurya Chandragupta, and Xandremes with Nanda.

The founder of the Mauryas, however, is not the only Chandragupta in Indian history, who was a king of Magadh and founder of a dynasty. In particular, there is Gupta Chandragupta, a Magadh king and founder of the Gupta dynasty at Pataliputra. Chandragupta Gupta was also not of "noble" birth and, in fact, came to power by deposing the Andhra king Chandrasri. That is, Megasthenes', Sandrocottus may well be Gupta Chandragupta instead of Maurya Chandragupta (and Xandremes the same as Chandrasri, and Sandrocryptus as Samudragupta). In order to determine which Chandragupta it is, we need to look further. It is, of course, a trifle silly to build one's history on this kind of tongue-gymnastics, but I am afraid we have no choice but to pursue the Megasthenes evidence to its end, since the currently acceptable but falsified history is based on it.

In order to determine at which Chandragupta's court Megasthenes was ambassador, we have to look further into his account of India. We find he was at Pataliputra. We know from the *Puranas* (which are unanimous on this point) that all the Chandravamsa king of Magadh (including the Mauryas) prior to the Guptas, had their capital at Girivraja (or equivalently Rajgrha) and not at Pataliputra. Gupta Chandragupta was the *first* king to have his capital in Pataliputra. This alone should identify Sandrocottos with Gupta Chandragupta. However, this point is a bit controversial because some 11th century A.D. sources call Pataliputra the Maurya capital, e.g., Vishakdatta in *Mudrarakshasa.*

Pursuing Megasthenes' account further, we find most of it impossible to believe. He appears to be quite vague about details and is obviously given to the ancient Greek writers' weakness in letting his imagination get out of control. For example, "Near a mountain which is called Nulo there live men whose feet are turned backwards and have eight toes on each foot" [See Solinus 52.36-30 XXX.B.] "Megasthenes says a race of men (exist in India) who neither eat or drink, and in fact have not even mouths, set on fire and burn like incense in order to sustain their existence with odorous fumes...." (Plutarch, Frag. XXXI). However, Megasthenes appears to have made one precise statement of possible application which was picked up later by Pliny, Solinus, and Arrian. As summarized by Professor K.D. Sethna of Pondicherry, it reads:

> "Dionysus was the first who invaded India and was the first of all who triumphed over the vanquished Indians. From the days of Dionysus to Alexander the Great, 6451 years reckoned with 3 months additional. From the time of Dionysus to Sandrocottus the Indians reckoned 6452 years, the calculation being made by counting the kings who reigned in the intermediate period to the number 153 or 154 years. But among these a republic was thrice established, one extending...years, another to 300 and another to 120. The Indians also tell us that Dionysus was earlier than Heracles by fifteen generations, and that except for him no one made a hostile invasion of India but that Alexander indeed came and overthrew in war all whom he attacked."

While there are a number of issues raised by this statement, the exactness with which he states his numbers should lead us to believe that Megasthenes could have received his chronological data from none else than the Puranic pundits of his time. To be conclusive, we need to determine who are the "Dionysus" and "Heracles" of Megasthenes' account.

Traditionally, Dionysus (or Father Bachhus) was a Greek God of wine who was created from Zeus's thigh. Dionysus was also a great king, and was recognised as the first among all kings, a conqueror and constructive leader. Could there be an Indian equivalent of Dionysus whom Megasthenes quickly equated with his God of wine? Looking through the Puranas, one does indeed find such a person. His name is Prithu.

Prithu was the son of King Vena. The latter was considered a wicked man whom the great sages could not tolerate, especially after he told them that the elixir *soma* should offered to him in prayer and not to the gods (*Bhagavata Purana* IV.14.28). The great sages thereafter performed certain rites and killed Vena. But since this led immediately to lawlessness and chaos, the *rshis* decided to rectify it by coronating a strong and honest person. The *rshis* therefore churned the right arm (or thigh; descriptions vary) of the dead body (of Vena) to give birth to a fully grown Prithu. It was Prithu, under counsel from *rshi* Atri (father of *Soma),*who reconstructed society and brought about economic prosperity. Since he became such a great ruler, the *Puranas* have called him *adi-raja* (first king) of the world. So did the Satapatha Brahmana (v.3.5 4.).

In the absence of a cult of *Soma* in India, it is perhaps inevitable that Megasthenes and the other Greeks, in translating Indian experiences for Greek audiences, should pick on adi-raja Prithu who is "tinged with Soma" in a number of ways and bears such a close resemblance to Dionysus in the circumstances of his birth, and identify him as Dionysus. If we accept identifying Dionysus with Prithu, then indeed by a calculation based on the *Puranas* (done by D.R. Mankad, Koti Venkatachelam, K.D. Sethna, and others), it can be conclusively shown that indeed 6451 years had elapsed between Prithu and a famous Chandragupta. *This calculation exactly identifies Sandrocottus with Gupta Chandragupta and not with Maurya Chandragupta.* The calculation also identifies Heracles with Hari Krishna (Srikrishna) of Dwarka.

This calculation must be necessarily long and tedious to counter the uninformed general feeling first sponsored by Western scholars, that the *Puranas* spin only fairy tales and are therefore quite unreliable. However, most of these people do not realize that most *Puranas* have six parts, and the *Vamsanucharita* sections (especially of Vishnu, Matsya, and Vagu) are a systematic presentation of Indian history especially of the Chandravamsa kings of Magadha. In order to establish these dates, I would have to discuss in detail the cycle of lunar asterisms, the concept of them according to Aryabhatta, and various other systems, and also the reconciliation of various minor discrepancies that occur in the *Puranas.* Constraints of space, however, prevent me from presenting these calculations here, but I would be quite happy to take it up in correspondence with readers.

On the basis of these calculations we can say that Gupta Chandragupta was "Sandrocottus" c.327 B.C. His son, Samudragupta, was the great king who established a unified kingdom all over India, and obtained from the Cholas, Pandyas, and Cheras their recognition of him. He also gave a beating to Seleucus Nicator, while his father Chandragupta was king. On this calculation we can also place Prithu at 6777 B.C.Derivation of other dates without discussion may also be briefly mentioned: Buddha's Nirvana 1807 B.C., Maurya Chandragupta c. 1534 B.C., Harsha Vikramaditya (Parmar) c. 82 B.C. Arun Bansal, who pioneered computer casting of horoscopes has, using astronomical data on planet positions given in the Puranas, determined that Lord Krishna was born on July 21, 3228 B.C and went back to his heavenly abode on February 18, 3102, when Kaliyug started. Western scholars accept the Puranic sequence of dynasty and Kings, so why not the dates?

Instead Western scholars have constructed an enormous edifice of dates to suit their contrived chronology of Indian history. A number of them are based on misidentification. For instance, the Rock Edict XIII, the famous Kalinga edict, is identified as Asoka's. It was, however, Samudragupta's. Samudragupta was a great conqueror and a devout admirer of Asoka. He imitated Asoka in many ways and also took the name Asokaditya. In his later life he too became a *sanyasi or monk. The Ceylonese Pali traditions leave out the Cholas, Pandyas, and Cheras from the list of Asoka's kingdoms, whereas Rock Edict XIII includes them. In fact, as many scholars have noted, the character of Asoka from Ceylonese and other traditions is precisely (*as R.K. Mukherjee has said) *what does not appear in the principal edicts. Facts which directly contradict Westerners theories, they have rather flippantly cast aside. We* *state here only two examples of such facts: (1) Fa-hsien was in India and at Pataliputra c.410 A.D. He mentions a number of kings, but makes not even a fleeting reference to the Gupta Kingdom, even though according to European scholars he came during the height of their reign. He also dates Buddha at 1100 B.C. (2) A number of Tibetan documents place Buddha at 2100 B.C.*

Thus, when we examine the accounts of ancient India as given in current history books still in use against the background of available data and the primary sources, we find a fundamental mismatch between scientific evidence and facts and historical theories propounded. As number of Indian scholars and institutions have begun to challenge the West-tutored falsified history. For example, Dr. N.S. Rajaram has admirably summarized this in his works debunking the bogus Aryan-Dravidian divide:

1. There is no Indian archaeological record of any invasion and/or massive migration from Eurasia in the Vedic period. If anything we find traces of movement in the opposite direction—to West Asia and even Europe.
2. The geography described in the *Rigveda* corresponds to North India in the fourth millennium BC and earlier and not Europe or Eurasia.
3. The flora and fauna described in the Vedic literature, especially those found in the sacred symbols, are tropical and subtropical varieties and not from the temperate climate or the steppes.
4. The climate corresponds to that found in North India.

The Aryan-Dravidian divide in the history taught in schools and universities is purely a conception of foreign historians like Max Mueller and has no basis in India historical records. This fraudulent history has been lapped up by many upper caste Indians, as their racial passport to Europe. Such has been the demoralization of the Hindu mind, which we have to shake off through a new factual account of our past.

The theory of the Aryan invasion, which is still taken as the foundation stone of the history of India, which was actual devised in the 18th and 19th centuries by British linguists and archaeologists, is that the first inhabitants of India were good-natured, peaceful, dark-skinned shepherds, called the Dravidians, who had founded what is called the Harappan, or Valley of the Indus civilization. They were supposedly remarkable builders, witness the city of Mohenjo-Daro in Pakistani Sind, but had no culture to speak of, no literature, no proper script even. They, around 1500 B.C., India is said to have been invaded by tribes called the Aryans: white-skinned, nomadic people, who originated somewhere in Western Russia and imposed upon the Dravidians the hateful caste system. To the Aryans are attributed Sanskrit, the Vedic or Hindu, religion, India's greatest spiritual texts, the Vedas, as well as a host of subsequent writings, the Upanishads, the Mahabharata, the Ramanaya, etc.

Thanks to this 'Aryan' theory, the British showed on the one hand that Indian civilization was not that ancient and that it was posterior to the cultures which influenced the Western world – Mesopotamia, Sumeria, or Babylon – and that whatever good things India had developed-Sanskrit literature, or even its architecture had been influenced by the West. Thus, Sanskrit, instead of being the mother of all Indo-European languages, became just a branch of their huge family. The religion of Zarathustra is said to have influenced Hinduism, and not vice versa. And on the other hand, it divided India and pitted against each other the low caste dark-skinned Dravidians and the high caste light-skinned Aryans, a rift which is till enduring.

But today, this theory is being challenged by two new discoveries, one archaeological and the other linguistic. Firstly, in the Rig Veda, the Ganges, India's sacred river, is only mentioned once, but the alleged 'mythic' Saraswati is praised fifty times. For a long time, the Saraswati river was indeed considered a myth, until the American satellite Landstat was able to photograph and map the bed of this magnificent river, which was nearly 14 km wide and took its source in the Himalayas. Archaeologist Paul-Henri Francfort, who studied the Saraswati region at the beginning of the Nineties, found out the Saraswati had "disappeared," because around 2200 B.C., an immense drought reduced the whole region to aridity and famine. "Thus," he writes, most inhabitants moved away from the Saraswati to settle on the banks of the Indus and Sutlej rivers." According to official history, the Vedas were composed around 1500 BC, some even say 1200 BC. Yet, the Rig Veda describes India as it was before the great drought which dried up the Saraswati, which means in effect that the so called Indus, or Harappan civilization, was a continuation of the Vedic epoch, which ended approximately when the Saraswati dried up.

Recently, the famous Indus seals discovered on the site of Mohenjo Daro and Harappa have been deciphered by Dr. N.S. Rajaram, a mathematician who worked at one time for the NASA and Dr Jha, a distinguished linguist. In the biased light of the Aryan invasion theory, these seals were presumed to be written in a crude Harappan (read Dravidian) script, although they had never been convincingly deciphered. But Rajaram and Jha, using an ancient Vedic glossary, the Nighantu, were able to prove that the script is of Sanskrit lineage and have so far deciphered 2000 seals. As the discovery of the Saraswati river, the decipherment of the Indus scripts also goes to prove that the Harappan civilization, of which the seals are a product, belonged to the latter part of the Vedic Age and had close connections with Vedantic works like the Sutras and the Upanishads.

Hence, it is becoming more and more clear that there never was an Aryan invasion in India, a theory which was imposed upon the subcontinent by its colonisers, is today kept alive by Nehruvian historians such as Romila Thapar, and missionaries (to convert the drowntrodden tribals and Dravidians, by telling them that Hinduism was a religion thrust upon them by the hated "Brahmin" invaders) and the Communists (who hate anything Hindu). But as long as India will not rewrite its history books and teach its children to be proud of its ancient and indigenous civilization, there will be others who will come and exploit India.

At a seminar on the 'History of Ancient India through Vedic Astronomy' held in 2003 in Chennai, organized by the International

Society for the Investigation of Ancient Civilizations (ISIAC), held in collaboration with Shri Chandrashekharendra Saraswathi Vishwamaha Vidyalaya (Deemed University), Kancheepuram, and Kupuswamy Sastry Research Institute, Chennai, there was a presentation on the dates of birth of Lord Ram and Lord Krishna.

Dr. N. Mahalingam, Chairman of ISIAC who heads Sakthi Sugars told the gathering that it was the culmination of an inquiry conducted at Ethiraj College, Chennai, since February 1979, ascertain the dates of ancient events using astronomical data available is the Vedas, the Puranas and Tamil Sangam literature.

A Tamil book by N.P. Ramadurai, a scholar from Thanjavur, whose findings were presented at the Chennai seminar, Ancient History Through Astronomy, concludes that the date of Ram's birth is 17-1-10205 BC, and Sri Krishna's is 23-7-3185 BC. "The findings have been based on information relating to astronomy culled from the Vedas, the Agamas and other ancient Sanskrit works," stated Mahalingam.

Saurabh Kwatia has observed, correctly that the ancient Indians had a perfect method of time measurement. They recorded the 'tithis'-days-according to the 'nakshatra' (stars) on which the moon prevailed, the months, the seasons, different Solstices and the positions of the astrologically relevant luminaries like the Sun, the Jupiter, the Venus and so on. In other words, the timings of the events were recorded in the astronomical format.

To convert this heavenly coded information into a simple calendrical timelines, all this is needed is a database of ephemeris. But cannot identical starry configurations occur in history. In general, the answer to this question is in affirmative, and the problem of timing reduces to a selection of a single date from the available solutions. It is similar to finding roots of an algebraic equation; there could be more than one roots or answers. However, this problem does not arise while timing events in Ramayana.

Sage Valmiki, the celebrated composer of Ramayana records the birth of Lord Rama as Chaitra Shuddha Navami (9th), on Punarvasu

Nakshatra and five plants were exalted then; Sun in Mesha upon 10 deg., Mars in Capricorn at 28 deg., Jupiter in Cancer at 5 deg., Venus in Pisces at 27 deg. And Saturn in Libra at 20 deg., the Sun, Mars and Rahu were in Dasharatha's nakshatra.

Calculating further backwards for the astral combination noted above, the date concludes to be only 4th December 7323 B.C. The starry configurations mentioned at the time of birth of Lord Rama are so unique that they have occurred only once so far in history, viz., on 4th of December, 7323 B.C. (however academically speaking, the date could well be before this date like some day in Treta Yug but the starry constellation would be very similar to the one of 4th December, 7323 BC.)

In another example of fixing dates, poetry comes as an additional help. Apart from providing the regular astronomical parameters at the time of Lord Rama's exile to the forests, Valmiki has beautifully described the sky at the moment. He states, "Crux (Trishankhu), Mars, Jupiter and Mercury have cornered the Moon. Vaishakha and Milky Way are shining in the sky." So poetically Valmiki describes the sketch as if the Moon was cornered by the planets. Using the additional input, Lord Rama's exile is fixed when he turned 17 years of ago.

In yet another example, confirmation of timing comes from another related event. Hanuman's return from Lanka after discovering Sita (in Sunderkanda, one of the most religious chapters of Lord Ramayana) is calculated using the previously mentioned tools; it comes out as a Pushya Pournima. Now, Hanuman had set out for Sita's search after the Ashwin masa as he himself says in Kishkindha. So he must have started the campaign in Kartika masa. One month, that of Margashirsha was spent in the cave of Swayamprabha. Some more time was spent in the search upto the South Sea (the present Indian Ocean), after which Hanuman entered Lanka, possibly on Pushya Shuddha, the 14th. Thus it highly probable that he returned on Pushya Paurnima, the next day of this entry.

Using the above techniques Kwatra has dated the following pivotal events of the Lord Rama at the following point in time:

Lord Rama's birth : 4th December 7323 B.C.,
Lord Rama's marriage with Sita : 7th April 7307 B.C.,
Lord Rama's exile : 29th November 7306 B.C.,
Hanuman's entry to Lanka : 1st September 7292 B.C.,
Construction of Setu (bridge) : 26-30th Oct. 7292 B.C.,
The beginning of the great war : 3rd November 7292 B.C.,
Ravana's killing by Lord Rama : 15th November 7292 B.C.,
Lord Rama's return to Ayodhya : 16th November 7292 B.C.,

As Dr. N.S. Rajaram has noted we now have the technical tools needed to unlock the secrets of our past, but it needs dedicated study and research in several disciplines. It is important, however, to familiarize oneself with the basics of human genetics to be able to make use of the wealth of ideas and data that are becoming available to historians. This calls for a new generation of historians that is more educated in science, as also less deferential towards anything handed down by Western academia. Humanities scholars in India need to catch up with the confidence developed by Indian scientists and technologists.

Sri Aurobindo wrote seven decades ago that "Indian scholars have not been able to form themselves into a great and independent school of learning is due to two causes: the miserable scantiness of the mastery in Sanskrit provided by our universities, crippling to all but born scholars, and our lack of sturdy independence which makes us over-ready to defer to European [and Western] authority." How true it is even today!

The history of no free country can be structured on foreign accounts of it. The time has come for us to take seriously our Puranic sources and to imbibe a de-falsified and well-founded history of ancient India, a history written by Indians about Indians. Such a history would bring out the amazing continuity of a nation, which nation asserted its identity again and again at times of war and political crises. It should focus on the fact that at the centre of our perception of Indian nation is the concept of the *Chakravartin* ideal—to defend the nation from external aggression while giving maximum internal autonomy to the *janapadas.*

A correct, defalsified history would record that Hindustan was conceptually one in the art of governance, in the style of royal courts, in the methods of warfare, in the maintenance of its agrarian base, and in the dissemination of information. Otherwise it was decentralized for autonomy of villages in self-administration. The Panchayat system is a manifestation of that.

An accurate history of course should not only record the periods of glory but the moments of degeneration, of the missed opportunities, and of the failure to forge national unity at crucial junctures in time that was required to confront and defeat foreign aggressors. It should draw lessons for the future generations from costly disunity errors in the past, for example when Baji Rao and Nizam-ul-Mulk failed to join force to defeat Nadir Shah in 1739. Similarly Madhav Rao and Haider Ali together could have crushed the corrupt East India Company, while Mahadaji Scindia failed to help Tipu Sultan against Cornwallis, thereby India was thoroughly defeated and conquered.

The same Cornwallis who miserably failed in the American War of Independence in the eighteen century was able to subdue a much larger population of India because of our inability to close ranks against the foreigner. Thus, it was not the much portrayed Hindu "submission" that was responsible for our subjugation but lack of unity and effective military strategy in a time of decadence and moral decay that had weakened our national resolve. Therefore, without such an accurate de-falsified history, India cannot develop the correct identity.

The correct perception of Indian identity is we are a people who have always constituted a nation living in a geographical location spanning from Kashmir to Kanyakumari, from Attak to Car Nicobar, bound together in a continuing civilization of more than 10,000 years, a people who are mostly of Hindu religious faith or of those others of separate but equally respected faith, whose ancestry is however Hindu. That is how the word Indian evolved.

At the center of the riddle of Indians' ancient past lies the famous Indus Valley (or Harappan) civilization, one of the world's oldest. It was certainly the most extensive by far, since it covered today's Punjab, Haryana, Gujarat, much of Rajasthan, Maharashtra and Kashmir, western Uttar Pradesh, the whole of Pakistan, even parts of Afghanistan; it was also one of the most sophisticated in terms of urbanization, industry, technology, trade and sailing. Its art and crafts were varied and refined, though much less abundant than in contemporary Egypt or Mesopotamia. However, its hallmarks were a remarkably peaceful civic organization based on cultural integration, and the care it bestowed on its humblest inhabitants. Its sanitation and water management, for instance, were of such a level that one wishes our municipal corporations would follow them today. In its fully developed phase (the "mature phase," as archaeologists call it), it lasted from about 2600 to about 1900 BC; its early phase dates back to at least 3500 BC (J.M. Kenoyer opts for 5000 BC). A few sites, such as Mehrgarh, even show a continuity of preceding cultures going back to 7000 BC. So far, over 2,600 sites have been identified, over half of them in India, with 700 along the dry bed of a mighty river to which we will soon return. While the best-known cites, Mohenjo-daro (on the Indus river) and Harappa (on the Ravi), now lie in Pakistan, Indian archaeologists have since Independence unearthed a number of important settlements, such as Dholavira and Lothal in Gujarat, Kalibangan in Rajasthan, Rakhigarhi and Banawali in Haryana.

When this civilization was discovered in the 1920s, the attempt was naturally to fit it into the accepted framework. It was therefore assumed that its inhabitants were Dravidians, that the invading Aryans destroyed its great cities, and that the surviving Dravidians fled south for refuge. But today, no one (except our Government's textbook writers takes this assumption seriously, since there is no evidence on the ground to corroborate it. Archaeologists, whatever their school of thought, whether Indian or Western agree at least on these three points:

First, as surprising as it may seem, there is no physical trace whatsoever of any invaders, Aryan or other, from the Northwest of elsewhere, and no findings have been made which could be associated with an Aryan people coming into India – neither pottery nor utensils nor tools nor weapons nor graves nor any form of art. It is hard to imagine how a people supposed to have conquered the subcontinent failed to leave the slightest physiocal trade! Not only that, there is also no trace of any major conflict in any of the cities, and no evidence of any southward population movement; the only clear movement, about the end of the Harappan civilization, is eastward and more precisely towards the Gangetic basic. B.B. Lal, former director-general of the Archaeological Survey of India observes:

> *"The supporters of the Aryan invasion theory have not been able to cite even a single example where there is evidence of "invaders" represented either by weapons of warfare or even by cultural remains left by them."*

J.M. Kenoyer, who is still pursuing excavations at Harappa, is even more categorical:

> *"There is no archaeological or biological evidence for invasions or mass migrations into the Indus Valley between the end of the Harappan Phase, about 1900 BC and the beginning of the Early Historic period around 600 BC."*

Second, experts analyzing the skeletons found in Harappan cities (especially in Sindh, Punjab and Gujarat) concluded that the physical traits of their inhabitants were not markedly different from those of the populations found today in the same regions. There is no sign of any sudden disruption in population patterns, only the gradual changes that one would expect to take place naturally over the centuries. Kenneth A.K. Kennedy, biological anthropologists at Cornell University, U.S.A., who has worked extensively on Harappan sites to study human skeletan remains, concludes unambiguously:

> *"Biological anthropologists remain unable to lend support to any of the theories concerning an Aryan biological or demographic entity.... What the biological data demonstrate is that no exotic races are apparent from laboratory studies of human remains excavated from any archaeological sites, including those accorded Aryan status {by the old school}. All prehistoric human remains recovered thus far from the Indian subcontinent are phenotypically identifiable as ancient South Asians.... In short, there is no evidence of demographic disruptions in the north-western sector of the subcontinent during and immediately after the decline of the Harappan culture."*

Third, as mentioned earlier, the highest concentration of Harappan settlements is found along a huge and now dry river, which follows with some precision (though more to the North) the traditional Sarasvati, and once flowed across Punjab, Haryana, Rajasthan, Sindh and Gujarat, joining the Arabian sea in Kutch. Its exact course has been plotted by geologists and confirmed by satellite photography; the Bhabha Atomic Research Centre has even found that in parts of Rajasthan, "in extreme desert conditions," the water of the Sarasvati "remains available at a depth of fifty to sixty metres," and radiocarbon measurements of some water samples have shown them to "range from 2400 to 7400 Before Present," with "no modern recharge discernible." Today, scientists agree that this river, whose bed was three to ten kilometers wide, could only have been the ancient Sarasvati – the same river which is often praised in the hymns in the Rig-Veda (This identification is accepted by most archaeologists, for instance Kenoyer, Raymond and Bridget Allchin, G.L. Possehl or D.P. Agarwal). But it so happens that this river dried up in stages, and its final disappearance has been scientifically dated to about 2000 BC. Then why did the supposed Aryans, who are said to have invaded India five hundred years later and to have composed the Rig-Veda still later, lavish so much praise on a long dried-up river? It stands to reason that the composers of the Vedic hymns lived near the Sarasvati while it was still in full flow, and that again fits perfectly well with the Harappan era.

In addition, had Dravidians fled to the South as was supposed, many scholars have asked why they should have forgotten the famous Indus script on the way, so that no trace of it is found in Southern India, and the oldest extant Tamil inscriptions had to wait another two thousand years, that too in the Brahmi script? Similarly, nowhere do we find in the South artifacts associated with Harappan culture, much less any trace of the urban skills found in Indus cities – in fact urbanization in the South grew only from the third century BC, probably under Mauryan and Roman influences.

Finally, it is increasingly recognized that there are strong links between the Veda and the Harappan culture: we find statues and seals depicting yogis and yogic postures, we find a Shiva-like deity, worship of a mother-goddess, fire altars, all of which are suggestive of Vedic culture. Harappan symbols include the trishul, the swastika, the conch shell (also used as a trumpet), the papal tree, all of which are central to later Indian culture. The Rig Veda itself is full of references to fortified cities and towns, to oceans, sailing, trade and industry, all of which are found in the Harappan civilization. Studying Harappan town-planning, R.S. Bisht, director at the Archaeological Survey of India and excavator of the well-known site of Dholavira in the Rann of Kutch, finds that city "a virtual reality of what the Rig-Veda, the world's oldest literary record, describes," {S.P. Gupta, Chairman of the Indian Archaeological Society, agrees: "Our analysis shows that ... the Indus-Sarasvati civilization reflects the Vedic literature."

So it is clear that objective data repudiate the old invasion theory. Archaeology completely fails to support the existence and arrival into India of any supposed Aryan people. On the other hand, there is much evidence to suggest that from a cultural point of view the Harappan civilization had a Vedic backdrop, which would make the Rig-Veda at least 5,000 years old.

Of course, many questions remain: For instance, what about the mysterious Indus script found on thousands of seals? The fact is that several scholars worked for decades trying to show that the language behind the script was some form of proto-Dravidian, but without any conclusive success at deciphering it. Most of them have now abandoned their attempt. Other scholars (such as S.R. Rao or N. Jha) worked on the opposite line, trying to show that the language was some form of Sanskrit, but their decipherments have not received general acceptance either. Only the discovery of a bilingual inscription, or a sufficiently long one (since most of the inscriptions on the seals are very brief) could clinch the issue.

So that is, briefly, what science has to tell us. One question: What does Indian tradition have to tell us on the same subject? Does it agree with science, or does it support the old Aryan theory? Does it also support the division between Aryans and Dravidians which comes as a result of the theory? The answer leaves no room to ambiguity: No Indian scripture makes any mention of an invasion from the Northwest or of a previous homeland outside India. In fact, the Vedic homeland most frequently referred to in the Rig-Veda is Saptasindhu, in other words, the Indus and Sarasvati basins, which is exactly where the Harappan civilization flourished.

Concluding, the Aryan-Dravidian myth has now been exploded and demolished by modern research on DNA of Indians. When Professor C. Panse of Newton, Mass. USA and other scholars published their research, the British Broadcasting Corporation (BBC) in it's October 6, 2005 service as the last citadel crumbling under the weight of evidence, completely debunked the Aryan-Dravidian race theory by stating that: "The theory was not just wrong, it included unacceptably racist ideas" {www.bbc.co.uk, religion and ethics homepage, Thursday, 6/10/05}. The damage done for two centuries still needs to be undone.

A rudderless India, disconnected from her past, as a consequence, has become a fertile field for religious poachers and neo-imperialists from abroad who paint India as a mosaic of immigrants much like a crowd on a platform in a railway junction. That is, it is clandestinely propagated that India has belonged to those who forcibly occupied it and gave it an identity. This is the theme around which the Islamic fundamentalists and fraud Christian crusaders are again at work, much as they were a thousand years ago, but of course in new dispensations, sophistication, and media forms.

Let me quote here Swami Vivekananda:

> *"There is not one word in our scriptures, not one, to prove that the Aryans ever came from anywhere outside India.... The whole of India is Aryan, nothing else."*

Some may say that this concerns the tradition of North India only. So let us take a look at the South. In the Sangam literature, we find the legendary origin of the Tamilians not in the North, but further South, in a now submerged island or continent called Kumari Kandam. This may be an embellished memory of the submergence of Poompuhar, the city described in the Shilappadikaram and Manimekhalai epics, a submergence confirmed by preliminary underwater explorations (note that marine archaeology in India is only beginning: we can hope for some major discoveries in the years ahead).

What about the so-called "Dravidian culture," then? No one will dispute the greatness and richness, even the distinctiveness of the Tamil genius, but I will certainly dispute what some like to call its "separateness." Early Tamil culture was no more "separate" than say, Bengali or Gujarati cultures. All of them have their own stamp and own original contribution, but all are branches of the same tree. If you take a look at the Shilappadikaram again, you will see vivid references to Indra, Shiva, Vishnu, Krishna, Durga, Lakshmi, and several mentions of the Veda; King Shenguttuvan is shown as bringing the stone for Kannagi's idol from the Himalayas, where his ancestors are said to have carved their emblem; he does fight North Indian kings, but there is no hint that their culture is regarded as different. In historical accounts, we find Chola and Chera kings proudly claiming descent from Rama or from kings of the Lunar dynasty – in other words, an "Aryan" descent. We are told that the greatest Chola king, Karikala, was a patron of both the Vedic religion and Tamil literature, while the Pandya king Nedunjezyn performed many Vedic sacrifices, and the dynasty of the Pallavas made their capital Kanchi into a great center of Sanskrit learning and culture. Another Pandya king is said to have fed the armies on both sides during the Bharata war. And let us now forget the reverence accorded in the South to Agastya, the great Rishi from the North. Countless similar examples could be cited from Sangam poetry or even the ancient Tamil grammar Tolkappiyam. {10} None of this suggests any clash of culture; rather the contrary, it was a mutual enrichment; while Vedic culture was welcomed in the South and harmonized with local elements, what has come to be called "Hinduism" owes much to the generous contribution the Tamil land made in return, for instance, in music, dance, architecture, or the bhakti movement.

Thus the Hindu unity of India has been seen from time immemorial. Sri Aurobindo never tired of stressing this essential unity:

> "In India," he said, "at a very early time the spiritual and cultural unity was made complete and became the very stuff of the life of all this great surge of humanity between the Himalayas and the two seas."

Sri Aurobindo said:

> *"A time must come when the Indian mind will shake off the darkness that has fallen upon it, cease to think or hold opinions at second and third hand and reassert its right to judge and enquire in a perfect freedom into the meaning of its own Scriptures. When that day comes we shall, I think, {.....} question many established philological myths – the legend, for instance, of an Aryan invasion of India from the north, the artificial and inimical distinction of Aryan and Dravidian which an erroneous philosogy has driven like a wedge into the unity of the homogenous Indo-afghan race."*

This intrinsic Hindu unity has thus been sought during the last two centuries to be undone by legitimizing such bogus concepts as Aryan-Dravidian racial divide theory, or that India as a concept never existed till the British imperialists invented it, or that Indians have always been ruled by invaders from abroad.

Modern India was portrayed by Marxist interests through this curriculum as a discontinuity in history, and as a new entity much as are today's Greece, Egypt or Iraq. That curriculum is largely intact today. On the contrary efforts are afoot to bolster the disparagement of our past in the new dispensation today. A rudderless India, disconnected from her past has, as a consequence, become a fertile field for religious poachers and neo-imperialists from abroad who paint India as a mosaic of immigrants much like a crowd on a platform in a railway station. That is, it is implicitly propagated that India has belonged to those who forcibly occupied it.

Thus the concept of intrinsic Hindu unity, and India's Hindu foundation are thus dangerously under challenge by these forces. Tragically most Hindus today are not even cognizant of it. Thomas Babington Macaulay who vowed that by change in India's educational system he would create a class of Indians in blood and colour, but English in taste, in opinions, in morals, and intellect, has eminently succeeded. The Hindutva movement based on Vedantic principles must undo this erroneous and dysfunctional assimilation.

Another deliberate misrepresentation of Indian history by the British was of the First War of Independence which the British re-named disparagingly as "Indian Mutiny."

On May 10, 1857, Indian soldiers of the regiments stationed at Meerut (U.P.) killed their British officers, marched to Delhi and liberated the city from British control. They then proclaimed the 82 year old Bahadur Shah Zafar as the "Emperor of Hindustan." The Emperor then appointed a Hindu as his 'Prime Minister' Mukund Ram just as Nana Saheb Baji Rao, the adopted son of the Peshawas and partner in the revolt, appointed a Muslim, Azimullah as his 'Prime Minister'. At Red Fort, the Bhagwa Dhwaj (saffron flag) was unfurled.

The uprising did not last long. In Delhi it was over by September 1857, and the domino effect in the country as a whole of the revolt was contained by end 1858. But the popular uprising fired the imagination of the nation and from the ashes of the burnt out revolution, sparks continued to ignite revolt in the country till Mahatma Gandhi led the nation finally to Freedom in 1947.

Exactly 148 years later today, however, the whole of India has become oblivious of this historic date and of the event that was the foreunner of India's freedom. No meetings, no TV discussions, no resolutions for this revolutionary day in a country which is ready to celebrate or mourn anything or anybody. Even for a Pope in far away Vatican we mourned for three days when the rest of the world except Italy did not see it fit to do so.

We forgot May 10, 1857 because we were programmed since then for nearly a century to delete it from out collective memory. After achieving Independence in 1947, the amnesia was not cured by Free India's government. Even the NDA government in the six years in office forgot about it, as they did mot other items of the nationalist agenda that had brought them center stage in the first place.

Time has however arrived to re-activate our memory and remember May 10, 1857 and put it on par with August 15, 1947. In one way, which I will explain shortly, the 1857 date is more significant for Indian nationhood and history than even the 1947 'date with destiny'.

The British imperialists who understood the significance and import of the 1857 uprising, had ensured that it be ridiculed and downgraded as a "Sepoy mutiny," as a sporadic and limited uprising of soldiers that was ignited due to obscurantist reasons such as aversion to 'pig fat' in the cartridges. Not only the Imperialists, but the Marxist thinkers as well sought to play it down as a 'reaction'. Writing in New York Daily Tribune in a series of articles in 1857, Karl Marx termed it as an army revolt, "a military mutiny" but of national proportion only because "the natives' apprehension" that Government may otherwise interfere with their religion. It was much later in 1957 a hundred year later that Marxist writer P.C. Joshi corrected the perspective of the party line. Others like Sir John Kaye, a prolific scribe, wrote that 1857 was due to the "fear on part of the Brahmins of the social changes" introduced by the British.

It was Veer Savarkar however who in 1909 challenged this diminution and degradation of the 1857 uprising. He wrote his account of 1857 under the title "The Indian War of Independence: 1857." It was printed in Holland, but nevertheless the British authorities proscribed it. Savarkar re-interpreted 1857 as a war of independence, and his magnum opus served to fire the imagination of the youth for years to come till 1947. His unfortunate involvement with those who conspired to assassinate Mahatma Gandhi dimmed the shine of his work, but in the end, Mrs. Indira Gandhi as Prime Minister commemorated his memory by issuing a special postal stamp in his honour.

Savarkar's contribution to nation building by his well researched and scientific analysis of 1857 uprising the First War of Independence shall remain everlasting and deserving of a Bharat Ratna. Only those brain washed by the British Imperialist can devalue it or detract from its seminal character. Savarkar saw the 1857 uprising as a national spirit that aroused "sepoy and civilian, king and pauper, Hindu and Mahomedan" to a revolution.

In his book the Indian War of Independence of 1857, he asks:

> "What, then were the real causes and motives of this revolution? What were they that for them men by the thousand willingly poured their blood year after year? What were they that Maulvis preached them, learned Brahmins blessed them that for their success prayers went up to Heaven from the mosques of Delhi and the temples of Benares?" And he answered this question as "These great principles were Swadharma (one's duty) and Swaraj {self-government}."

Savarkar approvingly quotes the newly installed 'Emperor of Hindustan's Proclamation' as stating:

> "Hindus and Mohamedans of India! Arise! Brethern arise ! Of all the gifts of God, the most gracious is that of Swaraj. God does not wish that you should remain idle. He has inspired in the hearts of Hindus and Mohamedans the desire to turn the English out of our country."

Thus Savarkar credits Nana Sahib, Bahadur Shah Zafar, Rani of Jhansi, and Khan Bahadur Khan of Rohilkhand along with the priests (Brahmins and Maulvis) of forcefully attempting a national consciousness of Hindustan to liberate the nation from foreigners.

The Hindustan, a term used by both Hindus and Muslims even today to describe India, would be 'Swadesh' for both Hindus and Muslims. Savarkar explains this adherence to the concept of Hindustan as follows:

"As long as the Mohamedans lived in India in the capacity of rulers, so long, to be willing to live with like brothers was to acknowledge national weakness. Hence, it was up to then, necessary to consider the Mahomedans as foreigners." And naturally so since no Muslim ruler adopted a secular state, and in fact adopted discriminatory taxes based on religion. Conversion to Islam was carried out by force, coercion and cruelty as evidenced in the tribulation suffered by Guru Teg Bahadur. So where was the question of brotherhood?

Savarkar then holds that after the heroism of Guru Gobind, Rana Pratap and the Maharattas, that grievance was no; more valid, and that the original distinction between the Hindus and Muslims "must be laid to eternal rest." Both communities, he adds in his *opus*, are children of the soil of Hindustan, children of the same Mother India and of the same blood. He exhorted all to "create a passionate desire in the Hindustan for this ideal, and make all the country to rise simultaneously for the purpose of achieving it."

The 1857 spirit and the magnificent articulation of it by Veer Savarkar stood us in good stead throughout the Freedom Struggle. It was ultimately detailed and destroyed by one "Himalayan Blunder" and two acts of treachery. The blunder was the Khilafat Movement of Mahatma Gandhi which he himself acknowledged as his Himalayan Blunder. By opposing the modernizing secular movement of Kamaal Ataturk in Turkey, Gandhi dignified reactionary conservative movement amongst Muslims of India, and rethroned the concepts of Darul Islam {Muslim ruled states} and Darul Harab {Muslims in violent rebellion in non Muslim ruled states} in large enough measure in the Muslim mind.

But it was the betrayal by Jawaharlal Nehru of the 1937 Lucknow electoral pact with Khaliq uz Zaman of the Muslim League that shocked the Muslims especially those Muslims who had wanted to be partners with Hindus in the Freedom Movement {by acknowledging that they were both children of Mother India seeking to liberate her}. Nehru wriggled out of a pre-election agreement with the Muslim League to share in power in the UP Government after finding that Congress Party had won majority on its own. This betrayal of a written pact swung emotional Muslims to demand Pakistan for the first time in 1940 at the Lahore session of the Muslim League.

Nehru again in 1946 by addressing a provocative press conference in Bombay sabotaged all efforts by Gandhi to effect a transfer of power from the British without Partition. Pakistan became a certainty that day, and the Hindu-Muslim brotherhood which flowered from 1857 onwards was subverted and finally laid to rest in 1947.

But the framework for Hindu Muslim brotherhood that Savarkar so brilliantly set out in his *The War of Independence 1857* needs to be revived. For that we must celebrate May 10, 1857 as equal to, if not more than August 15, 1947. The threat from the *Feringhi* {foreigner} is today as real as in 1857 and the nation must unite for it, without any appeasement or compromise on the ancient roots of Hindustan.

Partition became a fait accompli after the Jinnah-inspired terrorist attach on Hindus in Kolkata and other parts of Bengal leading to murder and rape of tens of thousands. Terror made Congress capitulate and Pakistan became inevitable.

But even today attempts are being made to 'whitewash' Jinnah's role.

Politicians nowadays are seen anxious to establish Jinnah's secular credentials. Both have ignored the crimes committed by Jinnah. They cite his speech on 11 August 1947 in the Constituent Assembly in the presence of Lord Mountbatten. Jinnah said that in a future Pakistan, everyone would be treated equally irrespective of their religion and non-Muslims would be free to practice their respective religion in Pakistan. Does that one speech make Jinnah a "secularist"? A close study of his speeches during 1934-48 shows that the word "secular" does not find mention in any of them, because acceptance of secularism means abandonment of the Shariah.

In 1910, Jinnah was elected to the Imperial Council on a reserved Muslim seat. He joined the AIML, formally in October 1913 and became its president in 1946. He gave up membership of the Congress in 1920, opposing Gandhi's decision to confront the British. One outcome of his efforts till then was the Congress-Muslim League Lucknow Pact of 1916, which settled the issue of separate electorate for the Muslims, paving the way for the birth of Pakistan. Jinnah married a Zoroastrian only after getting her converted to Islam.

In his meeting with Gandhi in September 1944, Jinnah demanded that the constituency for the plebiscite—to decide on the demand for Pakistan—would comprise only the Muslims, and not the entire population of the areas concerned.

After August 14, 1947 as head of the State of Pakistan, Jinnah talked of securing (a) "liberty, fraternity and equality as enjoined upon by Islam" (25 August, 1947); (b) "Islamic democracy, Islamic social justice and the equality of manhood" (21 February 1948); (c) "sure foundations of social justice and Islamic socialism which emphasized equality and brotherhood of man" (26 March 1948); (d) "the foundations of our democracy on the basis of true Islamic ideals and principles" (14 August 1948); (e) "the onward march of renaissance of Islamic culture and ideals" (18 August 1947). Are these pronouncements secular?

Earlier in his speech favouring the creation of Pakistan in the Muslim League conference in Lahore in 1940, he declared that "Islam and Hinduism – are not religions in the strict sense of the word, but are different and distinct social orders. The Hindus and Muslims belong to two different religious philosophies, social customs, literature, to two different civilizations they derive their inspiration from the different sources of history – (with) different epics, different heroes and different episodes."

In fact, less than one year before his August 11, 1947 speech, on 14th August, 1946, Jinnah called upon "the Muslims to get Pakistan by the sword." The result was the organized mass murder of at least 50,000 people of Kolkata and in the southern districts of East Bengal – Noakhali and Chittagong in particular. Jinnah never condemned the killings. But in the context of the ejection of Hindus from Noakhali in 1946, he said, that the transfer of population was in progress and that some sort of a machinery should be devised to carry it out on a large scale. Just on the eve of 15 August and after, when Jinnah was proclaiming his supposedly secular credentials in his speeches, the deportation of Hindus from Noakhali and elsewhere became an all out campaign. Jinnah, as the first Governor General of Pakistan, had the authority to control the situation. But he was then gearing up for the invasion of Kashmir, which took place on 20 October, 1947.

Thus the life of Jinnah and his activities illustrate that he was driven by the idea of an Islamic state for the Muslims even if it meant the destruction and displacement of hundreds of thousands of Hindus. Jinna's speech on 11 August 1947 was therefore fraudulent, a presentation designed to please temporarily the British elite. The constitution of Pakistan, which he had proposed and was implemented in 1955, was meant for an Islamic and not a secular state.

But Dr. Ambedkar never had any illusions. He wrote his famous book, Pakistan or the Partition of India in the year 1940. He asserted and pleaded that the partition of India into Islamic Pakistan and Hindu India was most desirable and necessary.

Dr. Ambedkar discussed the question of aggressions coming from the northwest side of India – Russia via Afghanistan. He observed, "*if the invasions came from Russia, it may be hoped that these gate-keepers of India will be staunch and loyal enough to hold the gate and stop the invader. But suppose the Afghans (now Pakistanis) singly or in combination with other Muslim States march on India, will these gate-keepers stop the invaders or will they open the gates and let them in? This is a question which no Hindu can afford to ignore. This is a question on which every Hindu must feel assured, because it is the most crucial question."*

The loyalty and dependability of NWFP Muslims in the army can only be tested by considering how it will behave in the event of an invasion by the Afghans (now, Pakistan). "*Will they respond to the call of the land of their birth or will they be swayed by the call of their religion, is the question which must be faced if ultimately security is to be obtained. It is not safe to seek to escape from these annoying and discomforting questions by believing that we need not worry about a foreign invasion."*

On the contrary, I should not be surprised if it was entered in the Constitution, when revised, as a safeguard for the Muslim Minority. The Musalmans are sure to make this demand and as against the Hindus, the Muslims somehow always succeed" How prophetic Dr. Ambedkar was.... Articles 29 and 30 of free India's Constitution are a testimonial to Minority appeasement, separatism and bloc voting power.

For our nation building therefore we need to clearly understand the political ideology embedded in Islamic theology. Otherwise Hindus will keeping coming to grief. The psychological change that Muslim undergoes from when he is in a minority to when he is in a majority is a paradigm change.

The Muslim-ruled municipalities have thereafter converted these areas into mini 'Darul Islams', in a Hindustan of 83% Hindus! The minority Hindu areas of the municipality were thus denied civic amenities, funds for schools, garbage clearing etc., and sent notices in Urdu. Hindus were bluntly told convert to Islam if they wanted civic facilities.

I could not believe this was possible in South India where Hindus are actually above national average at 90 percent of the population. I had visited Thondi and Rasathipuram Municipalities of Ramanathapuram and Vellore districts of Tamil Nadu respectively, and was truly shocked by what I saw. Both these municipalities are in Muslim majority areas, and the Local Bodies election had empowered the Muslims with their capture of the municipalities.

I know that in Kashmir valley, Muslims who are in majority have actively or passively connived in driving out half a million Hindus out of their homes and made them refugees in their own country. Temples have been demolished in the valley on a daily basis.

Thus, such atrocities are happening not only in Kashmir, but in other parts of India as well in pockets wherever Muslims are in majority, e.g., Mau and Meerut. In pocket boroughs of India thus, Darul Islam has today returned to India after two centuries. Considering that a demographic re-structuring is slowly but surely taking place, with Hindu majority shrinking everywhere, Darul Islam in pockets might indeed, like amoeba, proliferate, coalesce, and jell into a frightening national reality – unless we Hindus wake up and take corrective action now, actions for which we shall of course not get a Nobel Peace Prize.

Darul Islam is a Muslim religious concept of a land where Muslims rule, and the non-believers in Islam are termed as "Dhimmis." The term 'Dhimmi' was coined after the Jews were crushed in Medina {Khaybar to be exact}, and the defeated Jews accepted that if they did not convert to Islam, then they would accept second class status politically, culturally, and religiously. This included zero civil rights including the right to modesty of women, and the special tax jizya.

There is thus no scope for Muslims and non-Muslims uniting as equals in the political, cultural, or social system in a Darul Islam where Muslims rule. Secular order in India thus is possible only when Muslims are not in power. Thondi, Rasathipuram, and other places prove that the Muslim mind suffers from a dangerous duality – of seeking secularism when out of power and imposing a brutal demeaning theocracy for non-Muslims when in power.

It is this duality that patriotic Hindus must re-shape by modern education and other means, as also retain its demographic overwhelming majority in India. We do not have much time, in fact about 45 years, as the X-graph of statistical regressions estimated by

J.S. Bajaj and colleagues shows. 'X' represents the two trends – Hindu percentage declining and Muslim percentage rising, and intersecting in the year 2061.

The 'dhimmitude' of Jews in Medina and later in Mecca represents the beginning of religious apartheid inherent and basic to Islamic mores, and practiced long before what we saw in South Africa on the basis of colour and race, and that which became prevalent during the Islamic imperialist rule in parts of India. Hindus were dhimmis for six hundred years in those parts of India despite being a bigger majority in the country than even today. Hence, a majority is not enough. Hindus need also a Hindu mindset to be free.

In his Presidential address to the Muslim League in Lahore in 1940, Mohammed Ali Jinnah had articulated this concept of apartheid in his own inimitable way:

> "To visualize Hindus and Muslims in India uniting to create a common nation is a mythical concept. It is only a fancy dream of some unawakened Hindu leaders.... The truth is that Hindus and Muslims are two different civilizations ... since their thought process grow on different beliefs."

Large sections of Muslims in India then had rejected Jinnah and his concept of non-compatibility of Muslims with Hindus. But after Independence and Partition, instead of building on this rejection by many Muslims, the Nehru era saw increasing pandering precisely to the religious element that believed in this apartheid. Indira Gandhi vigorously continued this appeasement thereby nurturing the apartheid mentality of Muslim orthodoxy.

But the final undermining of the enlightened Muslim came when the government capitulated in the Shah Bano case. Thousands of Muslims had demonstrated on the streets demanding that the government not bring legislation that would nullify the Supreme Court's judgment in the Shah Bano case but in vain. Rajiv Gandhi, I learnt later, on counsel from his Italian Catholic family, had surrendered to the hard line clerics who protested that the Supreme Court had no right to interfere and to defacto amend the Shariat, the Islamic law code. These relatives on a directive from the Vatican thought that if secular law would be applied to Muslims, it can be to the Christians too.

This was a nonsense argument of the Muslim clerics, since the Shariat had already been amended, without protest, in the criminal law of India. The Indian Penal Code represents the uniform criminal code that equally applies to all religious communities. I therefore ask the clerics: if a Muslim is caught stealing, can any court in India direct that his hand at the wrist be cut off as the Shariat prescribes? If Muslims can accept a uniform criminal code what is the logic in rejecting the uniform civil code?

In India, Dhimmi status for Hindus during Islamic imperialist rule has had other social implications. Defiant Brahmins and Kshatriyas who had refused to convert and chose to remain Hindus, were forced to carry night soil and suffer great indignities for their women folk. Or it meant gross mental torture. Guru Teg Bahadur, for example, had to see his sons sawed in half, before the pious Guru's own head was severed and displayed in public.

The debasement of Hindu society then was such that those targeted valiant Brahmins and Kshatriyas who had refused to convert and thus made to carry night soil, were disowned by other Hindus and declared to be asparshya or "untouchable." The ranks of the Scheduled Caste community which was not more than 1% of the population before the advent of Islam in India, swelled to 14 percent by the time Mughal rule collapsed.

Thus, today's SC community especially those who are still Hindus, consists mostly of those valiant Brahmins and Kshatriyas who had refused to become Muslims but preferred ostracization and ignominy in order to remain Hindus. Hindu society today should offer koti koti prannams to them for keeping the Bhagwa Dhwaj of Hindu religion flying even at great personal cost and misery.

At this juncture let me add even though I oppose conversion as violence, as Swami Dayanand Sarasvati boldly wrote to the Vatican Pope, nevertheless if an Indian Muslim or Christian changes his religion to Hinduism today, I will not regard it as conversion because it is a return to the Hindu fold of those whose ancestors had been forcibly converted.

Islam is not only and merely what is stated in the Koran. Islam is a trilogy of Koran, Sira and Hadith. This trilogy defines a "true" Muslim or believer. Therefore those who sing praises of the Koran to prove that Islam is intrinsically humane have not read the Sira and Hadith. While Koran is a compilation of revelations of Allah to Mohammed through angel Gabriel, Sira is essentially a biography of Mohammed, while Hadiths are a collection of proverbs, poems, and practices of Mohammed. Thus Islamic theology is Koran plus what the Prophet said or did. This is borne by content analysis of the trilogy. Koran has 153,000 words, while Sira has 408,000 words, and Hadith compiled by Bukhari has 338,000 words. Hence, Koran is just 17% of Islam, while Sira and Hadith are 83% and about Prophet Mohammed.

Chapter VI

Integral Humanism and Economic Development

In 1969, I had presented a "Swadeshi Plan" at the Patna Session of the Bharatiya Jana Sangh which angered the Leftists. It was an instant national event. So much so, that Prime Minister Mrs. Indira Gandhi, who then held the Finance Portfolio, on March 4, 1970 took the floor of the Lok Sabha during the 1970-71 Budget debate to denounce the Swadeshi Plan, and me by name, as "dangerous". She was particularly irked by my thesis that if India gave up socialism for competitive market economic system, then India can grow at 10% per year, achieve self-reliance and produce nuclear weapons.

Those days in the 1970s, few dared to question socialism. The entire Left-wing academia therefore pounced on me because I debunked the Soviet economic model by describing it as a prescription for disaster for India. I was however proved right and vindicated later in 1991 financial crisis, when as Commerce Minister, I presented the first blue-prints for economic reform that was subsequently adopted by the Narasimha Rao government. Economic boom followed.

Hence, my Swadeshi Plan was noticed and discussed nationwide by intellectuals and the media following Mrs.Gandhi's outburst. Her Education Minister Mr. Nurul Hasan, then ensured that I lost my professorship at IIT, Delhi in 1972 [to which post I was re-instated twenty years later by a Delhi Court].

The Swadeshi Plan was influenced by Deendayal Upadhyaya's Integral Humanism, and by Dattopant Thengadi's commentaries on it. Guru Golwalkar, the Sarsanghchalak of the RSS, had also spoken to me about the best suited economic policy for India. Guruji motivated me when in 1970 I met him after I had returned to India from a long tenure as professor of economics at Harvard University USA.

Guru Golwalker, the RSS Chief (1940-1973) had long foreseen the debilitating effects of materialist outlook on human society, and long before the consumerism of globalization that we see today. He advocated the harmonization of material pursuits with spiritual and moral values to create an integral person. Guruji himself told me in 1970 that "swadeshi [self-reliance] and vikendrikaran [decentralization] are the two concepts which can summarise the economic policy suitable for our times." He added that economic policy thus designed must be consistent with the spiritual values of our ancient nation. It is this embryonic idea that Deendayal Upadhyaya developed into his thesis of *Integral Humanism.* To quote Deendayalji himself:

> "Both these systems, capitalist and communist, have failed to take account of the Integral Man, his true and complete personality, and his aspirations. One [system] considers him as mere selfish being, lingering after money, having only one law, th law of fierce competition, in essence the law of the jungle; whereas the other has viewed him as a feeble lifeless cog in the whole scheme of things regulated by rigid rules, and incapable of any good unless directed. The centralization of power, economic and political, is implied in both. Both therefore result in dehumanization of man" [*Integral Humanism,* Navchetan Press, Delhi, 1965, p. 76].

Deendayaiji also dismissed democratic or 'Gandhian' Socialism as failing to establish the importance of the human being [*op. cit.,* p.74-75]. He said: "The needs and preferences of individuals have as much importance in the socialist system as in a prison manual."

This is in keeping with Guruji's thoughts [Bunch of Thoughts, p. 13] that class struggle as a concept embedded in socialism, is anti-human, and instead, class harmony and conflict resolution are the basic instincts of the human. Guruji stated that the Communist concept of the dictatorship of the proletariat was nothing but "the dictatorship of the dictator of a dictatorial party."

Thus now well past the centennial year of Sri Guruji's birth, we can proudly assert that he gave the nation a new direction in economics by propounding the concept of integral outlook—namely that economic behaviour must blend with spiritual values to produce a happy society. We in this country have yet to incorporate this direction in our economic policy, but time will soon be at hand for us to do so when the people's mandate is given for a new system of governance.

Subsequently when I became Secretary of the Deendayal Research Institute (1971-75), it became clear to me that Guruji's ideas had been incorporated by Deendayal Upadhyaya in his *Integral Humanism* and also by Dattopant Thengadi in his *Ekatma Manavad. Ek Adhyan* [Rashtra Dharma Pustak Prakashan Lucknow 1970] and in his "Bharatiya Conception of Economic Order" [published in *The Perspectives*, Sahitya Sindhu Publishers, Bangalore, 1971]. Thengadi also summarized in point form the discourse he gave in a meet in Thane, Maharashtra in 1973 just before his demise. This was published in *Organizer* weekly and I am thankful to Dattreya Hosbale for retrieving it for me. Recently, I also had a discussion with the former Sarsangh chalak of RSS, Shri Sudarshan on what type of economic policy would suit our civilization and values. Sudarshanji gave me some valuable suggestions on the subject which I have incorporated here.

In 1977, at the invitation Dr. Mahesh Mehta, I presented a paper in New York titled "Economic Perspectives in Integral Humanism". This was later published in a volume [edited by Mahesh Mehta] titled: *Upadhyaya's Integral Humanism* (Edison, NJ, 1978).

Based on these works and researches, I have written this Chapter.

I. STRUCTURE OF ECONOMIC POLICY

Economic policy structured in a five dimensional framework, and may be thus defined by (i) Objectives (ii) Priorities (iii) Strategy (iv) Resource Mobilization Measures, and (v) The Institutional Architecture.

Let us take the first dimension, of objectives of economic policy of four main ideologies of Capitalism, Socialism, Communism and Integral Humanism. Theoretically, communism takes maximum production for the state as the goal, while capitalism considers that the jungle concept of *laissez faire* based on survival of the fittest will be guided by an Invisible Hand to achieve maximum profit for producers and maximum consumption of material goods for the worker. Socialism aims at maximum welfare measured by state guarantees against risks of disease, death and unemployment to the individual citizen. That is the concept of welfare under socialism.

However Deendayalji pointed out that all these goals are purely materialistic and derails human development. He said the human being's development must be viewed *integrally* and *holistically* (hence Deendayalji term 'Integral Humanism'). He advocated the blending of materialistic goals with spiritual imperatives as the primary goal of economic policy. Guruji in Chapter I of the *Bunch of Thoughts* (page 5), states: "All attempts and experiments made so far were based on 'isms' stemming from materialism. However, we Hindus have a solution to offer". And then he propounded that "the problem boils down to one of achieving a synthesis of national aspirations and world welfare." Guruji advocates that in this synthesis, "*swalambana* (or self-reliance) forms the backbone of a free and prosperous nation..." (p. 313), and that at the very minimum, "*atma poorti*" (or self-sufficiency) in food production is a must for our national defence...." (p. 316).

The difference between *swalambana* and *atma poorti* is this: the former requires that we must depend on our own resources, i.e., if there is a shortage of some commodity, we should earn enough foreign exchange by exports to buy it from abroad. That is, we should depend on our own resources. The latter concept of *atma poorti* requires that we produce in sufficient quantities in our own country so that we do not suffer in any shortage. That is, *we should* depend only on our own indigenous production.

Today we find that the nation has again moved from food self-sufficiency (*atma poorti*) to dependence on imports from abroad. Farmers are committing suicides, and land, due to use of chemicals and foreign seeds, are becoming of low productivity or going barren. Guruji warning thus was timely. We must re-orient the objective of our economic policy to re-gain self-sufficiency in food production, and must do it by environmental friendly means such as organic farming, wind energy, and cooperative endeavour.

Deendayalji thus has brought out how the 'Bharatiya' objective of economic policy is different from the objective in foreign ideologies of Capitalism, Socialism and Communism. Deendayalji propounded therefore the concept of 'Integral Man' as assimilating and harmonizing the *chaturvidha purushartha*, which he elaborated as a concept in his Integral Humanism. He added the concept of *Chiti*, the soul of the nation, which each nation must discover to decide the correct formulation of economic policy. The concept of *Chiti* of a nation is an original contribution of Deendayalji.

Thus the economic perspectives in *Integral Humanism* are fundamentally different from those contained in Capitalism, Socialism, and Communism. To quote Deendayalji himself,

> "Both these systems, capitalist as well as communist, have failed to take account of the Integral Man, his true and complete personality and his aspirations. One considers him as mere selfish being lingering after money, having only one law, the law of fierce competition, in essence the law of the jungle; whereas the other

has viewed him as a feeble lifeless cog in the whole scheme of things, regulated by rigid rules, and incapable of any good unless directed. The centralization of power, economic and political, is implied in both. Both, therefore, result in dehumanization of man." [*Integral Humanism*, Navchetan Press, Delhi 1965, p. 76]

Arguing that the so-called democratic socialism is no better, Deendayaji stated [p.74-75],

> "Socialism arose as a reaction to capitalism. But even socialism failed to establish the importance of the human being. The needs and preferences of individuals have as much importance in the socialist system as in a prison manual."

Therefore Upadhyaya stated for his Integral Humanism that: [p.76-77]

> "Man, the highest creation of God, is losing his own identity. We must re-establish him in his rightful position, bring him the realization of his greatness, re-awaken his abilities and encourage him to exert for attaining divine heights of his latent personality. This is possible only through a decentralized economy."

He went on to indicate: [p.78]

> "Swadeshi and Decentralization are the two words which can briefly summarize the economic policy suitable for the present circumstances."

Deendayalji's stress on the need to think in integrated terms is now fashionably called "systems analysis or holistic view in the West". He also emphasized the need to liberate man by recognizing "complemantarities" in life. Man is not on his own or alone. Deendayalji's plea for rejection of class struggle and the need to think in terms of conflict resolution and "class harmony" is now much in vogue today in the West—which is getting increasingly disillusioned with capitalism. In the same vein, Guruji ridiculed the Communist concept of 'dictatorship of the proletariat'. He said it is actually "dictatorship of the dictator of a dictatorial party." [p.13]. How true!

If we are not to suffer the social tensions of the West, then we have to break away from the path that we have chosen presently, viz., the Nehruvian path that needs to be completely abandoned. Partially is not enough for national good. The alternative to materialistic capitalism is not communism because even in Communist countries, there is a problem of "alienation" and "exploitation" as revealed recently from reports that have been received.

Deendayal Upadhyaya was also aware as early as in 1965, of the Communist degeneration. Logically for him, any system in which man does not receive primacy is bound to ultimately degenerate. Interestingly Deendayalji quotes M. Djilas the author of *The New Class* to prove that in Communist countries, "a new class of bureaucratic exploiter has come into existence."

Thus, by presenting his Integral Humanism, Deendayal Upadhyaya has placed before the world a new original alternative ideological framework. To appreciate the fundamentally different structure of economic policy imbedded in Integral Humanism, I have below in tabular form for ready reference, placed the various alternative competing ideologies in terms of its structural parameters of objectives, priorities, development strategy, resource mobilization, and institutional framework.

From the table we may note that the economic perspective of Integral Humanism is fundamentally different from the other ideologies. Capitalism and communism have similarities in matters of objectives and institutional framework. If cost of production is stabilized, then maximum profit and maximum production are identical.

Again, class struggle and annihilation and survival of fittest, are different only to the extent that communism envisages the survival of

IDEOLOGY

Dimension	Capitalism (Adam Smith)	Socialism (Harold Laski)	Communism (Karl Mars)	Integral Humanisam (Deendayal Upadhyaya)
1. Objectives	Maximum profit and Maximum consumption Energy-intensive	Maximum material welfare and bedge against risk	Maximum production Swalambana (self reliance)	Optimum synthesis of national development and global welfare. Swalambana (self
2. Priorities	Energy-intensive exploitation of resources	Guaranteed minimum material standards of pay, pension and unemployment	Primacy of the system based on coercion in the extraction of funds from the people for the state	Primacy of man through balanced development of Chaturvidha Purushartha [Artha, Kama, Dharma, and Moksha]
3. Development strategy	Primacy of labour saving capital-intensive technology that energy consuming Free trade globally	Nationalization of commanding heights and public distribution of essential commodities	Total ownership of all the means of production. Foreign trade discouraged	Conflict resolution and harmonisation through complemetaries
4. Resource Maobilization	Incentive and propensity to spend. Environment destructive	Taxation and controls and Licensing	Total control over incomes received and permitted consumption. Administered prices and terms and trade	Trusteeship and austerity, Four sources of wealth, vidya, sashtra, dhan, bhoomi distributed without concentration
5. Institutional	Survival of the fittest laissez faire in a free market. Invisible hand.	Administrative controls, licences and Government regulation in a quota system	Dialetical Materialism, Class struggle and Dictatorship of the Proletariat	Decentralization, Panchayati Raj, and self-employment of the people

Sources: Smith, Adam: *Wealth of Nations*
Laski, Harold: *Grammar of Politics*
Marx, Karl: *Das Kapital*
Upadhaya, Deendayal: *Integral Humanism*

the "fittest" class, whereas capitalism expects the "fittest" individual to engage in fierce competition and annihilate the other rivals. Similarly, socialism has only a difference of degree with communism—on the extent of coercion and control, and not fundamentally. That is why communism is often referred to as "scientific" socialism, although there is nothing scientific about it.

Since one socialism differs from another socialism only in degrees, therefore there are unlimited varieties of socialism varying from those of Hitler's Nazism, Uganda's Idi Amin's, Indira Gandhi's, to democratic socialism of Sweden. This has only caused confusion— and gives ample scope to hypocrisy. Thus we can see some people in India arguing on one hand for nationalization and austerity, and at the same time encouraging foreign collaboration while living in mansions. Such inconsistencies can be reconciled in some variety of socialism, interpreted at will.

From the above table it is also apparent that total humanity and growth, of man is nowhere under consideration in any ideology except in Integral Humanism. Humanity as a whole is in subservient to these systems either explicitly or implicitly. Under communism, man explicitly subserves the system. Coercion is legitimized "in the interest of the State." Even the choice of a career, location of work, and advancement are strictly directed by the State. Man in such countries has no room for choice or even any option to opt out of such a system because his freedom to travel out of the country is also completely curbed.

In capitalism, an individual may have technical freedom for his "pursuit of happiness", but the system fails to accommodate the varying capabilities and endowments of man. Since the law of the jungle ... the survival of the fittest ... prevails, therefore some achieve great advancement while others get trampled and disabled in what is called the "rat race". Since maximum profit is possible only in a newer and latest technology, man has to adjust to the terrifying demands of technology, rather than technology adjusting to the integral needs of man. So we witness today in an advanced capitalist country such as

USA, broken homes, high divorce rates and ruined family life have become common because technology has run riot there in making these eruet demands. So man has to adjust to it or perish. Such a development is inevitable in a system in which the "shortage of manpower (is) the guiding factor in the design of machines."

Thus in capitalism, under laissez faire, although man has technical freedom, but because the development strategy is to give primacy to technology, therefore implicitly man becomes subservient to the system. In such societies individuality is thus expressed in other outlets as crime, free sex, drunkenness, and rebel dropout movements. The recent craze in the West for our "Sadhus" and Hindu religion arises largely due to this search for individuality, to escape the mental tensions which this kind of technology demands from the people, and because their own religious preachers are ill-equipped to cope with it.

Just as survival of the fittest is dehumanizing, so is class struggle which is the foundation of Marxism. Under communism, classes are sought to be eliminated by the intensification of class struggle. Obviously such intensification will lead to hate and tension, consequently dehumanization. We saw the extent of such dehumanization in communist countries, In the USSR, for example, most prominent intellectuals such as Alexander Solzenitsyn, Andrie Sakharov had suffered severe punishment from the state because they had questioned this dehumanizating process. Marxism has in the end failed everywhere, even in the Soviet Union which has now unraveled. Comparing Marxist economic system with market economies of peers, the contrast is obvious.

It is important to recognize that a comparison of countries with a common history reveals that those countries which adopted the Soviet economic model performed much more poorly than their counterparts that had adopted the market economic strategy. Table below brings out this by comparing East with West Germany, and North with South Korea.

In India too as the data in the next chapter reveal, while India achieved a higher GDP growth under the Soviet economic strategy than that under British imperialist rule, it nevertheless remained at an unimpressive average rate of 3.5 per cent, of 5.6 per cent (1980-90) then to nearly 7 per cent (1992-97) and a decade average (1998-2003) of nearly 6 per cent per year, followed by nearly 9% during 2003-2008.

Table : Economic Indicators—South/North Korea (1995-96) and West/East Germany (1989) Compared

	South Korea	North Korea	South/North ratio	West Germany	East Germany	West/East ratio
1	2	3	4	5	6	7
Population Million	44.9	23.9	1.9	62.1	16.6	3.8
GNP Billion $	451.7	22.3	20.3	1,207	96	12.6
Per capita income $	10,067	957	10.5	19,283	5,840	3.3
Economic growth in % p.a. 1990-1995	+7.6	-4.5	—	3.0	-0.8	—
Government expenditure billion $	97.1	19	5.1	547.7	61.8	8.9
(as % of GNP)	(21.5)	85		(45.5)	(64.4)	
Defence expenditure billion $	14.4	5.2	2.8	28.5	11.2	2.6
(as % of GDP)	(3.2)	(23)		(2.5)	(11.6)	
per capita ($)	318	218	1.5	459	675	0.7
Foreign trade billion $	260.2	2.05	126.9	611.1	47.0	13.0
(as % of GNP)	(57.6)	(9.2)	(50.6)	(49)		
- Export of goods billion $	125.1	0.74	169	341.3	23.7	14.4
-Import of goods billion $	135.1	1.31	103	269.8	23.3	11.5
Foreign debt billion $	79	11.8	6.6	106.7	22	4.9
(as % of GNP)	(17.5)	(53)		(8.8)	(23)	
Life expectancy in years (1995)	72.0	70.5	1.02	75.0	74.0	1.01

Infant mortality Per 1,000 births (1995)	10	26	0.28	7.4	7.5	0.99
Rural population % of total (1995)	19	39	0.49	3.7	10.8	0.34
Radios[1] Per 1,000 Inhabitants (1989)	1,003	207	4.9	83%	99%	0.84
Televisions[2] Per 1000 Inhabitants (1989)	207	14	14.8	94%	57%	1.65

[1]For West and East Germany: percentage of households with ratio.

[2]For East and East Germany: percentage of households with colour television.

Source: National Unification Board, Bank of Korea; Statistisches Bundesamt, Statistisches Jahrnuchder DDR; Weltbank.

Thus, the results of this Soviet strategy have not anywhere been commensurate with either the resources mobilized from the public, or in terms of a nation's potential for growth. During the period since 1947 and till 1991 the Indian economy had grown at the average rate of less than four per cent per year, while countries adopting a different strategy have achieved development in the same period, growth 10-12 per cent per year. There is no reason for our low growth rate, considering that we have the world's third largest scientific and engineering manpower and a high savings rate of 23 per cent of GDP. The so-called "Four Tigers", namely South Korea, Taiwan, Hong Kong and Singapore, with less trained manpower and a lot fewer natural resources, have moved from the Third World category to First World status *(or Newly Industrialized Countries—NIC) in just one generation*! The per capita income of South Korea, for example, in 1962 was $82, comparable to India $70 at that time. Today South Korea's per capita income is about 13 times that of India's current level!

II. POSTULATES OF INTEGRAL HUMANISM

I need not dwell any further on the demerits of other ideologies, but consider in, concrete positive terms, what economic perspective Deendayalji's *Integral Humanism* offers. I would organize his thoughts in terms of basic economic postulates using modern theoretical terminology and jargon:

Postulate 1: The economy is a sub-system of the society and not the sole guiding factor of social growth. Hence no economic theorems can be formulated without first recognising that life is an integral system, and therefore whatever economic laws are deduced or codified, they must add or at least not reduce the integral growth of man. The centrality of Man's divine spark and his evolution is on the four *Purusharthas of dharma, artha, kama, moksha.*

Postulate 2: There is plurality, and diversity in life. Man is subject to several internal contradictions. The solution is to be based on the harmonization of this plurality, diversity, and internal contradictions. Thus laws governing this harmony will have to be discovered and codified, which we shall call *Dharma.* An economy based on *Dharma* will be a regulated one, within which man's personality and freedom will be given maximum scope, and be enlightened in the social interest.

Postulate 3: There is a negative correlation between the State's coercive power and *Dharma.* In the latter, the acceptance of regulation by man is voluntary because it blends with his individual and collective aspirations, whereas in the former regulations often conflict with aspirations and hence man is coerced to accept the regulation or suffer.

Postulate 4: A society of persons of common origin, history or culture has a *chiti* (soulforce). It is this *chiti* which integrates and establishes harmony. Each nation has to search out its *chiti* and recognise it consciously. Consequently, each country must follow its own development strategy based on its *chiti*. If it tries to duplicate or replicate other nations, it will come to grief.

Postulate 5: Based on the perception of *chiti* and recognition of *dharma,* an economic order can be evolved which rationalizes the mutual inter-balances of the life system, by seeking out the *complementarities* embedded in various conflicting interests in society. Such an order will reveal the system of social choices based on an aggregation of individual values.

Postulate 6: Any economy based on Integral Humanism, will take as given, besides the normal democratic fundamental rights, the Right to Food, the Right to Work, Right to Education, and the Right to Free Medical Care as basic rights.

Postulate 7: The right to property is *not* fundamental, but economic regulation will be based on the complementarity that exists in the conflicting goals of social ownership of property and the necessity for providing incentive to save and to produce.

These seven postulates represent the foundation of the *Integral Humanism* economic policy. Most of the established and popular slogans of Indian society emanate from one or more (in combination) of these postulates. For example, the electrifying call of the Freedom Movement for *Swadeshi,* or self-reliance is embedded in Postulate 4. The popular demand for *decentralization* finds its source in Postulate 3. The modern internationally fashionable slogan of environmental care and pollution control, follows out of Postulate 5. The widespread scientific consensus that optimum solutions can only be found in "systems analysis" is contained explicitly in Postulate 1. Mahatma Gandhi's advocacy of *Trusteeship* is implied in Postulates 2 and 7 read together. In other words, these seven postulates can singly or jointly conceptualize and synthesize the various goals which have stirred the soul of India (or its *chiti*).

With these postulates, we now need to derive the practical guidelines for our economic development. To do that, postulate 5 is very important.

First and foremost, we shall have to list out the various complementarities, second, work out a calculus of costs and benefits to integrate these various complementarities; and third, frame decision rules on how to make social choices based on divergent individual values.

An example of complementarities is that of an orchard farmer who has as his neighbour a honey producer. The bees of the honey producer can conveniently utilize the fruit blossoms of the orchard farmer with no cost to either but gain to both. This is an example of *positive complementarity.* An example of negative complementarity is that of pollution. For example, by setting up a fertilizer plant and oil refinery on an extensive scale employment in that area is certainly generated. But the toxic gases released by these factories adversely affect the health of the public and reduce the productivity of the workers of the entire region. So overall, the nation is the loser.

We have to select positive complementarities and eschew the negative ones, if *Integral Humanism* is to be followed. Therefore, we have to plan our urban habitation system in such a way that toxic creating machines are kept far from urban residential centres, or subject to strict environmental measures such as requiring CNG instead of diesel run public transportation buses. This means our transportation system will have to be integrated in location planning of industries as well. A good capitalist or a communist will look at the problem piece-meal. The capitalist would choose urban centres because profits are highest there. A communist would also pick urban centres because production will be maximum where a trained, industrial labour force resides, and an infrastructure is available. In a capitalist society, the "survival of the fittest" is the slogan so there are no complementarities to worry about.

In a communist society, the State is *so powerful* and coercive that no one questions its decision, in a democratic socialist society, the public will make a few noises, so the Government will order a few anti-pollution devices to be installed *but urban centres will* still be the location in the end.

However in an *Integral Humanist* society, the outlook will be systems-oriented, so the location would be "optimized", which will not be the urban centre. But a loss in monetary terms would have been suffered to the managers of the enterprise who would have preferred the maximum profit - area of the urban centre. So a "calculus" of incentives and compensation for effecting the complementarity is needed. Such a calculus is known to economists, but which for shortage of space, I shall not elaborate here. To do that here would make this paper unduly technical and mathematical.

It is not enough to have a calculus to aggregate the complementarities but also to frame decision rules on how to make consistent social choices based on individual values. It is not enough to say that in a democracy, social choices should be based on majority decision rule. The format for eliciting this majority needs to be spelt out, otherwise anamolies will result.

For example, suppose we divide society into three groups—A: Agriculturists, M: Manufacturers, S: Workers and those in services. Let us assume that the society consisting of A, M, and S has to rank the projects of X; Fertilizer plant; Y: Steel mill; and Z: Hospital, in order of preference. Thus agriculturists (A) will rank X most important of all, Y second most important, and Z as least important. Therefore a choice is offered to them between X and Y, they would choose X. If a choice is between Y and Z, then Y will be chosen. Obviously if X is preferred to Y, and Y is preferred to Z, then X will of course be preferred to Z for consistency. In notation, I shall write: '? ' for 'preferred to'

Assume: A : X → Y → Z
M : Y → Z → X
S : Z → X → Y

If a vote is taken on each pairs of projects, then we shall have:

X→Y A+S=2 M=1 X→Y i.e., choose X over Y
Y→Z A+M=2 S=1 Y→Z i.e., choose Y over Z
X→Z A=1 M+S=2 Z→X i.e., choose Z over X

This, in a majority decision without any format, a society may prefer with 2/3 majority, X over Y, Y over Z, and yet prefer over X ! To avoid such social inconsistency, we must ensure that A, M, and S consult each other and seek to find out their complementarity in choices, and then vote.

This is why format and creation of a basic consensus or harmony is so essential. Such a process is lengthy, cumbersome, and complicated. But this is the only way to optimize the nation's energies. But the process can be simplified by decentralization of political and economic authority. It cannot be achieved in a centralized society.

Once a decision is taken on the path of development, Deendayalji would advocate incentives, and realistic taxation to encourage saving, and to discourage conspicuous consumption as the only practical way to mobilize resources. This is contained in postulate 7. Most ideologies are weak when it comes to specifying resource mobilization, perhaps, because spelling it out means annoying one section or another. Therefore, the topic is either handled in a general way or indirectly. In Hindu way of life man must be encouraged to save, live simply and acquire wealth, but then it must be made socially prestigious to give away his wealth or manage it as a "trustee" for society. In western societies, the size of a person's wealth is the *most important* determinant of his social, cultural and national prestige. So he is encouraged to part with a portion of his wealth by urging him to spend more and on himself! This results in a fierce competition on who can spend more on himself "keeping up with the Joneses" leading to great waste. In Integral Humanism's scheme of things, social and cultural influences are integrated into a man's psyche, so that parting with his wealth for society becomes his own desire. In such a framework, there is no weakening of a person's resolve to have his income or pursue its immediate enlargement.

As a trustee, every individual also cares for the physical environment and pollution. He also treats animals humanely and where such animals are multiple assets to human civilization, such an integrally human person will even regard the animal as divine. The Cow is one such animal.

Traditional Hindu belief in the efficacy of the milk and products of the Indian breeds of cows and its sacred status has been divided by our Westernized elite that had led to the neglect of cow because it is held that milk from all breeds of cows and buffaloes is equally good; and to improve the present low milk yield of the Indian breeds of cows, cross breeding with Européan high yielding cows was recommended.

But recent researches suggest that that only the milk of *Bos Indicus* i.e. Indian breed of cows has the desired health promoting properties due to presence of Beta Casein A2 protein. European breeds of Cows are classified as Bos Taurus. Their milk contains the protein Beta Casein Al, which produces beta-casomorphin 7, which makes this milk diabetogenic relative to A2 milk. Medical researches have also linked Al milk with statistically higher incidence of Cardiac situations. In Australia, New Zealand, Korea Certified, A2 milk is already commanding the premium price of four times the price of non-certified A1A1-A1A2 milk.

Concomitantly cross breeding between the two breeds of the cow is being discontinued in these countries. Strategies are already being worked out to convert all the cows with the farmers to revert to Bos Indicus breeds for beta casein A2 protein in their milk.

Besides milk and dung, the ancient Hindu wisdom that cow's urine has medicinal properties and hence accessible at low cost to the rural poor, is borne out by Patents granted in United States.

Two US patents have been granted for cow urine distillate (US Pat. No. 6410059 and 6896907) for anti-micro-bial, anti-bacterial, anti-fungal, anti-cancer properties, also it is having a lot of anti-exidants. Since it has got immumomodulatory compounds in it, it is a very good bio-enhancer to facilitate drug availability to high extent in our body. Patent from China is also granted to cow urine distillate as a DNA protector.

One global patent has been granted for cow urine, neem and garlic as a pest repellent, fungicidal and growth promontory properties for all different crops (WHO 2004/087618A1).

Another US patent has been granted for strains obtained from Sahiwal cow milk for plant growth promoter phytopathogenic fungi controlling activity, abiotic stress tolerating capability, phosphatic solubilisation capability, etc. (US patent No. 7097830 dated 29/8/06).

Also CSIR has filed US patent for Amrit Pani (mixture of cow dung + cow urine + jaggery) from NBRI Lucknow for soil health improvement properties.

All the above claims had been made in Charaka Samhita, Sushrut, Vaghbhati and Nighantu, Ratnakar, etc.

The above examples very well prove the utility of cow dung and urine for sustainable agriculture as well as for almost curing or giving relief in many serious diseases like psoriasis, eczema, asthma, diabetes, blood pressure, renal failures and cancer, etc.

This confirms Vedic message: *Gomay Vaste Laxmi* i.e. cow dung is a source of wealth, whereas in western culture dung and urine are considered to be waste, even if their modern medical research has begun changing its view.

Cattle can be conveniently reared today only in villages because villages have open grazing lands and natural atmosphere and ponds, etc., which urban dwellings do not have.

But as the erstwhile Sar Sanghchalak of RSS Sri Sudarshan has observed at meeting of 'Gobhakta' industrialists in New Delhi recently, for rural economic development *cow-based* industries should be set up. An example of this is of Dr. Shrikrishna Mittal who successfully made tiles out of cow dung that could be used in rural housing.

Hence, a new fervour is necessary to create a *cow-renaissance* in the nation. As Bahadur Shah and Maharaja Ranjit Singh did, we should amend the IPC to make cow slaughter as a capital offence as well as a ground for arrest under the National Security Act, to give meaning and urgency to the total ban on cow slaughter.

The cow is thus a part of Hindutva, and we should defend it with all our might.

India has 150 million cows today, giving an average of less than 200 litres of milk per year. If they could be fed and looked after, then these divine animals can give an average of 11,000 litres of milk as the Israeli cows do. That could provide milk for the whole world.

The cow was elevated to the status of divinity in the *Rg. Veda* iself. In Book VI the Hymn XXVIII attributed to Rishi Bhardwaja, extols the virtue of the cow. In Atharva Veda (Book X, Hymn 10), the cow is formally designated as Vishnu, and "all that the Sun surveys." This divinely quality of the cow has been affirmed by Kautilya in his Arthsastra (Chapter XXIX).

The Indian society has addressed the cow with the appellation of 'mother'. "Tilam na dhaanyam, pashuvah na Gaavah" (Sesame is not a cereal, cow is not an animal). The Churning of the Sea episode brings to light the story of the creation of the cow! Five divine Kamadhenus (wish cows), viz, Nanda, Subhadra, Surabhi, Sushila, Bahula emerged in the churning.

Cow is there in the company of Bhagwan Dattatreya and Gopal Krishna. Cow is the vehicle of Shaillputri and Gowri—two of the nine manifestations of Goddess Durga. Umiya Mata's mount is cow. Without the blessings and help of the cow sinners cannot swim across the Vaitarani River of hell that administers retributive justice. Ancient coins with marks of bull/Nandi on them found in excavations, bull etched on Ashoka the Great's Lion Capital which is now the national emblem of Bharat, worship of the sacred Goverdhan hill's miniature replica made of cow dung. The Vatesdwaadashi celebration, adorning, worshipping and celebrating cows and bulls on Deepavali Day—these signify the central position that the cow and her progeny hold in Indian cultural traditions. It shows the cow culture of Bharat and our faith and love for this divine animal.

Thousands of names of places, persons and things and other words in our country have name of the cow: e.g. Gauhati, Gorakhpur, Goa, Godhra, Gondiya, Godavari, Goverdhan, Gautam, Gomukh, Gokarna, Goyal, Gochar etc. Having been prefixed by the term

"Go/Gow", signify the deep reverence and high ground reserved for the cow and her progeny in our culture.

In 2003, the National Commission on Cattle presided over by Justice G.M. Lodha, submitted its recommendations to the NDA Government. The Report (in 4 volumes) called for stringent laws to protect the cow and its progeny in the interest of India's rural economy. This is a Constitutional requirement under Directive Principles of State Policy. Article 48 of the Constitution says: "The State shall lendeavour or organize agriculture and animal husbandry on modern and scientific lines and shall, in particular, take steps for preserving and improving the breeds, and prohibiting the slaughter of cows and calves and other milchand draught cattle". In 1958, a 5-member Constitutional Bench of the Supreme Court {(1959) SCR 629} upheld Article 48 and the consequent total ban on cow slaughter as a reasonable restriction on Fundamental Rights.

When India fought the First War of Independence in 1857 and Bahadur Shah 'Zafar' was installed as Emperor by the Hindus in Delhi for a brief period, his Hindu Prime Minister, on the Emperor's Proclamation made the killing of cow a capital offence. Earlier in Maharaja Ranjit Singh's kingdom, the only crime that had capital punishment was cow slaughter. For a Hindu, the very appearance of a cow evokes a sense of piety. It is serene by temperament and herbivorous by diet. Apart from milk, cow dung known for its anti-septic value, is still used as fuel in its dried caked form in most Indian villages. It is also used in compost manure and in the production of electricity through eco-friendly gobar-gas. Thus, Mahatma Gandhi had declared: "Cow protection is more important than even Swaraj."

Even today, 75 per cent of Indians in villages derive the great benefits from cows and bullocks. Despite the compulsions of modernism, tractors are not suitable for the small Indian land holdings. In US, the land available to each person is around 14 acre; in India is around 0.70 acre. A tractor consumes diesel, creates pollution, does not live on grass nor produces dung for manure. Thus Albert Einstein, in a letter to Sir CV Raman, wrote "Tell the people of

India that if they want to survive and show the world path to survive, then they should forget about tractor and preserve their ancient tradition {bullock} ploughing."

The cow, according to Vedas provides the following four products for human society (The word *Kamadhenu* is the Sanskrit word for cow as the existing creature of almighty God).

1. *Godugdha* (Cow milk): As per Ayurveda, cow milk is useful in various disease as well as it increases energy and immune power of the person. Chemical composition wise it is having fat, carbohydrate, minerals, calcium, Iron and Vitamin B. Stroncin a even capacity for resist body again atomic radiation. Another contain Cerebrosides having good ability to improve and regenerate brain cell.
2. *Goghruta* (Cow Ghee): Best among all kind of ghee. As per Ayurvedic classics it is useful in various kind of systematic, physical and mental disorders as well as it sustain the age for long time and delayed genetic condition and maintain body bio-chemistry in it's optimum level (means increases Ojas). Gau ghruta also improves environment. When it is used in Yajna. It improves the level of oxygen and Ozon gases in surround areas.
3. *Gomutra* (Cow Urine): A total of 8 types of urine are used for medicinal purpose now-a-days. Among those, Cow urine is held to be the best. Anti-cancer, anti-bacterial, anti-fungal property is found in it. It is also having anti-oxidant and immune modulator property, which is very much useful for auto immune disease which are increasing now-a-day. In classics there are so many references available where cow urine is mentioned as a drug of choice internally as well as externally. It is also having germicidal property and it might be the chief reason why Gau *mutra* were used as a holy content on each and every occasion. Even Paris of Zoroastrian religion follow this practice.
4. *Gomaya* (Cow Dung): Gomaya is considered equally valuable as

Gau mutra and it is used to purify the environment. Cow dung has radium and it checks the radiation effects.

Furthermore, the common argument in the West for slaughtering cows is no more uncontested. Beef is not of high protein content as believed. Any dietician's chart shows that beef, with 22 per cent protein, ranks far below vegetable products like soyabeen (43), groundnut (31), pulses (24). Moreover, excess intake of protein is not good as it only contributes to obesity, a bane of modern civilization. Moreover, to procure 1 kg of beef (or for that matter any flesh) it takes 7 kg of crops and 7,000 kg. of water. This contributes to water shortage in regions where beef is prevalent.

Long back, scientist James Watson Scott had noted that if food shortages were to be banished from populous countries, the food habits of the people should be altered to vegetarianism, which is fast catching up in Europe. This protection of cow makes good economic and ecological sense. Swami Dayananda Saraswati, the scholar-sanyasi and Convenor of the Hindu Dharma Acharya Sabha, a body of all prominent Hindu religious heads has argued that non-vegetarianism indirectly contributes heavily to green house gases and other pollution.

A report from the United Nations in the year 2006 reveals the surprising fact that "raising animals for meat as food generates more green house gases than all the cars and trucks in the world combined." Ten of billions of animals farmed for good, release gases such as methane, nitrous oxide and carbon-di-oxide through their massive amounts of manure. Animals such as cows and sheep, being ruminant, emit huge amount of methane due to flatulence and burping. "The released methane", the report says, "has 23 times the global warming potential of CO". It is very alarming to note that the livestock industry alone is responsible for 37% of human induced methane emissions. To make room for these animals to graze, the virgin forests are cleared. The livestock industry also needs a vast stretches of land to raise mono-crops to feed the animals. The C02 that the trees and plants store escapes back into the air when they are destroyed.

Growng fodder for farmed animals implies heavy use of synthetic fertilizers produced with fossil fuels. While this process emits a huge amount of C02 fertilizer itself releases nitrous oxide (3) - a green house gas that is 296 times more potent than C02. Alarming though these facts are 1 see in them a reason for hope. All that the people all the world over has to do is to avoid meat eating. In the absence of demand for meat there is no more need for breeding millions of animals for daily slaughter. And then animals population would cease to be medicated for continuous breeding, thereby the population would be regulated.

A single individual by simply not consuming meat prevents the equivalent of 1.5 tons C02 emissions in a year. This is more than the one ton of C02 emissions prevented by switching from a large sedan to a small car. One needs to have an honest commitment to save the mother earth who has been relentlessly patient and magnanimous since she began bearing life. There are a number of reasons for one to be a vegetarian. People given to meat eating think that a pure vegetarian diet is optional. But now they have no choice if they are alive to what is happening to this life-bearing planet. There is no justification whatsoever for one to continue to be a non-vegetarian knowing the devastating consequences of meat eating.

As Swami Dayananda Saraswati has noted:

"Promotion of vegetarianism does not require any legislation from the State. It does require a change of heart on the part of meat eating individuals anywhere on this planet. I cannot appeal to the tigers and wolves. They are programmed to be what they are. Being endowed with freewill only a human being can make a difference by exercising responsibly his or her choice." If it is too much for one to switch to be a total vegetarian, then one needs to give up at least red-meat eating.

List of 14 Patents Granted/Filed on Cow Based Agri-Bioproducts with GVAK, Nagpur

Patents granted in India:

S. No.	Title	Country	Filed on	Granted on	Names of inventors
1.	Synergistic fermented plant growth promoting, bio-control composition	India	29/09/2004	12/01/2009	C.S. Nautiyal, S. Mehta, H. B. Singh, S. B. Mansinghka, S. H. Dawle, N.E. Rajhans, P. Pushpangadan

Patents granted abroad:

S. No.	Title	Country	Filed on	Granted on	Names of inventors
1.	Plant and soil health enhancer using cow urine and application thereof for promoting plant growth and controlling plant pathogenic fungi	Europe	18/10/2005	06/09/2006	C.S. Nautiyal, S. Mehta, S. Mehta, H.B. Singh, S. B. Mansinghka, S.H. Dawle, N. E. Rajhans, P. Pushpangadan
2.	Plant and soil health enhancer using cow urine and application thereof for promoting plant growth and controlling plant pathogenic fungi.	Netherlands	30/03/2004	06/12/2006	C.S. Nautiyal, S. Mehta, H.B. Singh, S. B. Mansinghka, S. B. Mansinghka, S.H. Dawle, N. E. Rajhans, P. Pushpangadan
3.	Synergistic fermented growth promoting, bio-control composition	USA	31/03/2004	20/11/2007	C.S. Nautiyal, S. Mehta, H.B. Singh, S. B. Mansinghka, S. B. Mansinghka, S.H. Dawle, N. E. Rajhans, P. Pushpangadan
4.	Plant and soil health enhancer using cow urine and application thereof for promoting plant growth and controlling plant pathogenic fungi.	Zimbabwe	29/09/2005	30/04/2008	C.S. Nautiyal, S. Mehta, H.B. Singh, S. B. Mansinghka, S.H. Dawle, N.E. Rajhans, P. Pushpangadan

Patents filed in India:

S. No.	Title	Country	Filed on	Granted on	Names of inventors
1.	Fermented bovine byproducts for enhancing plant growth, quality, shelf life and method of preparing thereof	India	30/03/2007	–	C.S. Nautiyal, P.S. Chauhan, S. Srivastava, H.B. Singh, S.H. Singh, S.H. Dawle
2.	A synergistic composition useful as bioinoculants	India	28/03/2006	–	H.B. Singh, A. Rehman, S. Srivastava

3.	Fermented bovine byproducts for enhancing plant growth, quality, shelf life and method of preparing thereof.	India	31/03/2006	–	C.S. Nautiyal, P.S. Chauhan, S. Srivastava, H.B. Singh, S.H. Singh, S.H. Dawle, S.B. Mansinghka
4.	Synergistic fermented plant growth promoting, bio-control composition.	India	29/09/2004	–	C.S. Nautiyal, S. Mehta, H.B. Singh, S. B. Mansinghka, S.H. Dawle, N.E. Rajhans, P. Pushpangadan

Patents filed abroad:

S. No.	Title	Country	Filed on	Granted on	Names of inventors
1.	Plant and soil health enhancer using cow urine and application thereof for promoting plant growth and controlling plant pathogenic fungi.	Japan	29/09/2005	–	C.S. Nautiyal, S. Mehta, H.B. Singh, S.B. Mansinghka, S.H. Dawle, N.E. Rajhans, P. Pushpangadan
2.	Plant and soil health enhancer using cow urine and application thereof for promoting plant growth and controlling plant pathogenic fungi.	Canada	29/09/2005	–	C.S. Nautiyal, S. Mehta, H.B. Singh, S.B. Mansinghka, S.H. Dawle, N.E. Rajhans, P. Pushpangadan
3.	Plant and soil health enhancer using cow urine and application thereof for promoting plant growth and controlling plant pathogenic fungi.	Italy	31/03/2004	–	C.S. Nautiyal, S. Mehta, H.B. Singh, S.B. Mansinghka, S.H. Dawle, N.E. Rajhans, P. Pushpangadan
4.	Plant and soil health enhancer using cow urine and application thereof for promoting plant growth and controlling plant pathogenic fungi.	Australia	31/03/2004	–	C.S. Nautiyal, S. Mehta, H.B. Singh, S.B. Mansinghka, S.H. Dawle, N.E. Rajhans, P. Pushpangadan
5.	Plant and soil health enhancer using cow urine and application thereof for promoting plant growth and controlling plant pathogenic fungi.	Brazil	31/03/2004	–	C.S. Nautiyal, S. Mehta, H.B. Singh, S.B. Mansinghka, S.H. Dawle, N.E. Rajhans, P. Pushpangadan

China Patent Information Center

Application Number	03826375
Application Date:	2003/03/31
Announcement Date:	2006/05/10
Pub. Date:	2009/04/08
Publication Number:	1771045
Announcement Number	100475221
Grant Date:	2009-4-8
Granted Pub. Date:	2009-4-8
Application Type:	Invention
State/Country:	IN
Agency Code:	11243
Agent(s):	zhong jing
Applicant Address:	
Postcode:	Field Classification

Title:	A composition (RCUD) for protecting and/or repairing DNA from oxidative damages and a method thereof.
IPC:	A61K 35/22; A61P 39/06
Applicant(s):	Council of Scientific and Industrial Research
Inventor(s):	Tapan Chakrabarti; Sivanesan Saravana Devi; Kannan Krishnamurthi; Dipanwita Dutta; Narain Singh Rishi; Balkrishna Mansinghka Sunil; Haribhau Dawle Suresh

Abstract:

A composition useful for protecting and/or repairing DNA from oxidative damages said composition comprising redistilled cow's urine distillate (RCUD) having components benzoic acid, and hexanoic acid, with ammonia content of the composition ranging between 5-15mg/L, and optionally along with anti-oxidants; and a method of protecting and/or repairing DNA from oxidative damages using composition of claim 1, said method comprising steps of estimating the amount of folded DNA in a sample, mixing the said composition to the said DNA either before or after the exposure of the DNA to the oxidatively DNA-damaging agent, and determining percentage folded DNA in the mixture showing protection and/or repair of DNA from oxidative damages.

Claim(s):

Priority:

PCT

National Entry Date:	2005/10/27
International Application No.:	PCT/IN2003/000125
International Filing Date:	2003/3/31
International Publication Date:	2004/10/14
International Publication No.:	WO2004/087176
International Publication Language:	English

Legal Status: *Declaration*

Chapter VII

Ram Rajya as Governance

It is generally assumed by our English-educated elite that the prevalent system of Government in ancient India was monarchy. The view is based on the assumption that since there were kings in ancient India, therefore system was monarchy. A deeper look suggests that the system in ancient India was more akin to a republic than a monarchy, though it was neither in essence. Perhaps the closest of the current systems is constitutional monarchy or much like India's ceremonial presidency. Mr. Anil Chawla, an activist based on Bhopal has made a deep study of Republics of Ancient India. Here I rely on his studies.

DEFINITIONS

Oxford English Dictionary defines *Republic* as follows:

1. A state in which the supreme power rests in the people and their elected representatives or officers, as opposed to one governed by a king or similar ruler; a commonwealth. Now also applied loosely to any state which claims this designation.

   On the other hand *Monarchy* is defined as follows:

2. A state having a form of government in which the supreme power is vested in a single person. Formerly, also, a nation or

state having dominating power over all other states. *Absolute or despotic m* absolute or despotic m., a government by the absolute will of the monarch. *constitutional m.* (see constitutional a. 4 b). *elective m.,* one in which the monarch is determined by election as opposed to heredity. *hereditary m.,* one in which the sovereign power descends by hereditary right.

Thus, a *Republic* involves *just one distinguishing condition* – the supreme power does not rest with any single individual. *Monarchy* is based on the concept that the *Sovereign power of the Crown is supreme,* and, the King's will is final, without any 'advice' from any person or body acting as a control or check on the King.

Moreover in governance of a country involves three institutions – Legislature, Judiciary and Executive, the King is the head of all three institutions. The King is the law-maker as well as the ultimate judge and is responsible for executive functions. On the other hand, the distinction between the three institutions is an essential feature of Republics. The supreme power which rests in the people and their elected representatives or officers in a republic is exercised through these institutions which are supposed to maintain an arm's length distance among themselves. In a monarchy, the Crown's will being Supreme, the distinction between the three institutions (if at all present) gets blurred since a single individual acts as the head of all three.

LEGISLATURE IN ANCIENT INDIA

To understand the systems prevalent at that time, it is interesting to look at the nature and origin of Hindu Law about which John Mayne said in July, 1878 "Hindu Law has the oldest pedigree of any known system of jurisprudence, and even now it shows no signs of decrepitude. At this day it governs races of men, extending from Cashmere to Cape Comorin, who agree in nothing else except their submission to it." It should be noted that the British who have always (erroneously) prided themselves on uniting India were forced to admit that even after almost eight centuries of foreign rule, the country "from Cashmere to Cape Comorin" was governed by a common set of laws and this was when the country was said to have been divided into hundreds of small kingdoms. Contrast this with Europe where there have never been more than a handful of countries, and yet there has never been a common set of laws. Each European King made his own laws and his freedom in this respect was said to be the concept of 'sovereignty'.

The situation in India was very different because no King had any legislative powers in ancient India. Legislative activity or Law making was done only at the Centres of Learning which can well be called the Universities of that time. Varanasi, Ujjain, Nalanda, Rameshwaram and almost all major temple towns were such centres of learning. The word Rishi used in Indian texts has often been translated as ascetic or sage but this creates a confusion and lends to the term a super-human aura, a sort of mysticism. An impression has often been created in public mind that the Rishis who framed laws did nothing else but sit meditating under a tree or in some cave in Himalayas. Nothing can be more removed from truth. Almost all rishis were married and lived a healthy family life. The best comparison of a rishi can be to the modern day university professor who lives in his university campus far removed from the din of the city and devotes himself to intellectual pursuits.

Laws in ancient India were codified in Smritis. It is interesting to look at Mayne's view in regard to Hindu law – "According to Hindu conception, law in the modern sense was only a branch of Dharma, a word of the widest import and not easily rendered into English. Dharma includes religious, moral, social and legal duties and can only be defined by its contents. The Mitakshara mentions the six divisions of Dharma in general with which the Smritis deal; and the divisions relate to the duties of the castes, the duties of orders of ASRAMAS, the duties of orders of particular castes, the special duties of kings and others, the secondary duties which are enjoined for transgression of prescribed duties; and the common duties of all men.

[Mitakshara on Yajn. I,1 (Setlur's Edn., p. 4); Varnadharma, asramadharma, varnasramadharma, gunadharma, nimittadharma and sadharanadharma....]"(emphasis added by author). The interesting feature that is central to our discussion is that the Smritis inter alia provided for the duties of Kings. This obviously implies that any king was governed by the Smritis that were drafted not by himself or by his predecessors but by bodies of intellectuals.

A king was prohibited from becoming a law-maker or even interpreting the law. However after the 10th century, when the invasion of Islam led to a destruction of the famous Universities of India, some kings, as an attempt to safeguard knowledge, either took upon themselves or encouraged their ministers to take up the task of writing Commentaries and Digests of the Smritis. "A commentary on the Code of Manu was written in the 11th century by Dhareshwava or King Bhoja or Dhara in Malwa. A little later, Vijnanesvara wrote his famous Mitakshara on the Smriti of Yajnavalkya under the auspices of King Vikramarka or Vikramaditya of Kalyan in Hyderabad. King Apararka of Konkan, wrote his commentary on the Yajnavalkya Smriti in the 12th century. Jimutavahana, the author of the Dayabhaga, which is as well-known as the Mitakshara, was, according to tradition, either a very influential minister or a great judge in the court of one of the Bengal Kings. Chandesvara, the author of the Vivada Ratnakara, was the Chief Minister of a King of Mithila in the 14th century. Madhavacharya, the great Prime Minister of the Vizianagar Kings, wrote his Parasara Madhaviyam in the same century. About the same time, Vivesvarabhatta wrote his Subodhini, a commentary on the Mitakshara and a treatise named Madana Parijata under the order of King Madanapala of Kastha in Northern India who was also responsible for the recovery of the commentary of Medhatithi on Manu. Lakshmi Devi, a Queen of Mithila, caused Mitramisra to compose his Vivadachandra just about the period. In the 15th century, Vachaspatimisra, who was himself a descendant of King Harasinha Deva of Mithila, wrote the Vivadachintamani under the auspices of King Bhairavendra, a ruler of Mithila. King Pratapa Rudra Deva of Orissa wrote the Sarasvati Vilasa. Nandapandita, the author of the Dattaka Mimamsa, wrote a commentary on the Vishnu Smriti, called the Vaijayanti under the auspices of an influential chief, Kesavanayaka alias Tammasansyaka. Nilakantha, the author of the Vyavyahara Mayukha, composed it under the orders of Bhagavanta Deva, a Bundella chieftain who ruled at Bhareha, near the Jumna. Mitramisra composed his Viramitrodaya by the command of Virasinha, the ruler of Orchcha and Datia."

Thus, during the period that is classified as ancient in Indian history i.e. upto 1000AD Kings and their ministers had neither the power to make any Laws nor the power to interpret Laws.

Even after the establishment of the Islamic rule in the country, the Smriti law continued to be fully recognized and enforced because the invader came with near zero skills for governance. In the 16th century for example, Dalapati wrote an encyclopaedic work on Dharmasastra called the Narasimha-prasada. He was a minister of the Nizamshah Dynasty of Ahmednagar which ruled at Devagiri (Dowlatabad) and wrote his work, no doubt, under the auspices of the Mohammadan ruler, who is extolled in several stanzas. Todarmalla, the famous finance minister of the Moghul Emperor Akbar, compiled a very comprehensive work on civil and religious law known as Todarananda."

JUDICIARY IN ANCIENT INDIA

"Both the Arthasastra and the Dharmasastras establish the fact that the King was the fountain of justice that is the monarch could forgive, commits or shorten sentences like today President of India. In addition to the King himself as a court of ultimate resort, there were four classes of courts. The King's court was presided over by the Chief Judge, with the help of counsellors and assessors. There were three other courts of a popular character called Puga, Sreni and Kula. These were not constituted by the King. They were not, however, private or arbitration courts but people's tribunals which were part of the regular administration of justice and their authority was fully recognized. Puga was the court of fellow-townsmen or fellow-villagers, situated in the same locality, town or village, but of different castes and callings. Sreni was a court of judicial assembly consisting of the members of the same trade or calling, whether they belonged to the different castes or not. Kula was the judicial assembly of relations by blood or marriage. Kula, Sreni, Puga and the court presided over by the Chief Judge (Pradvivaka) were courts to which persons could resort for the settlement of their cases and were a cause was previously tried, he might appeal in succession in that order to the higher courts. As the Mitakshara puts it, 'In a cause decided by the King's officers although the defeated party is dissatisfied and thinks the decision to be based on misappreciation the case cannot be carried again to a Puga or the other tribunals. Similarly in a cause decided by a Puga, there is no resort to Sreni or Kula. In the same way in a cause decided by a Sreni, no recourse is possible to a Kula. On the other hand, in a cause decided by Kula, Sreni and other tribunals can be resorted to. In a cause decided by Sreni, Puga and the other tribunal can be resorted to. And in a cause decided by a Puga the Royal Court can be resorted to'. These inferior courts had apparently jurisdiction to decide all law suits among men, excepting violent crimes."

ROLE OF KINGS AS EXECUTIVE ANCIENT INDIA

The following observations can now be made about the role of Kings in ancient India.

(a) A King in ancient India was responsible for execution of the legislative will and administration in his kingdom.
(b) A King had no direct or indirect legislative powers.
(c) A King was supposed to be the "fountain of justice" but he had no direct role in the judicial process where an elaborate system of judiciary consisting of royal courts and people's tribunals was operational.

(d) In ancient India, a King and his ministers could not even act as interpreters of law. However this changed in medieval times when Kings started patronizing the writing of commentaries and digests.

(e) King was responsible for defence of his kingdom from external aggression.

(f) Providing of public services like education, healthcare etc. was not a duty of King's employees but was done by persons who considered it their vocation or calling. Payment of charges for these services was a cess on agricultural and other produce directly from the farmers & producers to the service-providers. The rate of this cess was not decided by the King but was decided by the Smritis.

(g) Rate of taxes (payable to King) was also not decided by the King but was fixed by Smritis. The royal machinery was responsible for collection of taxes.

(h) A King was supposed to use the taxes in a manner provided by the Smritis but it is likely that the Smritis provided some freedom to the King in this.

The picture that emerges from the above observations is very different from the image of a King in Europe, where based on the theory of divine power of the King, *'Sovereignty of the Crown is supreme'* and *'A King is always right'* were the well-accepted rules. A ritual that was carried out at the time of coronation of any Hindu King (until very recently) illustrates the position of the King in ancient India. After the coronation, the crowned King declares that he is all powerful. As soon as he declares his acquired power, the Rajguru (the chosen representative of the rishis) hits him with a Dand (a wooden rod) and tells him that Dharma and not he is the most powerful. The act of hitting him with a Dand is a symbolic punishment to remind him of his subordination to the Law as decided by the intellectual class. This is unimaginable in the coronation of a European King.

While classifying the system as republic, we must keep in mind that a republic need not always be democratic. Fascist and autocratic regimes have also been classified as republics. *Compared to many of the modern day republics, the ancient Indian system was a true republic and classifying it as monarchy is a mistake that social and political scientists must correct without any delay.* This system of separation of powers and governance on principles of dharma is what we mean by Ram Rajya.

As nature abhors a vacuum, this void is being increasingly filled, using religious symbols India being 83 percent Hindu, and furthermore since the folklore in this religion has been pan-Indian, it is easy for the masses to understand the religious bonding. Ramayana narration traverses from the Punjab to Srilanka. Mahabharata covers incidents from Assam to Gujarat. Adi Shankara connected Kerala to Kashmir. The mutilation of Indian history by the British and later by the JNU cabal the absurd Aryan-Dravidian two-nation two race theory propounded by the British had been rejected by all Indian seers and patriots whether it was Swami Vivekananda, or Subramania Bharati, or Dr. Ambedkar. Yet till recently, the Nehru acolytes had assiduously propagated it and incorporated it into school curriculam. To reject it did not mean that one was an Hindutva fanatic. But was that was what the Nehru secularists precisely alleged. But now it is pathetic to see these very secularists capitulating in the face of recent facts uncovered by new scientific techniques such as DNA testing and lasers. For example, for decades Professor Romila Thapar of JNU propagated the Aryan-Dravidian two race theory. But in 2002, she has beaten a hasty retreat. In her book:-"Penguin History of Early India" she has disowned Aryan-Dravidian race/nation theory altogether! She states now that: "To refer to 'the Aryan' as a race is therefore inaccurate." Better late than never, but it is a pity that she has it after the avalanche of new data and discoveries leaving her no room to hide her bogus scholarship.

If we are to reject the Martin Luther, Marxist, Nehruvian how are we to positively structure a new concept that has appeal for the Indian masses?

To do that we have to recognize the process that the doyen of sociologists, Dr. M.N. Srinivas had termed as Sanskritization. This term has nothing to do with the ancient language. Instead it comes from the word 'Sanskrit!' which means culture. The learned scholar had told me years ago that the Indian masses first ape, then digest, and finally assimilate elite behaviour. He had decades of published research to prove this. The final co-option of the upward mobile sections of the masses for assimilation as elites happens with religions sanction. To see this in reality, one has to study how the Nadars in Tamilnadu, Ezhavas in Kerala, and Jats in UP became elites in society. The Thevars may be next caste to be so assimilated. The great seer Ramanujana assimilated well-educated Scheduled Castes into the socially prestigious priestly class.

It is my view that the real reason secularism as propounded by Nehru has floundered is that it became an obstacle to this process Sanskritization. Secularism as defined by Nehru froze the social order by either non-chalance or negative rebuke. It lacked the positive content of providing a process for assimilation.

The Hindutva propounded by the RSS has now attracted more the lower and deprived castes. In UP, the Yadavas, Kurmis, and Lodhs were the most enthusiastic adherents of Hindutva since it enabled Sanskritization through political empowerment.

Hence, Yadava leaders like Mulayam Singh, Kurmi leaders like Nitish Kumar and Lodh leaders like Kalyan Singh are feeling the heat of Hindutva and the pressure to conform. The RSS may be Brahmin dominated at the leadership level, but its cadre and front organisations like the Bajrangh Pal are mostly the Hindu proletariats.

The national patriotic intellectuals should redefine secularism. Considering the salutary effect our Hindu scriptures has on the people, we should by a Constitutional Amendments redefine secular state as "spiritual state" that advocates *sarva pantha sams bhava.*

For this sanskritization should be promoted by a call declaring the caste system as anti-Hindu. There is sufficient theological basis, as we saw in Chapter-III, for such a call.

Only such an approach in the interest of good governance can insulate the Indian mind from communal pollution and halt fascism. Indian governance needs modernization, but nor westernization. But we find today the opposite trend. The Muslim League nominee as the Central Minister of State for Railways E. Ahaamed has ordered the ban on the lighting of lamp and breaking of coconuts in public functions of inauguration of projects and conferences on the ground that it is against secularism!

The teaching of Sanskrit language with its Devanagari script is essential for reaching governance to the common people. As we saw in an earlier Chapter, Sanskrit is rapidly emerging as a language to be learnt for advanced computer science and thus receiving State patronage in US and Europe, while paradoxically it is being opposed in India as being communal and 'Hindu'.

The Supreme Court went into this question and ruled that it did violate any Constitutional provision of secularism to require teaching of Sanskrit.

In (1994) 6 SCC579 reported case before Justices Kuldip Singh and B. L. Hansaria, it was held:

"So far as we, the people of India are concerned they have always held in high esteem the cultural heritage of this ancient land. And to foretell our views, learning of Sanskrit is undoubtedly necessary for the protection of this heritage. The stream of our culture would get dried if we were to discourage the study of Sanskrit and that too on the most untenable ground that if the Central Board of Secondary Education (for short 'the Board') were to do so, it would have to make facilities also available for learning Arabic and Persian.

Sanskrit should be included by the Board as one of the elective subjects in the syllabus along with Assamese, Bengali, etc., which are the languages specified in the Eighth Schedule of our Constitution, mentioning about Sanskrit being also an Eighth Schedule language. The desire to keep Sanskrit does not stop here, as the submission also is that if Sanskrit comes, the Board shall have to bring in languages like French and German, even in the Lepcha, a language whose name many of the Indians might not have even heard.

We fail to appreciate *at all* the stand taken by a responsible body like the Board, which has been entrusted with the onerous duty of educating the youth of this country "in whose hands quiver the destinies of the future," as the same is wholly untenable. Without the learning of Sanskrit it is not possible to decipher the Indian philosophy on which our culture and heritage are based.

The question raised being important requires us to answer it appropriately, appraise ourselves about the place of Sanskrit in our educational ethos, and *shall finally see whether teaching of Sanskrit against secularism.*

It is well known that Sanskrit is a mother of all Indian languages and it is this language in which our Vedas, Puranas, Upanishads have been written and in which Kalidas, Bhavbhuti, Banabhatta and Dandi wrote their classics. Teachings of Shankaracharya, Ramanuja, Madhawacharya, Nimbark and Vallabhacharya would not have been woven into the fabric of Indian culture if Sanskrit would not have been available to them as a medium of expressing their thoughts.

The report of the Sanskrit Commission (set up by the Government of India) which was submitted in 1957 speaks eloquently about the importance of Sanskrit. We do not propose to burden this judgement with all that was said by the Commission in this regard.

The only objection which merits our close look is that if Sanskrit were to be included as an elective subject, Arabic and Persian shall also have to be so done. The two other objections, namely inclusion of French and German also in the syllabus and of language like Lepcha do not deserve any consideration for previous reasons.

We entertain no doubt in our mind that teaching of Sanskrit alone as an elective subject can in no way be regarded as against secularism. Indeed, our Constitution requires giving fillip to Sanskrit because of what has been stated in Article 351, in which while dealing with the duty of the Union to promote the spread of Hindi it has been provided that it would draw, whenever necessary or desirable, for its vocabulary, primarily on Sanskrit. Encouragement to Sanskrit is also necessary because of it being one of the languages included in the Eighth Schedule.

We, therefore, conclude by saying that in view of importance of Sanskrit for nurturing our cultural heritage, because of which even the official education policy has highlighted the need of study of Sanskrit, making of Sanskrit alone as an elective subject, *while not conceding* this *status to Arabic and/or Persian,,* would not in any way militate against the basic tenet of secularism. There is thus no merit in the first objection raised by the Board.

In the aforesaid premises, we direct the Board to include Sanskrit as an elective subject in the syllabus under consideration. Necessary amendment in the syllabus shall be made within a period of three months from today."

Having failed to black-out Sanskrit from the elective curriculum, the Westernized elite in our country has started a controversy over singing of Vande Mataram in official functions of the state.

The present controversy over the mandatory singing the song "Vande Mataram," is a return of the political discourse of the 1930s, that carries a message, of a lack of the integrity in our national identity. We must not yield to it.

The issue of a compulsion in signing was settled about 70 years ago, during 1937-39, when Mohammed Ali Jinnah purportedly gave vent to the 'anxiety' of the Muslim community, of its members that would be compelled to sing Vande Mataram in Independent India. Among the 'Quaid-e-Azam' papers in Pakistan, his *Discussion Note* of February 1, 1938, titled: "Vande Mataram must go" bears the out.

On March 1, 1938, in an article in *The New Times* of Lahore, Jinnah stated: "Muslims all over have refused to accept Vande Mataram or any expurgated edition of the anti-Muslim song as a binding national anthem." On April 16, 1938, in his presidential address at the special session of the All India Muslim League in Calcutta, he focused attention on the charge that the Indian National Congress "endeavoured to impose the Vande Mataram song in the legislatures." In his presidential address at the Sind Provincial Muslim League Conference, Jinnah reiterated the charge as indeed he did on many other occasions.

The "expurgated edition" of the song, which Jinnah refers to in his article, was the outcome of these harangues by Jinnah.

The abridged version of Vande Mataram is of the first two stanzas.

By a resolution of the Working Committee in October 1937, the Congress Party capitulated and reduced the celestial song to two stanzas.

The resolution was of vital importance for the Constituent Assembly in its decision to designate Vande Mataram as the national song, while "Jana-gana-mana" was given the status of the national anthem. It is evident from the draft Resolution that Gandhi wrote as a "Strictly Confidential: Not for Publication." Note that said: "As to the singing of the long established national song, Vande Mataram, the Congress, anticipating objections, has retained as national song only those stanzas to which no objection could be taken on religious and other grounds. But except at purely Congress gathering it should be left open to individuals whether they will stand up when the stanzas are sung. In the present state of things, in Local Board and Assembly meetings, which their members are obliged to attend, the singing of Vande Mataram should be discontinued."

There were some dissenting voices in the Congress. C. Rajagopalachari thought that such a "concession will not save the situation" (Rajagopalachari to Sardar Vallabhai Patel, January 7, 1939), and even G.B. Pant was quite lukewarm abut the idea (Pant to Nehru, January 8, 1939). Nevertheless Gandhi and Nehru, and more the latter who regarded the measure as essential. It was nevertheless a decision that Gandhi acquiesced but did not defend. He wrote a sort of apologia in *Harijan* later. (July 1, 1939): "... now we have fallen on evil days, although I will not risk a single quarrel over singing Vande Mataram at a mixed gathering. It [the song] will never suffer from disuse. It is enthroned in the hearts of millions."

Nehru was one of those Congress members who was not familiar with the song—in fact as late as October 20, 1937, he wrote, "I do not understand it without the help of a dictionary," but he had "managed to get an English translation." He read for the first time Bankim Chandra Chatterjee's novel in which the song features, only six days before the Working Committee meeting to decide the fate of the song. Vallabhai Patel and Rajendra Prasad had concluded their address as Congress Presidents, in 1931 and 1934, with the Vande Mataram slogan; Nehru did not in 1929 and 1936. Subhash Chandra Bose was vigorously in favour of Vande Mataram. Nehru's response to him was that considering that there was an outcry against the song and "people who have been Communistically (!) inclined" were watching the Congress actions in this regard. The Congress be added must "meet real grievances where they exist," without pondering to communalism (Nehru to Bose, October 20, 1937)—whatever that means.

Cornered, Nehru had sought a way out by appealing to Tagore, who ultimately decided the issue for the Congress. Tagore was the first person to sing Vande Mataram at a session of the Indian National Congress, in 1896 in Calcutta.

One of the governance issues is how to handle minorities, especially Muslims and Christians who are part of international religious networks. For India, Christians are by themselves peace loving and India-centric. But foreign missionaries tend, by their throwing money and fanning superstitions, derail this peace between Hindus and Christians.

When in a minority in a country Islamization begins when there are critically sufficient Muslims to noticeably agitate for their religious privileges. When politically 'correct' tolerant and culturally diverse but soft amorphous societies agree to Muslim demand for a particular religious privilege such as separate personal law other demands surface as well soon after.

Today's 1.5 billion Muslims make up 22% of the world's population. But their birth rates dwarf the birth rates of Christians, Hindus, Buddhists, and Jews, and all other believers. Muslims will exceed 50% of the world's population by the end of this century, if the present trends continue [Adapted from Peter Hammond: *Slavery, Terrorism and Islam: The Historical Roots and Contemporary]*. Hence, for us Hindus, the problem of conversion and infiltration from Bangla Desh is one of serious national security concern.

Thus, again today we are at a moment of history of our ancient nation when the Hindu foundation of the nation is could be gravely challenged, and sought to be undermined. But it is important to remember that never before in our history has the challenge been as dangerously deceptive, pernicious, and sophisticated as it is now. It is therefore difficult to respond to this challenge since it cannot be easily perceived by the common Hindu.

Hence, the response to this challenge and the implicit threat has to be as well thought out profound and simply explained to the people. But as before in our history, the response to be fruitful has to be designed and structured by the confluence of spiritual guidance and political resolve. Such a confluence has been the fundamental basis of our past responses to the such challenges in history, from the installation by *rishis* of Adi Raja Prithu as King of Bharatvarsh, Chanakya's founding of the Mauryan kingdom, the establishment of the Vijayanagaram empire at Hampi by Sringeri Shankaracharya, to inspiring the fighting armies of Shivaji by Swami Ramdass. Even Mahatma Gandhi and Jayaprakash Narayan in their respective struggles for independence of the nation from colonialism, and for the restoration of democracy in a nation that was drowned in the darkness of the Emergency, had followed this unique Hindu model of spiritually guiding a political movement without seeking the fruits of office for themselves.

Fortunately, an extraordinary gathering of revered and respected Hindu saints and spiritual leaders are being convened by His Holiness Swami Dayananda Saraswati under the auspices of Hindu Dharma Acharya Sabha. I have been privileged to address these august and holy gatherings on the topic of Hindu unity [see www.janataparty. org]. In those addresses I have focused on four dimensions of the current threat to the Hindu foundation of India and dealt briefly with the scope of each of the dimensions of the threat. I shall here elaborate in some detail the threat in one of the dimensions, that is, the threat arising out of the forced and deliberate demographic changes in the country caused by three factors: induced religious conversions, illegal migration into India, and differential application of family planning programmes.

The bottom line of my concern is that no matter what the threat is, India must remain a predominantly Hindu country to be the distinctive nation that it has been over the centuries. That distinctiveness includes the acknowledgment by the people of the nation that all religions, if practiced faithfully, are equally capable of leading to God. No other religion outside the Hindu family of theology holds forth thus. Hindus because of this enlightened secular outlook have a long tradition of being hospitable, accommodative and even to assimilate peoples of other religions who have come here seeking refuge. The Parsis, Jews, Syrian Christians and even Arabs [in Kerala] are examples of this hospitality and assimilation.

The Hindu foundation of modern India is why India has been and is even today referred to, in India and abroad, as Hindustan. Hindustan is defined as a nation of Hindus and those who accept that their ancestors are Hindus. The concept also includes refugee minorities who accept the core values of the Hindu culture and therefore recognized as a part of the Hindustan nation. Thus when the Dwarka Mutt Shankaracharya gave the arriving Parsi refugees in Sanjaan [Kutch coast] a five-point requirement for settling in the country, they readily accepted and have not deviated from it even today. These five points were: Giving up Persian language and adopting Gujarati; wearing Indian clothes instead of Persian; treating the cow as sacred; reciting some select Sanskrit slokas in their marriage ceremony; and laying down of weapons. Despite being the smallest minority, with disproportionate share in offices of power and national wealth, and perhaps also the wealthiest community, there is and has been no tension or conflict between Hindus and Parsis.

Parsis and Jews do not threaten the Hindu character of the nation. They do not seek to proselytize or convert Hindus by monetary inducements or by obscurantist preachings such as curing persons who convert, of incurable terminal diseases. But on the other hand, the preachings of the religious leaders of Islam and Christianity in India, altogether for a thousand years, had targeted Hindus and sought the religious conversions to their faiths by creating deprivation and loss of self-esteem, through the abuse of the power of the State against Hindus. They were not subtle about it. For example, in 1545, King John III of Portugal gave a command to the then Governor of Goa that neither public nor private 'idols' of Hindu heathens be tolerated on the island of Goa and that severe punishment be meted out to those who persist in keeping them. Thereafter, a terrible inquisition followed during which Hindus were killed, brutalized and their temples razed to the ground. Still we must not forget only a minority of Hindus converted to Christianity. No other religious community other than Hindus suffered such prolonged and atrocious persecution and survived as a religion of a vast majority on their own soil.

Today Hindus despite *de facto* in power and in the organs of the state are victims of that same targeting, but of course in a very subtle and sophisticated manner. In furthering the objective of this targeting, Islam and Christianity, more so the latter, have been able to leverage the influence of prominent Hindus themselves, who wittingly for money or unwittingly because of a programmed mindset of being defensive about being a Hindu [thereby ready to ape the West] are tools of this targeting.

What is the nature and scope of this targeting, and is there a way for us to end it by conciliation with Christians and Muslims? In other words, can we seek to end religious conversion in India today by the ancient Hindu way of *shashtrathas* as Hindu saints did, as for example Adi Sankara did with Buddhism and *Uttara Mimamsa* theologies and *Azhwars* and *Nayanars* saints in the south did with Jainism? Will indeed Christians and Muslims recognize the sanctity of *shashtratas*?

There is a serious problem here because as an interesting study of *Sarah Claerhout and Jakob De Roover* titled: "The Question of Conversion in India"! *Economic and Political Weekly*, July 9, 2005] concludes, Hindus and Christians have fundamentally different and mutually exclusive concepts of religion and thus also in their approaches to the question of conversion. Hence, say the authors, for Hindus and Christians to dialogue on conversion would be fruitless because they will have "great difficulties making sense of each other's statements and arguments." This is because Hindus do not consider any religion as wholly false, and as Gandhiji put it, all religions have some errors in them. Since all religions lead to God, hence there is no need for forcing a conversion. Christians [and Muslims] think that their's is the only true religion, and it is God's work to convert heathens and *kafirs* to their only true religion.

I have thus come to the conclusion after much study and observing what has been, and is happening in India, that *there is a fundamental disconnect between the religious outlook of Hindus and the Christians and Muslims which makes it impossible for a fruitful debate and mutual understanding on the Question of religious conversion.*

Therefore, either Hindus will have to capitulate on this question by permitting religious conversion in India, or in the alternative be united and assertive to ensure that laws are enacted and effectively enforced against religious conversion of Hindus. There is no third way.

It is urgent that Hindus be mobilized to assertively oppose any further conversion from Hinduism to any other religion. There is no room for indifference here. This is because that *status quo* is damaging to the Hindu faith, since the Christian missionaries and Muslim *mullahs* are already fully at work, funds being no constraint, to convert Hindus. If conversions are not explicitly opposed, then Hindus are implicitly acquiescing in the atrocity.

Reflect on the past trends: In 1000 A.D., Muslims and Christians in undivided India were in negligible numbers. By 1400, they had become 3.5 % of the sub-continent. In 1700, they rose to 11 %, and by 1891 to 13 %. By the time of Partition, they were 23 %, and today in South Asia the Christian and Muslim population is 36 %. What will it be in 2050 or 2150? This is an extraordinary rise, which has continued even after freedom from British colonial rule.

De facto power in the hands of Hindu majority has not changed the attitude of the proselytizers, only their strategy has changed and become invisible for most Hindus. And those Hindus who have been power in government have been soft on this issue entrapped by the lack of a Hindu mindset and bloc voting by the Muslims and Christians. And where Christian and Muslim interests are involved the government of the day rises to their defence. For example, in Mizoram there are about 7,000 persons who have been identified as members of B'nai Menashe, one of the 10 "lost" tribes of Israel. Having been discovered this tribe wanted to be formally recognized as Jews since even today they adhere to Jewish customs. However, they had been converted to Christianity during the British imperialist occupation of India. Hence, at the request of these Mizos, Israel's Chief Rabbinate decided to send a team, in November 2005, of Rabbis to India to perform religious ceremonies to re-convert them formally. However, when they applied for visas at the Indian Embassy in Tel Aviv, they were told that our Ministry of External Affairs had informed the Israeli government that the Indian government disapproves of the visit and will not permit religious leaders to come to India for proselytizing activities. But the Indian government permits Christian missionaries including those who have criminal cases pending against them in their own countries, to freely conduct conversion activities. Thus, it is clear that the present dispensation is acting as a patron for Christian aims and goals, and a subtly sponsoring them.

Hence, even the most secular Hindus should now worry about this demographic trend, because secularism is itself under threat if the Hindus lose their majority share in population. That is why even Gandhiji and Dr. Ambedkar [no Hindu fundamentalists but highly regarded secularists], during the freedom struggle had stoutly opposed religious conversions. In Mahatma's interview given to *The Hindu* in 1931 [see *Collected Works of Mahatma Gandhi,* Vol XLV, p.320] he stated: "Every nation's religion is as good as another. Certainly India's religions are adequate for her people. We need no converting spiritually."

Gandhiji went on to add that if foreign missionaries in independent India sought to convert by inducement such as by medical aid and in providing education, then he would ask them to withdraw from the country. Lest his remarks be treated as a misquote or off the cuff, Gandhiji later authored an article to reaffirm the same view in different language: "India stands in no need of conversions from one faith to another" *Young India (April 23. 1931 issue).*

When independent India debated the draft Constitution in the Constituent Assembly, enormous pressure was brought to bear within the Assembly and outside, to make the freedom to convert a fundamental right. Within the Assembly, the leader of Anglo-Indians, Mr. Frank Anthony, stated that the right to convert to Christian faith was the "most fundamental of Christian rights" [*Constituent Assembly Debates III;* pp. 489-90]. He and other Christian groups had wanted Article 25 to be so re-drafted as to make the right to carry on conversion activities as a fundamental right. But with the exception of a few, others did not agree. Dr. Ambedkar despite his own stated views against conversion as a right, was prevailed upon by Nehru to draft a hotch-potch Article 25, which meant all things to all persons, which then was adopted by the Constituent Assembly.

However, soon after Independence, the pinch of induced conversion began to be felt, and some State governments, notably Madhya Pradesh and Orissa Vidhan Sabhas, enacted laws banning induced conversions. In 1977, a ruling Janata Party MP, Om Prakash Tyagi, brought forth a Private Member's Bill in the Lok Sabha to seek parliamentary approval to get a law enacted to make induced conversions a national offence. Unfortunately, despite it having wide support, the Janata government did not last long enough to enact a law banning induced conversions.

In 1977, the Supreme Court clarified in a landmark judgment that Article 25 however worded did not allow for the right to convert. Chief Justice A. N. Ray opined that "if a person purposely undertakes the conversion of another to his religion that would impinge on the freedom of conscience guaranteed to all citizens of the country alike." Despite this clear ruling, governments that have come and gone have failed to translate the judgment into an explicit law. Since then the political play of secularism has continued to dilute the resolve of governments to stop induced conversions.

Now the freedom to convert has become of international concern. V. K. Shashikumar in an article titled: "Bush's Conversion Agenda for India" and published in *Tehelka* in February 2004 states that a project code named JOSHUA projects I&II was formulated by US Evangelical groups to map the 152,786 post offices in India and codified by PIN codes, and then identify who and how conversion may be planned. Based on this project, a recent September 2005 conclave in Dallas, Texas, targeted that 100 million converts from Hinduism should be achieved by 2020. Of course, knowing the US scene as I do, there are other Christian groups in the US who are apprehensive that these Evangelical groups may end up giving Christianity a bad name, and having been using the web blogs to expose these groups. One such concerned group, the Trinity

Foundation, had exposed Benny Hinn who had earlier been received almost as a State Guest in Bangalore to hold his fraud congregation to demonstrate his miracle cures. But India bears the brunt of the likes of Benny Hinn and not Trinity Foundation. And when we speak of Christian missionaries we mean those whose mission is to proselytize. And of course it is an international effort and we need to set our minds to have none of it.

Ms Jayalalitha as Chief Minister brought into law a statute titled Tamil Nadu Prohibition of Forcible Conversion of Religion, but soon she had to beat a hasty retreat when the US Consul General based in Chennai met her and apprised that the said statute violated US law on religious freedom. This was a sad capitulation for Tamils in particular and Indians in general. Ms Jayalalitha, claiming to be a staunch Hindu, was devoid of courage and had feet of clay. That is the mindset that we need to combat.

I must make clear here however that *I do not oppose voluntary and unforced conversion to Hinduism of those presently of the Semitic religions, such as Christians and Muslims of India*, because all Indians, except Parsis, Jews and Syrian Christians, are either Hindus or those whose ancestors are Hindus. Their becoming Hindus is re-conversion and a return to the Hindu fold. For most Christians and Muslims in India, the conversion of their ancestors in the past was coerced openly, crudely, savagely, or subtly, but it was not voluntary. One has to read what happened to Guru Tegh Bahadur to imagine what else must have happened in the country to make Hindus to convert. Today, every Muslim and Christian in India is a living example of that despicable violence against the Hindus. We may try to understand what and why it had happened in the past, but we should not forget the lesson embedded in the brutally forced conversions that did take place. We should, therefore, all be thankful to Swami Dayananda Saraswati for his open letter to the Pope of Vatican, John Paul II, during latter's visit to New Delhi to preach the Gospel. In that letter the Swamiji boldly stated: "Religious conversion destroys centuries-old communities and incites communal violence. *It is violence, and it breeds* violence" [www.hindunet.org/conversions/pope99/].

I am also not advocating that Hindus and other religionists must confront each other, and not interact or dialogue on any issue. Far from it, I advocate vibrant debate and discussion on most religious issues, but not on those issues which will erode or undermine the Hindu foundation of India. On the question of religious conversion, it should now be treated as a closed chapter. Hindus true to their legacy will not permit it. Either, true Hindus will prevail, or India will be deformed, twisted and ultimately, like Greece and Egypt, transformed beyond recognition. India as the world has known and admired would then be destroyed forever. Hence, instead Hindus must remain steadfast and make the Christians missionaries and Muslim *mullahs* see how they too can take pride in their great Hindu ancestry, and are welcome anytime of their choosing back to the Hindu fold. A Russian scholar, Alexander Zinoviev, of the Russian Academy of Sciences in Moscow, recently published an article in the *Organiser* that was titled: "For India's Survival Hinduism has to Prevail." He states:

> .... During the Renaissance, Western Europeans realized that they were successors of ancient Rome and Greece, and embraced their culture which for long centuries was being condemned by the Roman Catholic Church as "pagan" and "non-Christian," [hence] one day the Muslims on the Indian subcontinent will understand that they are inheritors of a great civilisation completely different from that of Arabs and the Middle East. This is a problem of education and knowledge.

Of course, before we can motivate and persuade the Indian Christian and Muslims to accept that their ancestors are Hindus and because of this fact they have the option of returning to Hinduism, *we Hindus have to set our house In order.* Over the centuries since Adi Shankaracharya, the Hindu religion has not undergone a renaissance. There have been valiant attempts, but these had been circumscribed by political compulsions of the time foisted on us by invasions and imperialism. Often these attempts at renaissance had to be aborted due to these compulsions. In 1947, however, we Hindus had an opportunity to usher a renaissance without compulsions, but the misfortune of a long tenure as Prime Minister of a *self-confessed agnostic and* the political culture imported from a God-less Communist Soviet Union thoroughly froze the distortions in Hindu religious practices. It is imperative, therefore, to create a new Hindu corporate awareness to confront these distortions frontally and remove them. Otherwise, the forces ranged against Hinduism today will succeed in their nefarious designs.

I am particularly concerned with the effect the *varna vyavastha* [caste system] is having in promoting religious conversions. It gives a talking point to the enemies of Hinduism. It is not that other religions do not have a stratification based on origin of the individual. Dalit converts to Christianity, for example, learn the hard way about their low status in their new religion, and hence are asking for reservation in jobs and education even after conversion! Of course, we should never agree to that because reservation is strictly a correction for the malfunction of the Hindu society in the past, and in fact reservations should have been confined to schedule castes and tribes only who have remained Hindus despite all the atrocities heaped on them for centuries. Christians and Muslims have been ruling classes in India for a thousand years and hence certainly not deprived or discriminated in any way. In that sense, scheduled castes are more steadfast Hindus than those of other castes, for having remained Hindus despite being deprived, humiliated and discriminated.

Moreover, I may add that I regard Dr. Ambedkar as the twentieth century intellectual who should be most admired by Hindu society for his profound perception of India's history which perception he has fortunately for all of us recorded in books and articles. Not only did he write like a Hindu patriot, but he can be regarded as a joint architect, with Mahatma Gandhi and Sardar Patel, of the geographical India of today. Had Dr. Ambedkar accepted the 1932 British imperialist offer for a separate electorate for scheduled castes, and Gandhiji had not staked his life on the line against it, India would have been completely balkanized before the British left in 1947. That was the imperialist plot and Dr. Ambedkar understood and a patriot refused to oblige. It is a great tragedy for India that personal jealousies led to his sidelining in politics after Independence and ultimately had frustrated him. It is not too late to venerate him even now by a campaign to demolish what is left of the caste system.

At this juncture in our history, nearly sixty years after securing freedom from successive oppressive regimes spread over a thousand years, empowered by a pluralistic democracy and on the verge of a major economic upsurge, Hindus are again finding themselves agonizing as to what the future holds for them as a religious community. Because of a greater readiness amongst Hindus to accept family planning and because effete governments over the years have failed to prevent illegal immigration of minorities from our neighbourhood, Hindus are in ratio of total population declining in numbers. More importantly, there are states of the Indian Union where Muslims and Christians are in majority, and Hindus are being denied their due in those states. In Kashmir, thousands and thousands of Hindus have been driven out in the despicably blatant ethnic cleansing. At this rate Hindus could become a minority with a hundred years. In Tripura, Hindu activists are being murdered every day by Christian terrorists. In the south, a Shankaracharya Mutt has been defiled by the state government filing false and bogus murder cases against venerated Holiness. The *acharya* was not permitted by a government official to perform his traditional *pujas* at the *Rameshwaram temple* because the *acharya* had this bogus case pending against him!! Even the carrying of the *dand* by the junior

Shankaracharya of Dwarka was opposed by the government-run Indian Airlines and the saint had to disembark from the plane he was sitting in. And all this is happening while Hindus are in power in the government.

Hence, Hindus need a new mindset the composition of which is in detail in my speech on "Fundamentals of Hindu Unity and the Concept of Hindustan" delivered before the Hindu Dharma Acharya Sabha conference held in Mumbai on October 16-18, 2005. As I have said before, Hindus are under a siege, and they do not even know it. There is a conflict on between "Om Shakti" and "Rome Bhakti" today through conversions.

Conversion activities are a symptom of the lack of a correct mindset among Hindus, and thus we must deal with this threat in that context. We can rectify this by proper governance based on a clear commitment to Hindutva.

Another art of governance that requires a Hindutva mindset is in dealing with terrorism. It requires a sophisticated balancing of crushing terrorism and safeguarding human rights.

COMBATING OF TERRORISM AND PROTECTION OF HUMAN RIGHTS

Human rights are the basic rights and freedoms entitled to any person, regardless of economic status, nationality, jurisdiction, age, ability, ethnicity, sex, and sexuality. These basic rights are the right to life, freedom, equality, justice, and freedom of thought and expression. However, in the Constitution of India all human rights including religious rights are subject to "reasonable" restrictions. Since these restrictions are not enumerated, hence courts under Article 32 and Article 226 decide it in a case to case basis.

Security of the individual is a basic human right and the protection of individuals is, accordingly, a fundamental obligation of Government. States, therefore, have an obligation to ensure the human rights of their nationals and others by taking positive measures to protect them against the threat of terrorist acts and to bring the perpetrators of such acts to justice. Thus there is a trade-off between human rights as well in this: some freedom for security, both being human rights.

In recent years, the security measures adopted by States to counter terrorism have often posed serious challenges to human rights. Some States have had to engage in torture and other ill-treatment to counter terrorism, while the legal safeguards available to prevent torture, such as regular and independent monitoring of detention centers, have been disregarded.

The question is whether sacrificing human rights beyond a point is not counterproductive to national and international security in combating terrorism? This requires a constant watch between what is a reasonable sacrifice or restriction of rights and what is excessive in the measures adopted to fight terrorism.

What are human rights?

Human rights are universal—in other words, they belong inherently to all human beings—and are interdependent and indivisible. The full spectrum of human rights involves respect for, and protection and fulfillment of, civil, cultural, economic, political and social rights, as well as the right to development.

In 1948, the UN codified these rights in the *Universal Declaration of Human Rights (Annexure 1).* In the Indian Constitution adopted by the Constituent Assembly on November 26, 1949, this was codified as Fundamental Rights.

International human rights law is reflected in a number of core international human rights treaties and in customary international law. These treaties include in particular the 1966 International Covenant on Economic, Social and Cultural Rights, and the International Covenant on Civil and Political Rights and its two Optional Protocols. India has ratified these two Covenants during the Janata Government tenure (1977-79) but the Protocols which establish the procedures have not yet been.

What is terrorism?

Terrorism is an act of violence that target civilians to overawe a legally constituted government and the people in the pursuit of political or ideological aims. In 1994, the General Assembly's Declaration on Measures to Eliminate International Terrorism, set out in its resolution 49/60, stated that terrorism includes "criminal acts intended or calculated to provoke a state of terror in the general public, a group of persons or particular persons for political purposes" and that such acts "are in any circumstances unjustifiable, whatever the considerations of a political, philosophical, ideological, racial, ethnic, religious or other nature that may be invoked to justify them."

Ten years later, the UN Security Council, in its Resolution No.1566 (2004), referred to "criminal acts, including against civilians, committed with the intent to provoke a state of terror in the general public or in a group of persons or particular persons, intimidate a population or compel a Government or an international organization to do or to abstain from doing any act."

The impact of terrorism on human rights

While we worry about the impact of counter-terrorism measures on human rights, terrorism has a direct impact on the enjoyment of a number of human rights, in particular the rights to life, liberty and physical integrity. The destructive impact of terrorism on human rights and security has been recognized at the United Nations, notably by the Security Council, the General Assembly, and the new Human Rights Council [the former Commission on Human Rights]. Specifically, Member States have set out that terrorism:

*Threatens the dignity and security of human beings everywhere, endangers or takes innocent lives, creates an environment that destroys the freedom from fear of the people, jeopardizes fundamental freedoms, and aims at the destruction of human rights;

*Has an adverse effect on the establishment of the rule of law, undermines pluralistic civil society, aims at the destruction of the democratic bases of society, and destabilizes legitimately constituted Governments;

*Has links with transnational organized crime, drug trafficking, money-laundering and trafficking in arms, as well as illegal transfers of nuclear, chemical and biological materials, and is linked to the consequent commission of serious crimes such as murder, extortion, kidnapping, assault, hostage-taking and robbery;

Hence, every government separately and collectively has a duty to take effective counter-terrorism measures, to prevent and deter future terrorist attacks and to prosecute those that are responsible for carrying out such acts. At the same time, the countering of terrorism poses grave challenges to the protection and promotion of human rights. As part of States' duty to protect individuals within their jurisdiction, all measures taken to combat terrorism must themselves also comply with States' obligations under international law, in particular international human rights, refugee and humanitarian law.

Today, every nation is being called upon to resolve the conflicting demands of combating terrorism and of protecting human rights. The relationship between the two is not "linear," but "non-linear." That is, *it is not true* that the less we protect human rights, the more we can combat terrorism. The converse is also not true. There is therefore a "optimum combination" of measures to combat terrorism and the level of safeguards that ensure human rights. The law of diminishing return operates on this trade-off.

The current position in terms of principles of combating terrorism are codified by the UN Human Rights Commission vide its Resolution No. 8 of 2005 (Annexure 2). The question before us how in India we go about combating terrorism, in light of our international commitments, and protecting fundamental human rights.

The fundamental question is that since in India we are the worst affected by terrorist attacks, even more than Iraq and Afghanistan, is how to formulate a policy to deal with terrorism. The cure we choose for terrorist attacks should not be worse in the long run than the consequences of these attacks as the Kandhahar IC-184 plane hijack has showed us. Terrorism in India worsened as a consequence of the deal made by the NDA government then to free the passengers and crew, but more innocent people have been killed in terrorist attacks since the release of Maulana Azhar, Umar Quereshi and Zargar in exchange for 159 passengers and crew in the Kandhahar case. These three upon reaching Pakistan after being freed in Kandhahar set up Jaish-E-Mohammed, LeT and Al Mujahedin which continue their terrorists acts even today including 26/11 in Mumbai.

Thus, terrorism affects human rights in three ways. The terrorist attacks deprive citizens of their lives, limbs and properties and hence their human rights. To combat these terrorists we place restrictions on human rights of the citizens, on privacy, freedom of travel and association so the victims of attacks suffer both way. Moreover, human rights questions are raised when the terrorists are apprehended on such issues as torture, deprivation of human dignity, the right to a free trial etc.

Thus we need a clear cut policy, which means a clear cut statement of objectives, defining the priorities of these objectives, the strategy to achieve the objective, and the commitment of necessary human, financial and infrastructural resources. In a nutshell, a government has to have the right to do what is sufficient but reasonable to combat terrorism for human rights. Present laws especially with Unlawful Activities Act after amendment is sufficient.

Objectives

Hindustan originally comprised the present-day India, Iran, Pakistan, Bangladesh, Nepal and Afghanistan. It may be recalled that Kaikeyi was from Iran, while Gandhari was from Afghanistan. It was a 100%

Hindu land till Muhammad bin Qasim's Arab army attacked Sindh in 711. But that attack was repulsed by the Chalukyas of Gujarat. The Turks then arrived in force 275 years later and then began the Islamic onslaught of Hindustan.

Despite fighting valiantly to defend their *dharma* and motherland during repeated Muslim invasions for over seven centuries thereafter, Hindus lost Afghanistan in 987, Iran in 1011; and present-day Pakistan and Bangladesh in 1947 to Muslims. After 1947, truncated India, i.e. Bharat has seen genocide and eviction of Hindus from Muslim-majority Kashmir, not to mention Pakistan and Bangladesh.

Alert Hindus today apprehend that because of higher Muslim population growth rate and infiltration from Bangladesh, they will be outnumbered soon by Muslims (in a few decades) and face the same fate of Hindus in Afghanistan, Pakistan and Bangladesh, which also was once a land of Hindu.

It is ironic that despite repeated waves of foreign invaders for over 1,200 years, Hindus resisted converting to Islam and Christianity. But now we are acquiescing in a demographic invasion.

Hindu civilisation today is a demographically challenged civilisation. Many districts in India bordering Bangladesh have seen abnormal increase in Muslim population because of infiltration. The nature of Islam as a religious theology is such that wherever Muslims are in majority they behave most intolerantly and violently towards Hindus and other minorities. Within India, we see this not only in Kashmir but even in pockets like Mau in UP and in 40 nagar panchayats in Tamil Nadu where Muslims are in majority. Hence, one aspect of terrorism we face is the Islamic demographic invasion from Bangladesh which is compounded by a higher population growth of all Muslims in India. By 2061, at this differential rate of population growth, India would become a Hindu-minority and Muslim-majority nation. So the *first anti-terrorist objective* is to check this infiltration and impose uniform family planning on all communities.

By its judgment dated July 12, 2005, Supreme Court had struck down the Illegal Migrants (D.T.) Act, 1983 as unconstitutional; and termed Bangladeshi infiltration as "external aggression" and directed that "Bangladeshi nationals who have trespassed into Assam or are living in other parts of the country have no legal right of any kind to remain in India and they are liable to be deported."

But, instead of deporting the infiltrators, on Februaty 10, 2006, UPA government brought in the Foreigners (Tribunals for Assam) Order to nullify the apex Court's judgment. On December 5, 2006, Supreme Court quashed this Order also as unconstitutional, and called for implementation of its earlier judgment dated July 12, 2005 for deporting illegal immigrants.

Despite this judgments, hardly any infiltrator has been deported by the government. Instead of being deported, infiltrators are being quietly acquiring voting rights, since the government is busy with terrorist and infiltrator-friendly 'confidence building measures' like soft borders, peace talks, Indo-Pak and Indo-Bangladesh bus and rail links, which are bringing more and more Pak-Bangla nationals into India everyday.

What did the despicable terror and mayhem in Mumbai on November 26th signify for India? Shorn of the human tragedy, wanton destruction, and obnoxious audacity of the terrorists, it fundamentally signifies a challenge to the true identity of India from radical Islam securely based in Pakistan. Pakistan is a Muslim-majority country and, therefore, by definition cannot be a secular peace-loving country. It is to be regarded instead as Darul Islam where minorities have no place. Islam commands Muslims of Darul Islam to wage *jihad*, and hence India will continue to be attacked by terrorists from Pakistan. To end this, patriotic Indians must force them to sign a *Al Taqqiya* contract.

For this any patriotic Indian government, as *a second anti-terrorist objective*, must not permit any area of India, from State to district to town panchayat, to be a Muslim-majority area because then it will become a breeding ground for *Jihad* based terror.

The *third anti-terrorist objective* is straight forward—prevent terrorists attacks.

Priorities

First priority is the third objective. We need a strategy of deterrence. Second priority is the first objective; and third priority is the second objective.

As regards the first priority, i.e., third objective, what to do, for examples, against terrorist attacks against Hindus of Kashmir who have been driven out? They number 5 lakhs, mostly in 'refugee' camps since 1989.

A nationalist government must as a strategy ensure a population re-settlement to restore the Hindu-Muslim balance in J&K. The Indian government must thus resettle 10 lakh ex-service personnel of the armed forces to reconstruct the population ratio of Hindus in Kashmir.

Secular intellectuals may wax eloquent about the "true Islam" being humane and peaceful on TV programmes, but it is clear that they have not read any authoritative translations of the *Koran, Sira* and *Hadith* which three holy books together constitute the theology of Islam.

Hence, instead of talking about the "correct interpretation" of Islam, those who call themselves as "moderates" in the Islamic community, ought instead to urge for a new reformed Islamic theology that is consistent with democratic principles. Of course, then like Salman Rushdie and Taslima, they will have to run for cover to escape fanatic murderous Muslims. In 2003, two years after the 9/11 perfidious Islamic assault on USA, resulting in killing of more than 3,000 persons within two hours, and which crime of terror was perpetrated by leveraging the democratic freedoms in USA, the Saudi Arabian Embassy in the website of its Islamic Affairs Department [www.iad.org] laid down what a "good" Muslim is expected to do. In that site it is stated:

"The Muslims are required to raise the banner of *jihad* in order to make the word of Allah supreme in this world, to remove all forms of injustice and oppression, and to defend the Muslims. If Muslims do not take up the sword, the evil tyrants of this earth will be able to continue oppressing the weak and helpless."

The above quote is what in substance is being taught in every *madrassa* in India, and can be traced back to the sayings of Prophet Mohammed. I can quote a plethora of verses from a Saudi Arabian translated *Koran* [e.g. verses 8:12, 8:60, and 33:26] which verses justify brutal violence against non-believers. If I delved into *Sira* and *Hadith* for more quotes, then I could risk generating unbearable shock, so it will suffice to say that Islam is not only a theology, but it spans a brutal political ideology which we have to combat in realm of ideas sooner or later.

Some may quote back at me verses from *Manusmriti* about brutality to women and scheduled castes. But as a Hindu I have the liberty to disown these verses if such verses exist [since it is a *Smriti*] and even to seek to re-write a new *Smriti* as many, for example, *Yajnavalkya* have done to date.

Reform and renaissance is thus inbuilt into Hinduism. But in Islam, the word of the Prophet is final. No true Muslim can disown these verses, or say that they would re-write the offensive verses of the *Koran.* If they do, then they would have to run for their lives. Leave alone re-writing, if anyone draws a cartoon of Prophet Mohammed, there will follow world-wide violent rioting. But if Hussein draws Durga in the most pornographic posture, the Hindus will only groan but not violently rampage.

We Hindus have a long recognized tradition of being religious liberals by nature. We have already proved it enough by welcoming to our country and nurturing Parsis, Jews, Syrian Christians, and Moplah Muslim Arabs who were persecuted elsewhere, when we were 100 per cent Hindu country. But today's systematic infiltration of Muslims from Bangladesh and Pakistan is not because of persecution of Muslims in these two countries, but for *jihad* in India.

Despite a 1,000 years of most savage brutalization of Hindus by Islamic invaders and self-demeaning brain washing by the Christians, even then, Hindus as a majority in 1947 had adopted secularism as a creed. We have not asked for an apology and compensation for these past atrocities. But the position of Hindus in this land of *Bharatmata,* where Muslims and Christians locally are in majority, in pockets—such as in Kashmir and Nagaland, or in small enclaves such as town panchayats of Tamil Nadu, is terrible and despicable. Even in Kerala where Hindus are 52 per cent of the population, they have only 25 per cent of all the prime jobs in the state, and are silently suffering their plight at the hands of 48 per cent who vote as a vote bank. Recently, out of 37 new engineering colleges given state clearance, 19 or more than 50 per cent were given to Muslims. Hindus got only 6 per cent! If the proposed Islamic Bank comes through and $50 billion in funds West Asia Arab nations are capitalized in this bank, it will be made available as loans more easily to Muslim youth. Those Hindus who want a loan will be quietly told to convert.

Strategy

This means we have to deal squarely with the incubator of Islamic terror namely Pakistan. Today Pakistan's civil and democratic society is impotent. They are paying the price of Benazir Bhutto who as Prime Minister helped Taliban to strike roots and infected Kashmir with the call for *azadi.* Time has come for us to stand up against all this.

What does it mean in the 21st century for Hindus to stand up? I mean by that a mental clarity of the Hindus to defend themselves by effective deterrent retaliation, and also an intelligent co-option of other religious groups into the Hindu cultural continuum. Mental clarity can only come if we are clear about the identity of the nation. What is India? An ancient but continuing civilization or is it a geographical entity incorporated in 1947 by the Indian

Independence Act of the British Parliament? What then does it means to say "I am an Indian"? A mere passport holder of the Republic of India or a descendent of the great seers and visionaries of more than 10,000 years? Obviously, our identity should be of a nation of an ancient and continuing Hindu civilization, legatees of great *rishis* and *munis,* and a highly sophisticated *sanatana* philosophy.

If Hindu culture is our defining identity then how can we co-opt non-Hindus, especially Muslims and Christians? By persuading them by *saam, dhaam, bheda* and *dand* that they acknowledge with pride the truth: *that their ancestors are Hindus.* If they do, then it means that they accept Hindu culture and its liberal enlightened mores. That is, change of religion to Islam does not mean change from Hindu culture. Then we should treat such Muslims and Christians as part of our Brihad Hindu family, and even welcome them to re-convert.

For a clear strategy we need to learn lessons from our own history.

The first lesson to be learnt from recent history, for tackling terrorism in India is that the Hindu is the target and that Muslims of India are being programmed to slide into suicide against Hindus. It is to undermine the Hindu psyche and create fear of civil war that terror attacks are organized. And hence since the Hindus are the target, they must collectively respond as against the terrorists and not feel individually isolated or worse, be complacent because he or she is not personally affected. If one Hindu dies merely because he or she was a Hindu, then a bit of every Hindu also dies. This is an essential mental attitude, a necessary part of a *virat* Hindu.

Therefore, we have to have a collective mindset as Hindus to stand against the terrorists. In this response, Muslims and Christians of India should join us. However, the Islamic terrorist outfits, e.g. the SIMI being the latest has already resolved that India is *Darul Harab,* and they are committed to make it *Darul Islam.* That makes them free of any moral compunction whatsoever in dealing with Hindus.

The second lesson for combating the terrorism we face today that we need to learn is: since demoralising the Hindu and undermining the Hindu foundation of India in order to destroy the Hindu civilization, is the goal of all terrorists in India we must never capitulate and never concede any demand of the terrorists. Terrorists are encouraged by appeasement but never satisfied by it.

In fact, the earliest terror tactics in India were deployed in Bengal in 1946 by Suhrawady and Jinnah to terrorise Hindus to give in on the demand for Pakistan. The Congress Party claiming to represent the Hindus capitulated, and handed 25 per cent of India on a platter to Mohammed Ali Jinnah.

Therefore, no matter how many Hindus have to die for it, the basic policy has to be: never yield to any demand of the terrorists. That necessary resolve has not been shown in our recent history. Instead ever since we conceded Pakistan in 1947 under duress, we have been mostly yielding time and time again.

In 1989, to obtain the release of Mufti Mohammed Sayeed's daughter, Rubaiyya, who had been kidnapped by terrorists, five terrorists in Indian jails were set free by the V. P. Singh's government. This made these criminals in the eyes of Kashmiri separatists and fence-sitters as heroes, as those who had brought India's Hindu establishment on it's knees. To save Rubaiyya it was not necessary to surrender to terrorist demands.

In 1991, when Chandrashekhar was PM, and I was his senior Minister handling the Law and Justice portfolio, Saifuddin Soz's daughter was kidnapped by the JKLF. They too made the same demand [release of four terrorists in jail], but we refused. We also took some secret retaliatory action which made the JKLF frightened and hence Soz's daughter was put on a autorickshaw and sent home unharmed. This toughness was shown at a time when our government was tottering and about to fall! The difference with the V. P. Singh's government was in our mindset: it had become clear from day one to the JKLF that we meant business as also that two can play the game of terror.

We also showed similar grit and guts when we received information that LTTE had established a parallel establishment in Tamil Nadu. Most of the senior bureaucrats of our government had warned that we risked bloodshed and rise of separatist Dravidian movement if we applied Article 356 of the Constitution to remove the DMK government. But we dismissed the DMK government, sacked the Governor for inaction, and smashed the terror infrastructure in the state. Had we not done that, then Tamil Nadu would have been worse today than Kashmir. Thus toughness on both occasion was rewarded.

The third lesson to be learnt is that whatever and however small the terrorist incident, the nation must retaliate—not by measured and "sober" responses but by massive retaliation. For example, when Ayodhya Temple was sought to be attacked, or the Institute of Science in Bangalore was targeted, these were not big terrorist incidents but we should have massively retaliated. Our intelligence agencies keep telling me in private that we have clinching proof of terrorist training camps in PoK and Bangladesh, and if that is so, we should bomb them by despatching our Air Force. There is some evidence that the US agency, the FBI, has presented to a district court in California satellite photos that do establish that terror training camps exist in near Balakot in northeast Pakistan. Indian government claims proof which has not been made public that there are 57 camps in Pakistani-held territory and 36 camps in Bangladesh.

If instead of being supportive, Pakistan and Bangladesh protest or retaliate if India bombs these camps, then it means that they are sponsors and not unwilling hosts to free lancing terrorists, and hence we should be ready for war. We could retaliate then by fulfilling our pre-1947 commitment to NWFP, and openly help the Baluchis and the Sindhi to meet their legitimate aspirations. We could demand territory from Bangladesh for all those illegal Bangladeshis settled in India. After all, Partition was for those Muslims who could not bear to live with Hindus. Hence, the territory of Bangladesh should be reduced in proportion to millions of Bangladesis that have come to

India *and* the Hindus pushed out since 1947. Strategically, northern one-third of Bangladesh could then be annexed if Bangladesh goes to war with us.

Otherwise, what is the alternative? Walk meekly to death expecting that our "sober" responses will be rewarded by our neighbours and their patrons? We will be back to 1100 AD fooled into suicidal credulity. We should not be ghouls for punishment from terrorists and their patrons. This is *Kaliyug*, and hence there is no room for *sattvic* responses to evil people. Hindu religion has a concept of *apat dharma* and we should invoke it.

What then should be our measured retaliatory response to terrorist attacks, viz. our strategy to deter terrorists? It is argued by secular, "liberals" that no retaliation against terrorists can be effective because of the motivation of terrorists.

What motivates the Islamic terrorists in India? Many are advising us Hindus to deal with the root "cause" of terrorism rather than concentrating on eradicating terrorists by retaliation. And pray what is the root "cause"?

According to bleeding-heart liberals, terrorists are born or bred because of illiteracy, poverty, oppression, and discrimination. They argue that instead of eliminating them, the root cause of these four disabilities in society should be removed. Only then terrorism will disappear. Moreover they argue, terrorists cannot be deterred by force since they are irrational, willing to commit suicide, and have no "return address." Before replying to this, let us understand that I have serious doubts about the integrity of these liberals, or more appropriately, these promiscuous *Supari*. They seek to deaden the emotive power of the individual and render him passive. A nation state cannot survive for long with such a capitulationist mentality.

The fourth lesson to learn is that more than the overt threat of the terrorists in India, the more sinister corrosion of our nation state occurs from within. This corrosion provides "a force multiplier" to the terrorists. That is, the terrorists are able to leverage the influence of highly placed individuals in the government, media and academia, who have been compromised by the terrorists and blackmailed on sex, drug money and illegitimate favours, into collaborating with them.

The widow of Rajiv Gandhi, Ms. Sonia Gandhi, for example, finds nothing wrong with having political alliance with pro-LTTE parties. Furthermore, Ms Gandhi wrote to the President that the four LTTE/DK criminals to be hanged on the orders of the Supreme Court [May 12, 1999], should be given a lesser sentence of life imprisonment. Is this her concept of zero tolerance for terrorism?

It is rubbish to say that terrorists who master-mind the attacks are poor. Osama Bin laden, for example, is a billionaire. Islamic terrorists are patronized by those states that have grown rich from oil revenues. In Britain, the terrorists arrested so far for the bombings are all well-to-do persons. Nor are terrorists uneducated. Most of terrorist leaders are doctors, chartered accountants, and teachers. Islamic terrorists certainly do not face discrimination and oppression in their own countries. In fact, in these countries it is the non-Islamic religious minority which is discriminated and oppressed. In Kashmir valley, where Muslims are in majority, not only Article 370 of the Constitution provides privileges to the majority but it is the minority Hindus who have been slaughtered, or raped, and dispossessed. They have become refuges in squalid conditions in their own country. The gang of nine persons which hijacked four planes on September 11, 2001 and flew them into the World Trade Towers in New York and other targets were certainly not discriminated or oppressed in the United States. Hence it utter rubbish to say that terror is the outcome of the poverty of terrorists.

It is also a ridiculous idea that terrorists cannot be deterred because they are irrational, willing to die, and have no "return address." Terrorist master-minds have political goals and a method in their madness. An effective strategy to deter terrorism is, therefore, to defeat those political goals and to rubbish them by counter-terrorist action. How is that strategy to be structured? In a brilliant research paper published by Robert Trager and Dessislava Zagorcheva this year["Deterring Terrorism," *International Security*, vol. 30, No.3, Winter 2005/06, pp. 87-123] has provided the general principles to structure such a strategy.

Applying these principles, I advocate the following strategy to negate the political goals of Islamic terrorism in India.

Political Goal 1: Overawe India on Kashmir.

Strategy: Remove Article 370, and re-settle ex-servicemen in the Valley. Create Panun Kashmir for Hindu pandit community. Look or create opportunity to take over PoK. If Pakistan continues to back terrorists, assist the Baluchis and Sindhis to struggle for independence.

Political Goal 2: Blast our temples and kill Hindu devotees.

Strategy: Remove the masjid in Kashi Vishwanath temple complex, and sequentially 300 others in other sites as a tit-for-tat retaliation.

Political Goal 3: Make India into Darul Islam.

Strategy: Implement Uniform Civil Code, make Sanskrit learning compulsory and singing of *Vande Mataram* mandatory, and declare India as *Hindu Rashtra* in which only those non-Hindus can vote if they proudly acknowledge that their ancestors are Hindus. Re-name India as Hindustan as a nation of Hindus and those whose ancestors are Hindus.

Political Goal 4: Change India's demography by illegal immigration, conversion, and refusal to adopt family planning.

Strategy: Enact a national law prohibiting conversion from Hindu religion to any other religion. Re-conversion will not be banned. Declare caste is not birth based but code of discipline based. Welcome non-Hindus to re-convert to the caste of their choice provided they adhere to the code of discipline. Annex Bangladesh territory in proportion to the illegal migrants from that country. At present, northern one-third from Sylhet to Khulna can be annexed to re-settle the illegal migrants.

Political Goal 5: Denigrate Hinduism through vulgar writings and preaching in Mosques, *Madrassas,* and Churches to create loss of self-respect amongst Hindus and fit for capitulation.

Strategy: Propagate the development of a Hindu mindset.

India can solve its terrorist problem within five years by such a deterrent strategy, but for that we have to learn the four lessons outlined above, and have a Hindu mindset to take bold, risky, and hard decisions to defend the nation. If the Jews can be transformed from lambs walking meekly to the gas chambers to fiery lions in just ten years, it is not difficult for Hindus in much better circumstances [after all we are 83 per cent of India], to do so in five years. Guru Gobind Singh has shown us the way already, how just five fearless persons under spiritual guidance can transform society. The Vijayanagaram empire was founded by two re-converted[from Islam] persons Bukka and Hakka under the spititual guidance of Shankaracharya of Sringeri. So did Krishnadevaraya, Rana Pratap, Shivaji, Rani Jhansi, Kattaboman, and Netaji Subhash Bose inspire the nation to greatness. But since 1947 and so far we Hindus have meekly followed Jawaharlal Nehru and his imitations in other parties.

Today the Hindu *dharamacharyas* have to play a similar role to forge an instrument to implement the above strategy to deter terrorism in India. Swami Dayananda Sarasvati has already taken a big step in forming the Hindu Dharma Acharya Sabha of Shankaracharyas, Muttadeeshs, Mahamandaleshwars and Akhadas, and adopting the Tirupati Declaration calling on Hindus not to vote for those who work as against the Hindu religion. Even if half the Hindu voters are persuaded to collectively vote as Hindus and for a party sincerely committed to a Hindu agenda, we can forge an instrument for change. *And that ultimately is the bottom line in the strategy to deter terrorism in a democratic Hindustan*: to develop a Hindu vote on the basic of a Virat Hindu identity.

That is, India is not Darul Harab to be trifled with. It is in the interest of the Muslims of India to accept this reality. Hindus must persuade by the time-honoured methods, the Muslims and Christians to accept this and its logical consequences.

This identity was not understood by us earlier because of the distorted outlook of Jawarharlal Nehru who occupied the Prime Minister's chair for seventeen formative years after 1947, and for narrow political ends, had fanned a separatist outlook in Muslims and Christians.

Without a resolution of the identity crisis today, which requires an explicit clear answer to this question of who we are, the majority will never understand how to relate to the legacy of the nation and in turn to the minorities. Minorities would not understand how to adjust with the majority if this identity crisis is not resolved. In other words, the present dysfunctional perceptional mismatch in understanding who we are as a people, is behind most of the communal tension and inter-community distrust in the country and our failure to deal with Pakistan.

To deal with Islamic terrorism and infiltration and culturally assimilate Muslims of India has to be our strategy. India thus needs a Hindu renaissance that incorporates modern principles, e.g. of the irrelevance of birth antecedents, fostering gender equality, ensuring equality before law, and accountability for all. It is also essential to integrate the entire Indian society on those principles, irrespective of religion. Uniform civil code, for example, is something that the vast majority of Muslim women want. But the Muslims think that this is the first step in several to subjugate them or wipe out their identity. But Muslims have quietly accepted Uniform Criminal Code [the IPC] even though it contradicts the Sharia.

In other words, Hindutva has two components—one that Hindus can accept [such as caste abolition, eradication of dowry etc.] without any other religion's interests to consider. The other is the embracing by minorities of the core secular Indian values which have Hindu roots. This would require, particularly Muslims and Christians, to acknowledge that their ancestry is Hindu, and thus own the entire Hindu past as their own legacy, and to thus tailor their outlook on that basis. This would integrate Indian society and make the concept of an inclusive [Brihad] Hindutva and rooted in India's continuing civilization.

Once Indianness means Virat Brihad Hindutva, we can tackle terrorism of Pakistan by an effective strategy of defence. The components of that strategy has to be formed by taking Pakistan as a failed state, a sponsor of terrorism, and hence, we need to dismember it unless there is evidence that Pakistan's civil society is ready to reform Islam in keeping with modern principles of civilisational values and age old dharma of Akhand Hindustan.

We can manage infiltration from Bangladesh by either assimilation into the Hindu cultural mainstream or by asking Bangladesh to part with territory in proportion to the Bangladeshis in India (which is about one-third of that country), since partition of Indian territory was on the basis of population ratio of Hindus and Muslims. If we draw a line from Khulna to Sylhet and annex all territory above it, it will be just compensation as also a great boon for our military to go from Bengal to Assam. Of course, Bangladesh can avoid this by taking back their infiltrators without our having to deport them.

Resources

Terrorism can be fought only with generous allocation of resources that need to be closely monitored in its uses. The recent disastrous corruption in the purchase of bullet proof fests for Mumbai police that sent brave officers to their death on 26/11 terrorist attack is a case in point.

Hence, it is important that the Supreme Court direction {in (1998) 1 SCC 226} on Police Reforms be carried out so that the present trends in the Police towards corruption will not only waste resources but actually enable terrorists to infiltrate it ... a dangerous development indeed.

Conclusion

The conflict resolution between the sufficiency of response to terrorism and the protection of human rights has to be worked out in India in Indian context, which is that the main terrorists confronting us today are Islamic by religion and swear by it.

The *jihad* that terrorists have launched against India is stated to "complete the Islamization of India" and to make India "part of the Caliphate." That Islamic terrorism is for "unfinished business" to make India a *Darul Islam* from the present *Darul Harab*.

Impact of Infiltration on Governance

Indian mainstream media and most political parties are silent spectators when bit by bit Pak terrorists and Bangia infiltrators everyday are placing the nation in a precarious position by invading demographically. India is facing the terrorist cum illegal immigrant pincer today.

Despite the Supreme Court's judgments on how to deal with infiltrators, no significant number has been deported by the government. Rather, instead of being deported, infiltrators are *de facto* being given voting rights! At the other end, Pakistan-trained terrorists are crossing at will into India, with ISI-printed Rs.1000 rupee notes in crores, and setting up local cells for a future attack on vital installations. But appeasement has become the hallmark of Indian politics. Hence, this perfidious development is threatening to become a terminal cancer on our nationhood.

Hindustan originally comprised the present-day India, Iran, Pakistan, Bangladesh, Burma, Nepal and Afghanistan. It may be recalled that Kaikeyi was from Iran, while Gandhari was from Afghanistan. It was a 100% Hindu land till Muhammad bin Qasim's Arab army attacked Sindh in 711 and laid the foundation for the take-over of Iran and Afghanistan.

Despite fighting valiantly to defend their *dharma* and motherland during repeated Muslim invasions for over a thousand years, Hindus lost Afghanistan in 987, Iran in 1011; and the present-day Pakistan and Bangladesh in 1947 to Muslims. After 1947, truncated India, i.e. Bharat has seen genocide and eviction of Hindus from Muslim-majority Kashmir and heavy oppressive discrimination in localized Muslim majority areas.

Alert Hindus today apprehend that because of higher Muslim population growth rate and infiltration from Bangladesh, they will be outnumbered soon by Muslims (in a few decades) and face the same fate as the Hindus did in Afghanistan, Pakistan and Bangladesh.

Hindu civilisation today is a demographically challenged civilisation. Many districts in India bordering Bangladesh have seen abnormal increase in Muslim population because of infiltration.

By its judgment dated July 12, 2005, Supreme Court had struck down the Illegal Migrants (D.T.) Act, 1983 as unconstitutional; and termed Bangladeshi infiltration as "external aggression" and directed that "Bangladeshi nationals who have trespassed into Assam or are living in other parts of the country have no legal right of any kind to remain in India and they are liable to be deported."

But, instead of deporting the infiltrators, on February 10, 2006, UPA government brought in the Foreigners (Tribunals for Assam) Order to nullify the apex Court's judgment. On December 5, 2006, Supreme Court quashed this Order also as unconstitutional, and called for implementation of its earlier judgment dated July 12, 2005 for deporting illegal immigrants.

Despite this judgment, hardly any significant number infiltrators have been deported by the government. Those that were, just crept back Instead of being deported, infiltrators have been quietly acquiring voting rights, since, the government is busy with infiltrator-friendly 'confidence building measures' like soft borders, peace talks, Indo-Pak and Indo-Bangladesh bus and rail links, which are bringing more and more Pak-Bangla nationals into India everyday.

It is ironic that despite repeated waves of foreign invaders for over 1,200 years, Hindus valiantly resisted converting to Islam and

Christianity. But now we are acquiescing in a demographic invasion of Islam and conversion activities of Christian missionaries.

Islamic Terrorism

Did the despicable terror and mayhem in Mumbai on November 26th signify for India to wake up? It fundamentally signifies a challenge to the true identity of India from radical Islamic fundamentalists, who securely based in Pakistan.

Pakistan is a Muslim majority country and, therefore, by definition cannot be a secular peace loving country. It is to be regarded instead as *Darul Islam* where minorities have no place. Islam commands Muslims of *Darul Islam* to wage *jihad* into countries which are *Darul Harab,* and hence India will continue to be attacked by terrorists from Pakistan and infiltrated from Bangladesh. In *Darul Harab,* the non-Muslim majority is expected to be flabby and amorphous as the Hindu majority are today. If the majority is united and cohesive then it is *Darul Ahad* where minority Muslims are to enter into a peace agreement with the majority. This is called *Al Takkiya.*

Therefore today, patriotic Indian government must require Muslims to sign an Al *Takkiya* contract. For this, Indians must not permit any area of India, from State to district to town panchayat, to be a Muslim majority area because then it will become a breeding ground for *jihad* based terror and a mini *Daru Islam.* A nationalist government thus must ensure a population re-settlement to make this happen.

In Kashmir, the Indian government must resettle 10 lakh ex-service personnel of the armed forces to reconstruct the population ratio of Hindus in Kashmir that had been changed despite Article 370.

Secular intellectuals may wax eloquent about the "true Islam" being humane and peaceful on TV programmes, but it is clear that they have not read any authoritative translations of the *Koran, Sira* and *Hadith* which three holy books together constitute the theology of Islam.

Hence instead of talking about the "correct interpretation" of Islam, those who call themselves as "moderates" in the Islamic community, ought instead to urge for a new reformed Islamic theology that is consistent with democratic principles. Of course, then like Salman Rushdie and Taslima, they will have to run for cover.

In 2003, two years after the 9/11 perfidious Islamic assault on USA, resulting in killing of more than 3000 persons within two hours, and which crime of terror was perpetrated by leveraging the democratic freedoms in USA, the Saudi Arabian Embassy in the website of its Islamic Affairs Department [www.iad.org] laid down what a "good" Muslim is expected to do. In that site it is stated:

"The Muslims are required to raise the banner of *jihad* in order to make the word of Allah supreme in this world, to remove all forms of injustice and oppression, and to defend the Muslims. If Muslims do not take up the sword, the evil tyrants of this earth will be able to continue oppressing the weak and helpless."

The above quote is what in substance is being taught in every *madrassa* in India, and can be traced back to the sayings of Prophet Mohammed. I can quote a plethora of verses from a Saudi Arabian translated Koran [e.g., verses 8:12, 8:60, and 33:26] which verses justify brutal violence against non-believers. If I delved into Sira and Hadith for more quotes, then I could risk generating unbearable shock, so it will suffice to say that Islam is not only a theology, but it spans a brutal political ideology which we have to combat in realm of ideas sooner or later.

Some may quote back at me verses from Manusmriti about brutality to women and scheduled castes. But as a Hindu I have the liberty to disown these verses if such verses exist [since it is a Smriti] and even to seek to re-write a new smriti as many, for example, Yajnavalkya have done to date.

Reform and renaissance is thus inbuilt into Hinduism. But in Islam, the word of the Prophet is final. No true Muslim can disown these verses, or say that they would rewrite the offensive verses of the Koran. If they do, then they would have to run for their lives. Leave alone re-writing, if anyone draws a cartoon of Prophet Mohammed, there will follow world-wide violent rioting. But if Hussein draws Durga in the most pornographic posture, the Hindus will only groan but not violently rampage.

We Hindus have a long recognized tradition of being religious liberals by nature. We have already proved it enough by welcoming to our country and nurturing Parsis, Jews, Syrian Christians, and Moplah Muslim Arabs who were persecuted elsewhere, when we were 100% Hindu country. But today's systematic infiltration of Muslims from Bangia Desh and Pakistan is not because of persecution, but for *jihad.*

Despite a 1000 years of most savage brutalization of Hindus by Islamic invaders and self demeaning brain washing by the Christians, even then, Hindus as a majority in 1947 had adopted secularism as a creed. We have not asked for an apology and compensation for these past atrocities. But the position of Hindus in this land of Bharatmata, where Muslims and Christians locally are in majority, in pockets—such as in Kashmir and Nagaland or districts such as Malapuram in Kerala, or in small enclaves such as town panchayats of Tamil Nadu, is terrible and despicable. Even in Kerala where Hindus are 52% of the population, they have only 25% of all the prime jobs in the state, and are silently suffering their plight at the hands of 48% who vote as a vote bank. This factor make infiltration and change in the population ratio lethal for our civilization.

If we do not stand up now to this Islamic explicit and terrorism and implicit then India will end up like Beirut, a permanent battlefield of international terrorists, buccaneers, pirates and missionaries, or in the end a Darul Islam of Muslim majority.

This means we have to deal squarely with the incubator of Islamic terror namely Pakistan. Today Pakistan's civil and democratic society is impotent. They are paying the price of Benazir Bhutto who as Prime Minister helped Taliban to strike roots and infected Kashmir with the call for "azadi." Time has come for us to stand up against all this.

A Possible Solution

What does it mean in the 21st century for Hindus to stand up? I mean by that a mental clarity of the Hindus to defend themselves by effective deterrent retaliation, and also an intelligent co-option of other religious groups into the Hindu cultural continuum.

Mental clarity can only come if we are clear about the identity of the nation. What is India? An ancient but continuing civilization or is it a geographical entity incorporated in 1947 by the Indian Independence Act of the British Parliament? What then does it means to say "I am an Indian"? A mere passport holder of the Republic of India or a descendent of the great seers and visionaries of more than 10,000 years? Obviously our identity should be of a nation of an ancient and continuing Hindu civilization, legatees of great rishis and munis, and a highly sophisticated sanatana philosophy.

If Hindu culture is our defining identity then how can we co-opt non-Hindus, especially Muslims and Christians? By persuading them by *saam, dhaam, bheda* and *dand* that they acknowledge with pride the truth: *that their ancestors are Hindus.* If they do, then it means that they accept Hindu culture and its liberal enlightened mores. That is, change of religion to Islam does not mean change from Hindu culture. Then we should treat such Muslims and Christians as part of our Brihad Hindu family, and even welcome them to re-convert.

This identity was not understood by us earlier because of the distorted outlook of Jawarharlal Nehru who occupied the Prime Minister's chair for seventeen formative years after 1947 and for narrow political ends, had fanned a separatist outlook in Muslims and Christians.

Without a resolution of the identity crisis today, which requires an explicit clear answer to this question of who we are, the majority will never understand how to relate to the legacy of the nation and in turn to the minorities. Minorities would not understand how to adjust with the majority if this identity crisis is not resolved. In other words, the present dysfunctional perceptional mismatch in understanding who we are as a people, is behind most of the communal tension and inter-community distrust in the country and our failure to deal with Pakistan. This is why Hindutva is crucial for governance of the nation.

We can manage infiltration from Bangladesh by either assimilation into the Hindu cultural mainstream or by asking Bangladesh to part with territory in proportion to the Bangia Deshis in India (which is about one-third of that country), since Partition of Indian territory was on the basis of population ratio of Hindus and Muslims. Of course, Bangla Desh can avoid this by taking back their infiltrators without our having to deport them.

To deal with Islamic terrorism and infiltration and culturally assimilate Muslims of India, India thus needs a Hindu renaissance that incorporates modern principles, e.g., of the irrelevance of birth antecedents, fostering gender equality, ensuring equality before law, and accountability for all. It is also essential to integrate the entire Indian society on those principles, irrespective of religion. Uniform civil code for example, is something that the vast majority of Muslim women want. But the Muslims think that this is the first step in several to subjugate them or wipe out their identity. But Muslims have quietly accepted Uniform Criminal Code [the IPC] even though it contradicts the Sharia.

Once Indianness means Virat Brihad Hindutva, we can tackle terrorism of Pakistan by an effective strategy of defence. The components of that strategy has to be formed by taking Pakistan as a failed state, a sponsor of terrorism, and hence, we need to dismember it unless there is evidence that Pakistan's civil society is ready to reform Islam in keeping with modern principles of civilisational values and age old dharma of Akhand Hindustan.

Chapter VIII

CONCLUSIONS

The main thrust of the previous chapters is that we need a new Hindutva ideological framework for modernity that can unite the nation, if every individual be motivated by equipping him with fundamental concepts of Brihad Virat Hindutva, with an overriding concept of national identity, and empowered by adequate modern education to inculcate the scientific spirit of inquiry, thus to bring about a national renaissance, and to *make the Indian people strive for global greatness and for world power.*

The ideological framework to achieve such a national renaissance the following parameters are essential.

(a) The State is to be *minimalist* in regulatory interventions in social and economic matters, *maximalist* in the maintenance of law and order, in opposing, terrorism, and *optimalist* in providing the quality of life needs, *while being politically accountable to the people in a democracy.*

(b) A social ethos based on the concepts of trusteeship of wealth, philanthropy and voluntary group action is encouraged by religious sanction for the better distribution of income and for minimizing economic contradictions and deprivation.

(c) The key goal of the state is to empower the individual through a modern education that blends the essential concepts of spiritual commitment with material pursuits to extol and venerate the pursuit of knowledge, to enable the individual to be self-reliant and yet have strong character derived from *Sanatana Dharma.* This requires the adoption of integral Humanism as a model.

(d) The individual is to be persuaded by the State through incentives and not by coercion. The State will hence make no promise to the people without specifying the sacrifices to be made for delivering on the promise.

(e) India will make rapid economic progress to become a developed country only through a globally competitive economy that requires assured access to the markets and technological innovations of the United States and its allies. This will have concomitant political obligations that must be accepted as essential for national renaissance.

(f) Such rapid progress would require a national security strategy for attaining a peaceful environment which necessitates strong security ties with such of those countries with which India has no intrinsic clash of interests.

(g) The citizen must have a mindset to bond collectively with others in the nation. At present, generally the Indian has loyalty to the family but is apathetic to the community where he lives. The Indian does not easily acknowledge the accomplishment of others. He respects intellectual endeavour but not dignity of labour, and is more concerned with form than content in personal and professional discourse. Moreover, an Indian feels less accountable for his actions the higher he or she rises m authority. These character flaws have come from ten centuries of deprivation feudalism and colonialism. These flaws are incompatible with a people forming a great nation, and can be rectified by developing a strong and coherent concept of national identity, i.e., Brihad Virat Hindutva, whose defining characteristics can be culled from a correct perception of our history and values in *Sanatana Dharma*.

These parameters define a perimeter of reconstruction of the Indian mindset and outlook, and hence is an enormous but essential task that we must undertake to do to earn the right to be a legatee of our glorious past when we had become the world's most developed nation by the then prevailing standards.

Based on the Hindutva concepts elaborated in the previous chapters therefore the *necessacity* today is first and foremost for undiluted unity of Hindus, a unity based on a mindset that is nurtured and fostered on Hindutva as essential for a renaissance. Only then Hindus can meet the challenge of missionaries and fundamentalists. I can do no better here than quote Swami Dayananda Sarasvati:

"Faced with militant missionaries. Hinduism has to show that its plurality and all-encompassing acceptance are not signs of disparateness or disunity. For that, a collective voice is needed."

Since the task to defeat the nefarious forces ranged today against Hindu society is not going to be easy, we cannot therefore trust those amongst in our midst whose commitment to the motherland is ambivalent or *ad hoc* or those who feel no kinship to the Hindu past of the nation. We partitioned a quarter of Hindustan to enable those Muslims who could not live with Hindus in a democratic' framework of equality and fraternity. Hence, we have to ensure by our persuasive powers of *Saam, Dhaam, Bheda,* and *Dand* to foster in all citizens Hinduness or Hindutva.

With this in mind, I suggest the following Agenda for Action:

First, the concept of Hindustan defines the identity of India. That is, Hindustan is a nation of Hindus and those others who proudly accept that their ancestors are Hindus. Muslims and Christians shall be part of the Hindustan if they accept this truth and revere it. *That is the first dimension of Hindutva, that is of a Brihad Hindutva. Therefore, the first item of a Hindutva Agenda has to be to establish the overriding Hindustani identity of all citizens of Bharat, that is India based on the concept of Brihad Hindutva.* In this inclusive concept of Hindutva we have to examine and determine if the present divisive caste system can be considered as sustainable.

Second, Sanskrit and the Devanagari script, in addition to the mother tongue and its script, will one day in the future, be Hindustan's link language. All the main Indian languages have already a large percentage of their vocabulary common with Sanskrit. Even Tamil which is considered as ancient, has 40 per cent words in common with Sanskrit. The scripts of all Indian languages are derived or evolved from Brahmi script. *Hence, the second item of the Hindutva Agenda has to be a commitment to re-throne Sanskrit with Devanagari script as Hindustan's link language,* which is to be achieved through a compulsory 3-language formula of mother tongue, Hindi, and English in all schools, and *by a steady sanskritization of Hindi's vocabulary till Sanskritized Hindi becomes indistinguishable from Sanskrit.*

Third, Hindus, and those others who are proud of their Hindu past and origins, must learn the correct history of India. That history which records that Hindus have always been, and are one; that caste is not birth-based nor immutable but a code of discipline by choice and adherence. India is a continuum, *sanatana.* That is, ancient Hindus and their descendents have always lived in this area from the Himalayas to the Indian Ocean, an area called *Akhand* Hindustan, and did not come from outside; and that there is no truth in the Aryan-Dravidian race theory. Instead Hindus went abroad to spread learning. Also fresh perspectives have to be given to chronology including recognizing that the Vijaynagaram Dynasty lasted 300 years reigning over a larger area than the Mughals from Akbar to Aurangzeb which lasted about 150 years. But most all this history must record the valiant and continuous struggle against the foreign invaders whether Islamic or Christian and the ultimate victory in 1947 and never having had capitulated. *So the third item of the Hindutva Agenda item has to be a total and complete re-writing of history text books, that are then prescribed in educational institutions.*

Fourth, the virat Hindutva mindset is to retaliate when attacked. The retaliation must be massive enough to deter future attacks. If terrorists come from training camps in Pakistan, Bangladesh or Sri Lanka, Hindus must seek to carpet bomb those training camps, no matter the consequences. If 5 lakh Kashmir! Hindus are driven out of the Valley by Islamic terrorists, we must arm and financially equip 10 lakhs of the able-bodied ex-servicemen to go with their families and settle in the former residences of the driven-out Hindus. If Bangladesh permits its population to infiltrate into Hindustan, then our armed forces should annex the northern parts of Bangladesh [above the line from Khulna to Sylhet] as compensation within the meaning of the Indian Independence Act of June 1947 passed by the British Parliament to legitimize Partition. The Act was framed on the principle that territory in proportion to Muslims not wanting to live under what Jinnah called as the 'hegemony' of the Hindus, be carved out as Pakistan. One-third of Bangladesh has already infiltrated into Hindustan to live under Hindu 'hegemony' so one-third of Bangladesh territory must be reclaimed, or Bangladesh should take their people back.

Thus, virat Hindutva minded Indians must prefer to lose everything they possess rather than submit to treachery, tyranny or to terrorism. Today those in India who submit to terrorists and hijackers hence must be vehemently despised as anti-Hindus. They cannot be good Hindus just because they are pious or go regularly to the temple, or good Hindustanis just because they are citizens of India or even tom-tom religious slogans.

Today's so-called self proclaimed "good" Hindus have however failed to avenge or retaliate for the attack on Parliament, Akshaya Mandir, Ayodhya, and even a former Prime Minister's [Rajiv Gandhi's] assassination. On the other hand those who defend these assassins and praise the terrorist organization behind them, are central government Ministers today.

Thus, the fourth item of the Hindutva Agenda has to be a commitment of 'zero tolerance' for terrorists, also for those who forcibly or by inducements seek to convert Hindus to other religion, and to never negotiate with them unless they surrender, and to retaliate against the political objectives of these enemies. *This is virat Hindutva.*

At this juncture I would like to add a basic axiom that we must always remember. While we may adhere to the principle of Hindu secularism, i.e., *sarva pantha sama bhava,* we must never forget one fundamental tenet of Islamic behavior: Islam teaches that Muslims must behave differently when in majority, from when in strong minority [if majority waffles or appeases], and in weak minority [if majority is united and clear sighted]. Saudi Arabia is in the first category, termed as *Darul Islam,* India, UK and Germany is in the second category called *Darul Harab.* Australia, China, and US is in the third category held to be *Darul Ahad* or *takkiyya.* This categorization applies even within countries. Kashmir is held to be *Darul Islam,* and hence Hindus have to be driven out or killed as *kafirs,* or brutalized as *dhimmis,* their temples razed, and their women publicly raped. Even in Tamil Nadu where Muslims state-wise are less than 5 per cent of the population, and culturally very close to Hindus, there are 40 Town Panchayats where Muslims are in majority, and there the Muslim psychology undergoes a complete transformation. Thus, what happens in Kashmir happens also in these elected Town Panchayats but in more subdued forms for the hapless minority Hindus of these Town Panchayats. Similar is the fate of Hindus in Mau and Azamgarh, Meerut, and good parts of Assam.

Darul Islam is a Muslim religious concept of a land where Muslims rule, and the non-believers in Islam are termed as *Dhimmis.* The term *Dhimmi* was coined after the Jews were crushed in Medina [Khaybar to be exact], and the defeated Jews accepted that if they did not convert to Islam, then they would accept second-class status politically, culturally, and religiously. This included zero civil rights including the right to modesty of women, and the special tax *jizya.*

There is thus no scope for Muslims and non-Muslims uniting as equals in the political, cultural, or social system in a *Darul Islam* where Muslims rule. *Secular order in India thus is possible only when Muslims are not in power.* Thondi, Rasathipuram, Malapuram, and other places prove that the Muslim mind suffers from a dangerous duality—of seeking secularism when out of power and imposing a brutal demeaning theocracy for non-Muslims when in power.

It is this duality that patriotic Hindus must re-shape by modem education and other means, as also retain its demographic *overwhelming* majority in India. We do not have much time, in fact about 45 years, as the X-graph of statistical regressions estimated by J.S. Bajaj and colleagues shows. 'X' represents the two trends—Hindu percentage declining and Muslim percentage rising, and intersecting in the year 2061.

The 'dhimmitude' of Jews in Medina and later in Mecca represents the beginning of religious apartheid inherent and basic to Islamic mores, and practiced long before what we saw in South Africa on the basis of colour and race, and that which became prevalent during the Islamic imperialist rule in parts of India. Hindus were *dhimmis* for six hundred years in those parts of India despite being a bigger majority in the country than even today. Hence, a majority is not enough. Hindus need also a Hindu mindset to be free.

In his Presidential address to the Muslim League in Lahore in 1940, Mohammed Ali Jinnah had articulated this concept of apartheid in his own inimitable way to suit his patrons, viz., the British colonialists:

> To visualize Hindus and Muslims in India uniting to create a common nation is a mythical concept. It is only a fancy dream of some unawakened Hindu leaders.... The truth is that Hindus and Muslims are two different civilisations .... since their thought process grow on different beliefs.

Large sections of Muslims in India then had rejected Jinnah and his concept of non-compatibility of Muslims with Hindus. But after Independence and Partition, instead of building on this rejection by many Muslims, the Nehru era saw increasing pandering precisely to the religious element that believed in this apartheid. Indira Gandhi vigorously continued this appeasement thereby nurturing the apartheid mentality of Muslim orthodoxy.

But the final undermining of the enlightened Muslim came when the government capitulated in the Shah Bano case. Thousands of Muslims had demonstrated on the streets demanding that the government *not* bring legislation that would nullify the Supreme Court's judgment in the Shah Bano case but in vain. Rajiv Gandhi, I learnt later, on counsel from his Italian Catholic family, had surrendered to the hard line clerics who protested that the Supreme Court had no right to interfere and to defacto amend the *Shariat,* the Islamic law code. These relatives on a directive from the Vatican thought that if secular law would be applied to Muslims, it can be to the Christians too.

This was a nonsense argument of the Muslim clerics, since the Shariat had already been amended, without protest, in the criminal law of India. The Indian Penal Code represents the uniform criminal code that equally applies to all religious communities. I therefore ask the clerics: if a Muslim is caught stealing, can any court in India direct that his hand at the wrist be cut off as the Shariat prescribes? If Muslims can accept a uniform criminal code what is the logic in rejecting the uniform civil code?

In India, *Dhimmi* status for Hindus during Islamic imperialist rule has had other social implications. Defiant *Brahmins* and *Kshatriyas* who had refused to convert and chose to remain Hindus, were forced to carry night soil and suffer great indignities for their women folk. Or it meant gross mental torture. Guru Tegh Bahadur, for example, had to see his disciples sawed in half, before the pious Guru's own head was severed and displayed in public.

The debasement of Hindu society then was such that those targeted valiant *Brahmins* and *Kshatriyas* who had refused to convert and thus made to carry night soil, were disowned by other Hindus and declared to be *asprashya* or "untouchable." The ranks of the Scheduled Caste community which was not more than 1 per cent of the population before the advent of Islam in India swelled to 14 per cent by the time Mughal rule collapsed.

Thus, today's SC community especially those who are still Hindus, consists mostly of those valiant *Brahmins* and *Kshatriyas* who had refused to become Muslims but preferred ostracization and ignominy in order to remain Hindus. Hindu society today should offer *koti koti pranams* to them for keeping the *Bhagwa Dhwaj* of Hindu religion flying even at great personal cost and misery.

Here I suggest therefore that we Hindus must understand the true nature of Islam before we can formulate a strategy to defeat those who threaten us. The true nature of Christianity is different in sophistication in presentation, but no less is their menace of religious conversions of Hindus.

At this juncture let me add even though I oppose conversion as it is indeed violence, as Swami Dayanand Sarasvati boldly wrote to the Vatican Pope, nevertheless if an Indian Muslim or Christian changes' his religion to Hinduism today, I will not regard it as conversion because it is a return to the Hindu fold of those whose ancestors had been forcibly converted.

Islam is not only and merely what is stated in the *Koran.* Islam is a trilogy of *Koran, Sira* and *Hadith.* This trilogy defines a "true" Muslim or believer. Therefore, those who sing praises of the Koran to prove that Islam is intrinsically humane have not read the *Sira* and *Hadith.* While *Koran* is a compilation of revelations of Allah to Mohammed through angel Gabriel, *Sira* is essentially a biography of Mohammed, while *Hadiths* are a collection of proverbs, poems, and practices of Mohammed. Thus Islamic theology is *Koran* plus what the Prophet said or did. This is borne by content analysis of the trilogy. *Koran* has 153,000 words, while *Sira* has 408,000 words, and *Hadith* compiled by Bukhari has 338,000 words.

For 13 years in Mecca, Mohammed preached the *Koran* and managed to convert just 150 persons. But in Medina, Mohammed did and said what is contained in *Sira* and *Hadith.* Within 10 years he became the King of Arabia, and converted 100 per cent of the people who survived the sword of Islam.

To enforce his revelations, Mohammed resorted to *jihad,* which meant sacred violence as a process of spreading Islam. Holy war is just one phase of *jihad,* because *jihad* is a process. It is in *Sira* that one finds a detailed manual of the complete strategy of *jihad* and political dimension of Islam. *Sira* is about how Mohammed dealt with those who disagreed with him.

While *Koran* is personal to every Muslim or believer, *Sira* and *Hadith* affect non-believers. Islamic theology is obsessed with what to do with unbelievers and non-believers. Unlike Hinduism, which says not a word against non-believers, in fact says that other religions also lead to God, Islam is harsh on them, and justifies violence against them as sacred. The choice to non-believers in Islam is: convert or accept dhimmitude. Hence, the explanation for Thondi, Rasathipuram, Mau etc., and the duality in ethics practiced by Muslims everywhere.

Hindus should also not be defensive about mosques built on where temples stood because, as the Supreme Court has held in the *Faruqui vs. Union of India case [(1994)6 SCC360]* that a *masjid* is not an essential part of Islamic theology, and have been, and can be demolished for public good. Of course, because of this no one in a democracy can take law into his own hands to demolish these *masjids.* But a Government can do so with the cooperation of Muslims.

Therefore, one basic axiom for *virat Hindutva* is: never permit Hindus to become a minority anywhere in Hindustan. For any kind of secularism, genuine, pseudo, or Hindu, we Hindus have to be necessarily in majority. We cannot blame Muslims for this—their mind is clear and set by Islam. We Hindus are at fault—our mindset is of the numerous goats in a forest or of lions in a circus. *We lack today a virat Hindutva mindset.*

Fifth, our Hindutva ideology has to be based on Ekatma Manavad or Integral Humanism. Deendayal Upadhyaya recognized as far back as 1965 that the world cannot be a happier place merely by material progress. There has to be a harmonisation of material progress with spiritual development of any human being. This reality has dawned after centuries on Christians and even Communists. No wonder, the *News-week* article [Annexure 4] states that Americans feel increasingly that they logically "are all Hindus today." The Chinese President Hu Jintao actually got a resolution passed in a special session of the Communist Party of China in October 2006 that Chinese progress is sustainable only if China adopts the concept of "Harmonious Society" in which blending of material progress with spiritual values [drawn from Confucious and Buddha] is the only way to progress for China. In 2007 China ruled by the atheistic Communist Party convened an international conference on Buddhism!

Thus, the far-sighted Dcendayaiji advocated the concept of the 'Integral Human', which concept is squarely within the Hindu ethos and based on Hindutva. Ekatma Manavad or Integral Humanism as he termed it. contrasts this harmonization as it differs from capitalism and communism. [The tabular presentation in Annexure 3 brings this out].

Political Action for Implementation of the Agenda: Three Steps

These five items together constitute the *Brihad Virat Ekatma Hindutva Agenda,* which if followed and sincerely implemented will lead to a bonding that Hindus need today to confront the challenge that Hindu civilization is facing from Islamic terrorists, fraud Christian missionaries from abroad, and a gang of Marxists and Macaulayist intellectuals in the academia and media, who are also aided and abetted by confused Hindus within the country.

Without such a Hindu unity based on the implied mindset in the Agenda we will be unable to nullify and root out the subversion and erosion that undermine today the Hindu foundation of India. This foundation is what makes India distinctive in the world, and hence we must safeguard this legacy with all the might and moral fibre that we can muster, for and with Hindutva, and thus seek the implementation of this five-point Hindutva Agenda.

In the implementation of this Agenda we will get great moral support from Hindus resident abroad because of their sheer commitment to the Hindus. I refer not only to skilled professionals in US and Europe, but in equal measure if not more to the valiant indentured and brutalized labour taken forcibly from India by British colonialists to far away Guyana, Fiji, Mauritius and Africa, who despite being isolated and cut off from contact with the motherland fiercely fought for generations to keep their Hindu identity. The motherland must now own them as its dear tested children, and co-opt them in our struggle to establish Hindutva in Hindustan to achieve Hindu Rashtra. Moreover, we must also welcome anyone who becomes a Hindu whatever his pedigree and blood as Swami Vivekananda, Veer Savarkar [as exemplified by his attitude in the Sister Nivedita case], and Deendayalji made clear: no discrimination between Indian and foreigner Hindu.

Free from economic constraints and aching for an identity, and well educated. I have seen the Hindus abroad *able* to organize and effectively challenge the attempts to slander Hindu religious symbols and icons. Overseas Hindus have contributed during our Freedom Struggle, the fight against the Emergency, and in enabling our *acharyas* to spread the message of the Hindu religion abroad. Our final goal has to be to spread Hindutva and Hindu theology abroad, but by example and not by inducing conversion. This has to been done without demeaning other religions.

At home since in a democracy the war is in fighting of elections, we must therefore resolve to foster a Hindu consciousness that leads to a cohesive vigorous Hindu unity and mindset, so that the Hindustani voter, will cast his ballot in an election only for a Front that will be loyal to the Hindutva Agenda, We cannot afford to be tolerant anymore of past excuses for failure to implement a Hindutva Agenda. Hence, to use the Quit India cry: *We must do or die in the effort. Therefore the time fur political action is now.*

From my personal experience as a Minister in a minority government, I can say that lack of majority in Parliament is no excuse for implementing any agenda. As a Minister of Law in the minority Chandrashekhar government I got made K. M. Pandey, the Sessions Judge of Faizabad. a High Court judge despite the fact that the previous V. P. Singh's three-legged government had issued orders on file that since Pandey had directed the locks on the so-called Babri

Masjid to be removed, he should never be made a High Court judge. Mulayam Singh was our Chief Minister of UP, and I however got his protests sufficiently moderated. He cooperated because he knew I would do it anyway make Pandey a judge of the High Court. The same clarity enabled the Chandrashekhar government to get Saifuddin Soz's kidnapped daughter freed without releasing any dreaded terrorists. There are methods for doing that—mostly based on retaliation. In each case it is the mindset of those elected to high office that matters. It was this mindset that enabled the Chandrashekhar government to nearly solve by an agreement the question of building of a Ram temple in Ayodhya. The government however fell before it could be clinched.

But it is easier said than done to expect that politicians would do or die for the Hindutva Agenda. As our rudderless democracy has drifted, we are today in a "match-fixing mode" even in electoral contests. In Tamil Nadu, the DMK and AIADMK are bitter enemies, but in most crucial constituencies, a match-fixing arrangements for money had been worked out between Sasikala of the AIADMK and Arcot Veerasamy of the DMK, who are *alter egos of their respective top leaders, and determined to keep out the Hindutva forces from Tamil Nadu.* The same match-fixing disease has spread to other parties nation-wide. We have to cure it before it completely debilitates and destroys our democracy as it has done in Latin American countries such as Colombia and Peru.

Therefore, to meet this challenge, the second step, after the electoral battle is over, is **to** form a Hindutva Parliamentary and Legislative Forum of hopefully 50 or more MPs and likewise 10% of the Legislative Assemblies. These Forums must use every rule in the parliamentary procedure to make the government accountable for the Hindutva Agenda and to speak, debate and get implemented the five agenda items of Brihad Virat Ekatma Hindutva. For the efficacy of this, a staff of retired Lok Sabha and Vidhan Sabha Secretariat officials should be created, with remuneration, to draft, file and get listed Motions, Call Attention Notices, Questions and Petitions.

The third step necessary arises from the reluctance today to confront and expose the anti-Hindu personages in Parliament, Academia and media because of this disease of "match-fixing." It is said that such attacks would be personal and counter-productive. There is, as is being argued, however nothing "personal" in such directed and organized attacks. Just as the world focused on Hitler or Mussolini, without thinking of it being personal, or our Hindutva enemies today focus on persons in our ranks without being apologetic, therefore, we should identify and expose especially the persons who have emerged as the fountain-head of the anti-Hindutva campaign today.

These above-noted steps are thus the essential political actions for the implementation of of Brihad Virat Ekatma Hindutva Agenda to weld Hindustanis again into vibrant citizens of a *Hindu Rashtra.*

INDEX